ENCYCLOPAEDIA OF INDIAN GOVERNMENT: PROGRAMMES AND POLICIES

ENCYCLOPAEDIA OF INDIAN GOVERNMENT: PROGRAMMES AND POLICIES

ENCYCLOPAEDIA
OF
INDIAN GOVERNMENT:
PROGRAMMES AND POLICIES

Vol. 13

Natural Resources

Edited by

Satish Tiwari

ANMOL PUBLICATIONS PVT. LTD.

NEW DELHI - 110 002 (INDIA)

ANMOL PUBLICATIONS PVT. LTD.
4374/4B, Ansari Road, Daryaganj
New Delhi - 110 002

Encyclopaedia of Indian Government: Programmes and Policies

First Edition, 2000
ISBN 81-261-0515-1 (Set)

PRINTED IN INDIA

Published by J.L. Kumar for Anmol Publications Pvt. Ltd., New Delhi - 110 002 and Printed at Mehra Offset Press, Delhi.

Contents

Preface

Encyclopaedia of Indian Government: Programmes and Policies contains authoritative information on about fifty departmental policies and their future developmental programmes.

Organised to be completed in 40 volumes, this gigantic work covers Agriculture; Atomic Energy; Chemicals and Fertilizers; Coal; Commerce; Communication; Culture; Defence; Education; Environment and Forests; External Affairs; Finance; Food & Consumer Affairs; Food Processing Industries; Health and Family Welfare; Home Affairs and Internal Security; Human Resources; Industry; Information and Broadcasting; Labour; Law, Justice and Company Affairs; Non-conventional Energy Sources; Ocean Development; Parliamentary Affairs; Personnel, Public Grievances and Pensions; Petroleum and Natural Gas; Planning and Programme Implementation; Planning and Statistics; Posts and Telegraphs; Power; Rural Development; Science and Technology; Social Justice and Empowerment; Space; States Affairs; Steel; Steel and Mines; Sugar and Edible Oils; Surface Transport; Textiles; Tourism; Urban Development; Water Resources; Women and Child development etc.

Based on the information derived from authoritative sources, this work contains authentic facts and figures. I am deeply beholden to all the scholars whose writings are cited or substantially made use of in the present work. I am also thankful to Anmol Publications Pvt. Ltd. for undertaking publication of this encyclopaedia. I am solely responsible for shortcomings in presentation of matter.

Encyclopaedic in nature, this will prove a dependable reference work for scholars and academics besides those appearing for different competitive examinations.

—Satish Tiwari

1

Natural Resource Development

Current Status of Indian Forests

India has a total geographical area of 3287263 sq. km. The officially recorded forest area is 765210 sq. km., which constitutes 23.8% of the total geographical area. Over 45000 species of plants occur in the country and several thousand species of them are endemic to India. Their range of distribution is confined only to this country and not reported from any other part of the world. India is equally rich in fauna. The country has about 350 species of birds and qmqore than 20,000 species of insects.

Various sources give different figures of the land use pattern in the country. However, the task of reconciliation of these figures has been assigned to National Remote Sensing Agency (NRSA) and in all probability it would be completely reconciled in the beginning of Ninth Plan, which is to begin from April 1997. Presently, the land use pattern have been quoted from the report published by Directorate of Economics and Statistics, a nodal agency in the country to compile the data related to various departments in the country.

The total area recorded as forest in 1950-51 was 404800 sq. km. Over the years recorded forest area continuously rose and touched the figures of 765210 sq. km. This was on account of unoccupied government lands being declared as the Forest area by state/UT governments. Most of these lands were non-productive and came under the category of wastelands. A unique situation exists in the North-Eastern states of the country.

These forest lands are unclassed i.e. without any legal status. In India the total unclassed forest is 125385 sq. km. which constitutes 3.8% and 16.38% of the geographical area and recorded forest area of the country respectively.

The transfer of forest land to non-forest uses is also one of the important factors which has depleted India's natural forest ecosystem. In between 1951 to 1980, 4.328 million ha. of forest land were officially diverted for non-forestry uses. It would be proper to mention here that the transferred forest lands were highly productive lands and would have contributed much towards enrichment of forest ecosystem, if retained.

While analysing the state-wise forest cover of India it is revealed that owing to specific problems the country may be broadly divided into two regions namely, North Eastern region and rest of the country.

North Eastern region consists of seven states. There has been a decrease in the dense forest and open forest cover in almost every state and there is an alarming proportion of forest degradation in this region.

The loss of forest cover in N-E region because of the practice of shifting cultivation accounts for 1526 sq. km. and for other reasons the loss is 377 sq. km.

In most of the states as mentioned in preceding para, the dense forest cover has shown a deslining trend thereby setting in a chain reaction in the degradation of ecosystem.

In 1995 assessment (fifth cycle) the State wise and above forest category wise detail are not given but it has shown that in totality there has been an increase in the dense forest and Mangrove but open forest has shown a declining trend. Presently, the Forest ecosystem is under tremendous pressure on account of excessive removal of biomass in all forms including diversion of forest lands to non forest uses.

Forest policy and land management in India

Our forest cover has dwindled notwithstanding three successive National Forest Policies. A scientific land use policy alone can ensure sustained production, ecological balance and environmental benefits. It is time that the Forest Policy is reviewed and a new strategy adopted keeping in view that conservation includes preservation, maintenance, sustainable utilization, restoration and enrichment of the environment. Man depends on natural resources from his forest environment for all his basic needs. No doubt, the majority in the industrialized countries is no longer dependent on the natural living resources but the bulk of the rural and a section of the urban population in India and the rest of the developing world continue this dependence, especially for their fuel, fodder and timber needs. The forest serves many valuable functions as has been reflected in the national forest policies. Moreover, forest plays an active role as a storehouse of living organisms of potential use and as a regulator of rainfall, soil and water regime, source of many basic needs of the weaker sections of the rural population. The relationship between land, climate and forest is such that if the soil is allowed to deteriorate or lost, degradation of both land and vegetation becomes inevitable. Unfortunately, in the developing countries like India, biotic pressures are intense.

Problems with India's forests

The situation is worsening in spite of the lofty aims propagated by the three successive national forest policies. In India, although the first policy is nearly a century old, the present forest cover is worse than when it was originally proposed. The failure of the national forest policies is perhaps due to their focus on government forests rather than to the land and soil in general. There has been a lack, of scientific land use policy having legal backing and public support. For these reasons, the definition of 'forest' has come to imply land area constituted as reserve forests and not general tree cover.

Biotic pressure

The tremendous increase in human population, the resultant poverty nd the heavy dependence on agriculture have resulted in the use of wood as the main fuel. India's ecology is today no better with the deficit of firewood at 145 million m^3 and 43 million ha of land brought under the plough between 1951 and 1976 for the extension of agriculture. The loss of forest area for various purposes during 1951-76 was substantial. The situation has still remained the same and the condition has not changed as is evident from the cases of some of the States. The problem has worsened due to excessive grazing coupled with forest fire. About 52 per cent of India's forests are incapable of regenration largely due to the combined effects of biotic pressures. In a developing country like India, forests have suffered badly because of the failure in land management practices. To what extent can we put the blame on forest policies? Are the policies wrong or inconsistent or is it that the policies have remained merely ceremonial documents devoid of the will to implement or people's support? An analysis of the forest policies of India would reveal that the main cause of failure has been, perhaps, viewing forests in isolation rather than taking into consideration the country's soil as a whole. It is after all the soil which supports all kinds of plant life in the biosphere.

Forests are a renewable source and contribute substantially to economic development. They play major role in enhancing the quality of environment. The country has an area of 752.3 lakh hectare notified as 'forests, of which 406.1 lakh hectare is classified as reserved and 215.1 lakh hectare as protected. Unclassified forest area is spread over 131.1 lakh hectare. About 19.47 per cent of the total geographical area of the country is under actual forest cover.

Forest policy and law

India is one of the few countries which ahs a forest policy since 1894. It was revised in 1952 and again in 1988. Main plank of the revised forest policy of 1988 is protection, conservation and development of forests. Its aims are: (i) maintenance of environmental stability through preservation and restoration of ecological balance; (ii) conservation of natural heritage; (iii) check on soil erosion and denudation in catchment area of rivers, lakes and reservoirs; (iv) check on extension of sand dunes in desert areas of Rajasthan and along coastal tracts; (v) substantial increase in forest/tree cover through massive afforestation and social forestry programmes; (vi) steps to meet requirements of fuel wood, fodder, minor forest produce and soil timber of rural and tribal populations; (vii) increase in productivity of forest to meet the national needs; (viii) encouragement of efficient utilisation of forest produce and optimum substitution of wood, and (ix) steps to create massive people's movement with involvement of women to achieve the objectives and minimise pressure on existing forests.

The entire gamut of forest activities are being given a new orientation in the light of the National Forest Policy of 1988. Some of the important areas for immediate and effective protection of forests include afforestation and development of wastelands, reforestation and replantation in existing forests, settlement, restriction on grazing, encouragement for wood substitutes and supply of other kinds of fuel, elimation of forest contractors, discouragement of monoculture practice etc.

Forest conservation

Increasing destruction and degradation of forests and treelands especially in the Himalayas and other hilly areas, is contributing to heavy erosion of top soil, erratic rainfall and recurring floods. It is also causing acute shortage of firewood and loos of productivity due to eroded and degraded lands. The Forest (Conservation) Act, 1980 enacted to check indiscriminate deforestation/ diversion of forest lands for non-forestry purpose was amended in 1988 to make it more stringent by prescribing punishment for violations.

Another area of concern has been degradation of forests due to biotic pressure. Guidelines have been framed for preparation of working plans and felling in forests. Some of the salient features are: (i) working plans shoudl be up-to-date and stress conservation; (ii) preliminary working plan should have multi-disciplinary approach; (iii) tribal rights and concessions should be highlighted and with control mechanisms; (iv) grazing should be studied in detail and specific prescriptions should cover fodder propagation; (v) shifting cultivation and encroachments need to be controlled; (vi) clear-felling with artificial regeneration should be avoided as far as possible and clear felling blocks should not exceed 10 hectare in hills and 25 hectare area in plains, and (vii) banning all felling above 1,000 metre altitude for a few years should be considered to allow these areas to recover. Critical areas in hills and catchment areas prone to landslides, erosion etc., should be totally protected and quickly afforested.

Guidelines have been issued in June 1990 to state governments for involving village communities and voluntary agencies for regeneration of degraded forest lands on usufruct shraing basis. As a follow up of these guidelines, 14 states have issued appropriate orders. These states are: West Bengal, Orissa, Bihar, Madhya

Pradesh, Rajasthan, Gujarat, Maharashtra, Tripura, Himachal Pradesh, Haryana, Jammu and Kashmir, Andhra Pradesh, Karnataka and Tamil Nadu. Other states are being persuaded to issued such orders.

Firewood

Firewood occupies a predominant place as an energy source in rural areas. As against the estimated requirement of about 15.7 crore tonnes of fuelwood per annum, recorded production is only 5.8 crore tonnes. Due to scarcity of firewood, considerable quantities of cowdung and agricultural residues are burnt as fuel leading to air pollution. It is expected that programmes of renewable energy sources and augmenting fuel growth in wastelands will help in closing the gap.

Forest fire control

Fire is one of the major factors responsible for destruction of forests in the country. In India, most of the fires are man-made and are generally deliberate and on rare occasions accidental. The causes of deliberate fire incidences are grazing, mahua seed and flower collections, tendu leaf collection, poaching and shifting cultivation, etc. In order to reduce the incidents of fire in India, the following steps have been undertaken by the forest department: (i) development of firelines and (ii) establishment of watch towers besides employing fire watchers during fire seasons. In order to develop the techniques for detection, prevention and suppression of fire in the country, a UNDP assisted Modern Forests Fire Control Project was initiated in 1984 in Chandrapur, Maharashtra and Haldwani/Nainital, U.P. Techniques like development of better communication network and effective use of hand tools and other equipments developed under the projects have proved successful in reducing the fire damage. In addition, fire danger rating system, wireless network, fire reporting system and hand tools etc., were designed. This scheme is being continued in 11 states of the country.

Wildlife

The National Wildlife Action Plan adopted in 1983 provides the framework of strategy as well as programme for conservation of wildlife. At present the protected area network comprises 80 national parks and 441 sanctuaries covering 4.5 per cent of the total geographical area of the country. The Wildlife (Protection) Act, 1972 adopted by all states except Jammu and Kashmir (which has its own Act), governs wildlife conservation and protection of endangered species. The Act prohibits trade in rare and endangered species. India is also a signatory to the Convention on International Trade in Endangered Species of Wild Flora and Fauna. Under this, export or import of endangered species and their products is subject to strict control. Commercial exploitation of such species is prohibited. The Centre provides finanacial and technical assistance to states for: (i) development and improved management of national parks (ii) protection of wildlife and control of poaching and illegal trade in wildlife products; (iii) eco-development in areas around national parks and sanctuaries; (iv) conservation of elephant and its habitat; and (v) conservation of rhinos in Assam. The Wildlife (Protection) Act, 1972 has been amended to make the provisions more effective. Endangered species of plants and animals have been brought under the purview of the Act. A Central Zoo Authority has been set up to look after the management of zoological parks in the country. The Authority has since notified rules for recognition of zoos which stipulates the standards for upkeep, maintenance and veterinary care of animals. It coordinates the activities of over 200 existing zoos and also supervises the exchange of animals on a scientific basis. Project Tiger, one of the premeir conservation efforts of the country has completed 20 years in April 1993. Under this scheme 21 Tiger Reserves have been set up all over the country. A Global Tiger Forum has been set up for Tiger Range countries and an interim secretariat has been set up at New Delhi. A Tiger Crisis Cell has been set up to obtain all the information essential for conservation of the tiger.

Animal welfare

The Animal Welfare Board of India, established in 1962 under the provisions of the Prevention of Cruelty to Animals Act, 1960 is an autonomous organisation of the Ministry of Environment and Forests working for the cause of animal welfare in the country. A series of camps for training the members of SPCAs and Animal Welfare Organisations are being held all over the country, in collaboration with the Royal Society for Prevention of Cruelty to Animals, London. The Board also celebrates Animal Welfare Fortnight from 14 January every year.

National forest policy

Forest policy—precedence of agriculture: The first National Forest Policy initiated nearly a century ago, while stressing the important role played by forests in conserving the ecology of the country, had expressed in no uncertain terms that the role of forests was secondary to that of agriculture. However, it suggested that, except for the reserved forests (the preservation of which was essential on climatic and physical grounds), if the demand for permanent agriculture arose, forests should give place to it and even in the case of economically rich forests, the considerations of forests income were to be subordinate to that of satisfying the needs of the local population for forest produce. Further, the areas excluded from reserved forests should be managed in the interests of the local population for forest produce as distinct from the general public.

The National Forest Policy of 1952 was framed at a time when pressure on land had begun to be exerted and the slogan 'grow more food' was at the cost of forest covered areas. It stressed that a system of balanced and complementary land use was of permanent importance,and contradicted the considerations that neighbouring areas and agricultural requirements should be entitledto a prior and preferential claim over forests. It supported the necessity of forest not only on the slopes but also in flat areas with dry conditions.It countered demands for the clearance of forests for extension of agriculture, saying that the solution to the food problemof an increasing population lay in intensive cultivation. It suggested that India should aim at maintaing one-third of its land area under forests.

The current National Forest Policy (1988) recommneds increased afforestation in view of the wide gap between demand and supply and the evident allround degradation of the land, and the desire that the mountainous region should have forests over 66 per cent of the land area. The policy also stresses that the poorer people should be encouraged in the afforestation programmes, and that land grant rules and land ceiling laws should not be subverted. Giving first priority to the local needs, the policy recommends sharing of forest revenues with local communities from social forestry plantations. It is also against the supply of forest raw materials from natural forests to industry, implying mismanagement in the forestry sector, and holding forest-based industries and contractors partly responsible for the deterioration of forests.

The only aspects of land use touched upon are the afforestation of denuded wastelands nd the ban on diversion of good agricultural land to forestry plantations. The policy generally refers to blocks legally constituted as reserve forests with no recommendations or restraints on the use of the remaining 77 per cent of the land area outside the reserve forests. There is no suggestion on prohibition of cultivation on steep slopes in the Himalayas on the Western Ghats, or in the semi-arid and arid regions. Tree-covered government land not classified as reserve forest continues to be released for cultivation. This includes government land in the mountain belt also.

Regularisation of encroachment on government land is a priority issue with the Centre and many State governments. It recommends that revenue from forestry plantations should be shared with the local people. While acknowledging that 29 per cent of all energy consumed in the country is from firewood, compared with 55 per cent from commercial energy, the document has pointed out that the share of the forestry sector in the VII plan was around three per cent of the commercial energy sector. The afforestation contemplated in the 1988 policy is more in the nature of poverty alleviation schemes rather than through development of forests. While the policy advocated strict grazing practices, entry of cattle into reserve forests continues to be free and unregulated.

Perceptions differ

In the developing countries like India, classification of land use is adopted with the focus on conservation and prevention of forest sites being used for agriculture rather than for promoting afforestation in sites unsuited for agriculture. Hence the extent under forests invariably refers to the area of the government forest, the minor distinction being reserved forest and unclassified forests. It does not necessarily imply are under tree cover. The position is different in the developed countries where the areas designated as forest are fully clad with tree growth and can belong to government, companies, co-operatives or private individuals. The imperative of wage structure as in Canada; tax incentives and agricultural pricing policies as in the UK; strong tax support as in Brazil, legal requirements with tax incentives as in Sweden, or simply the requirement by law as in Switzerland has promoted private forests mainly in land unsuited for agriculture in these countries. Presently, Japan is promoting increased use of wood for house construction. Such wood, mainly produced through private enterprises, will far exceed its consumption and Japan does not wish the afforestation programme to suffer a set-back for economic reasons. Development has unfortunately implied increased agricultural production, mainly through the expansion of the area under agricultural crops. In many regions and terrains, soil and climate may not be suited for sustainable agriculture. Therefore, proper scientific land classification alone can provide for sustained production, ecological balance and environmental benefits.

Our economic and ecological sustenance can be ensured only through the care of the soil involving several factors including population growth and poverty. Redemption from poverty cannot be through indiscriminate extension of agriculture in unsuitable areas but through intensification of production. This could be through industry, handicrafts or production of the best suited crop for the site. A forest policy has more meaning if it prescribes specific scales for the use of land based on site factors, rather than deliberating on the advantages of ecological equilibrium. The government must devise measures and means to implement the land use policy with as much concern as it devotes to the protection of the country's frontiers. Wherever a tree crop is the best alternative, it should be grown.

It is time to assess the results of the 1988 policy, because of the steady decline in both the extent and quality of forests, occurrence of floods and droughts, which result in the national loss of 600 million tonnes of soil annually and the widening gap between demand and supply for firewood which will increase from 144 million m^3 to 300 million m^3 in the next evolve a new strategy of forest conservation keeping in mind that conservation includes preservation, maintenance, sustainable utilization, restoration and enhancement of the natural environment.

Forestry is one of the cheapest option to bring about a change in rural economy of the country. Forests not only give fuelwood, small timber, timber, and fooder to the people but it also conserves water and soil moisture for the agro-eco system. Development and conservation of forest area will help rural people to improve their level of loving. The forest wasteland has immense potential in this respect. Degradation of forest has been going on because of various pressure groups on the forest eco-system. Today, various agencies give different figures for the extent of waste land avaliable in the country. Forest Survey of India has given 31 million hectares of degraded forest in the country, though the actual figure may be higher. The Ministry of Environment and Forest considers and extent of forest wasteland around 35 million hectares. The problem of increasing wasteland becomes more complex if the non-forest wasteland is also taken into consideration. The National Commission on Agriculture (1976) has given a figure of 176 million hectares of wasteland available in the country while Society for Promotion for Wasteland Development has given 129 million hectares as wasteland in the country. To arrive at the actual figure the job for assessing wasteland in the country has been assigned to National Remote Sensing Agency (NRSA) and it is believed that a conclusive figure would be provided in the beginning of Ninth Five Year Plan (1997-98).

Regardless of the extent of wasteland available in the country, it becomes all the more important to develop them on priority basis so that the basis requirement of the local populaltion is fully met. The total annual availability of fuelwood and small timber from the forest is 26290 thousand cum. and 8 million cum. respectively whereas the total requirement of fuelwood, fooder and small timber of the country has been estimated and found to be much higher than their annual availability.

All eco-systems develop a set of specialised and integrated structural and functional properties which are in delicate balance. In a stable ecosystem, all the system variables may return to the initial equilibrium, if the disturbance is moinor. The stability of a system, however, may be exclusively or collectively determined by the extent of its resistance and/or resilience. Exploitation of natural resources beyond the threshold limits imposed by the resistance and resilience of the ecosystem warrants immediate attention. Any further mismanagement can lead to damages beyond repair. For example, tropical moist forests, rich in genetic resources, are continuously under biotic pressure resulting in soil erosion, floods,l loss of species, loss of biomass and many others. Therefore, the management of each ecosystem should be site and problem specific if the forests have to be conserved an developed on the principle of sustainability. This has also been seen after a very careful review of the various schemes in the Forestry sector that this sector has not been dealt with adequate attention from planning point of view. For example, the scheme titled "control of forest fire" covers only five states in the country though it is a menace which not only disturbs the existing ecosystem but also leads to extinction of many flora and fauna. Likewise, control of poaching, rhino conservation, forest protection, natural regeneration are many areas where regular efforts or schemes are needed to strengtrhen the infrastructure in general and capacity building in particular.

Management of non-wood forest products

Non-timber forest products (NTFP) and non–wood forest production (NWFP) are terms that are being widely used currently to denote what was termed minor forest produce earlier. The term NTFP as is used now broadly includes fuel and fooder, biomass, bamboo, cane, grasses, fibre, oil, tannin and dyes, gums, resins, medicinal plants, barks, leaves flowers, fruits, tubersl, mushrooms, seeds, mammals, birds, reptiles, fish and insects etc. The term minor forest produce clearly indicates that the produce was not of any great economic importance to merit serious consideration. However, recent facts and figures give altogether a different picture. NTFPs accounted for nearly "two fifths of forest department revenue and three fourths of net exporet earnings from forest produce. About 70% of the NTFPs are collected from the five states of Maharashtra, Madhya Pradesh, Bihar, Orissa and Andhra Pradesh (World bank, 1991). Sixty five per cent of India's tribgal population live in these five states.

It is estimated that employment opportunities through collection of NTFP can be increased from 0.8 million to 3.3 million persons/year. Again it is estimated that out of approximately 571.85 women days of women's employment generated in forest based enterprises, 90% is in small scale enterprises using NTFP as raw material. It is worth recalling here, the figures for NTFP have been derived from forests which are already degraded. With the improvement of the protection status of the forests through JFM it is expected that barring a few items like bidi leaves, production of most other items will increase significantly and the total turn over in terms of money will fare exceed timber. Consequent potential as well as the export earinings will also go up. Despite all this, adequate attention has not been paid to NTFP either at the national or at the state level. Sustainable extraction of NTFPs together with processing and marketing can generate significant income and economy. In fact, in terms of employment as well as income, NTFP in many instances have been found to give better return than commercial.

India is a country of vast diversity lying at the juncture of the biogeographic provinces of Afro-Eurasia and orient. Due to its wide ranging environmental regime and diverse biological communities, it has been recognised as one of the world's top twelve mega diversity nations. There are 3000 plant species in India which yield NTFPs. But only 126 have developed marketability. According to E.O.Wilson there may be 100 million species of plants and animals in tropical forests. It is estimated that about 1.7 million species, formally identified and classified represent only 5% of the total number of species now present on earth. Though extinction of species also has been a predictable feature of evolution since life appeared on each some 3.6 billion years ago byt man has been major cause in this extinction. Species which are of MFP value only have suffered more in this regard.

The scope of NWFPs is so wide and fruitful that if properly managed the return from these products can well outweigh the losses in the revenue due to the ban on felling of trees and can help as most powerful tool for poverty alleviation of rural masses. The royalty realised through the disposal of NWFPs extracted from government forests was over Rs. 100 crore in 1985—86, which has gone up during subsequent years. The contribution of NWFPs to the total value of forest based export is over 70 per cent. Similarly out of total employment of 2—3 million man years generated by forestry sector, employment of 1.6 million man years is available from NWFP, by way of collection, processing and sale. At present, only 0.32 million tonnes of NWFPs are being collected against the production of 1.25 million tonnes. In case arrangements to extract the totsal available NWFPs are made employment on this account shall go up to 4 million man years from the present 1.6 million man years. this will not only improve the economy of poor inhabitants living in and around forests but also boost the state revenue as well as export earning of the country. Management of NWFPs has therefore, gained renewed importance in India for sustainable development.For environment and ecological security restrictons, regulations and restraints are the fundamental requirements. But the socio—economic compulsion of the socially and economically less or unprivileged people with their exploding population necessitates and culminates into unrestricted, unrestrained and unregulated use of the forest ecosystem. Both these also these also need the resource to comprise a variety of floral and faunal richness. Just contrary to these, commercial and industrial economies are concerned with the bulk production of a few commercially and industrially relevant commodities to be produced in bulk and specific sizes.

Management perspectives with regard to forest have to accomodate these situations ina balancing way. For tree species there has been bias (at least) towards commercial and industrial economies. But NTFP have so far not been adequately and properly managed even for these economies. There is urgent need to develop proper management perspective for forests in general and NTFPs in particular. NTFPs can be harvested without damaging the forest ecosystem. It should be possible to develop a management system to meet demand of certain mix of products. The trio of tribal–forest–ecology needs an urgent change in the management approach. The change should put the NTFP in forefront. First step is intimacy with the forest ecosystem and the people in and around. Optimum levels of interference patterns should be worked out. Forest ecosystem should include the resource base adiacent to forests. Assessment of what, where and how much in respect of NTFPs should be done. National, regional and local level lists of NTFPs should be prepared. Ecological, socio—economic, harvesting, storage, processing, value addition and marketing studies of listed items should be done. Forest working Plans should deal with NTFPs seperately and adequately. NTFP stock maps should be prepared.

In aerial photographs and satellite imageries layers below tree canopies should be interpreted. NTFP atlas of the country should be prepared. Management should be prescribed for species mix both horizontally and vertically. Canopy manipulations should be prescribed for yielding NTFPs. Fodder should be recognised as NTFP. Zoning based on the richness of particular NTFP should be done and maps prepared. Local and internal consumption should be recorded. Prevailing prices at different salepoints should be accurately surveyed.

Deforestation

The human population in India has increased from 361 million in 1951 to 844 million in 1991 and is likelyk to cross 1.18 billion by 2010. The danger of population pressure is lurking on unguarded forest and it may be totally wiped out if the present trend continues.

Similarly, the livestock population not only destroys forest ecosystem completely but stops its natural regeneration capacity. Unfortunately, livestock population has also shown a phenomenal rise over the years as it has increased from 155.3 million in 1951 to

429.60 million in 1987. The goat population has shown the maximum increase amongst all the livestock from 47.1 million in 1951 to 99.4 million in 1992. It is expected to cross 152.7 million by 2001 A.D. It is a widely accepted fact that goats disturb the forest ecosystem more seriouly than other animals. The other factor which has led to illegal felling of valuable timber from our forest ecosystem is primarily economic and its related market forces. The problem is of such a gigantic dimension that its impact would be felt in times to come, if it is not realised today. In Uttar Pradesh, the most populous state of India, approximately 5000 young poles of 0-10 cm. diameter class are cut illegally everyday. It is not only a serious problem from socio-economic angle but from silvicultural point of view also as the forest ecosystem is being depleted from natural regeneration and these forests are gradually turning out to be dead forest.

2

Biological Diversity

There are manifold causes for the loss of bio-diversity. Among these are the rapid expansion of industry, agriculture, urbanisation and large scale development of projects like dams, highways, mining and increased expansion and intensification of human activities. About 20 species are categorised as possibly extinct as these species have not been sighted during last 6 to 10 decades. Cheetah has become extinct during this century 0. The pressure on many mega-fauna like tiger, rihnos etc. is so intense that nothing could be estimated as yet about their future. Tiger census of 1993 has very clearly indicated a declining trend in their population. Similarly, 81 species of mammals, 47 birds, 15 reptiles, 3 amphibians and a large number of butterflies, moths and beetles, besides 1500 plant species are considered vulnerable and endangered. Unfortunately, illegal trade still continues in ivory, rhino's horns, bones of tigers and many other threatened plant species. There are many government programmes which are aiming at conservation of ecologically fragile forest ecosystem buyt their forceful implementation is lacking in the absence of forceful legislation. Biodiversity conservation was the focal point after Earth Summit held at Rio in 1992. A concrete Action Plan is the need of the hour.

Timber production

FAO estimates that in 1994, the world produced 3,419.9 mcum of round wood, out of which India's share was only 293.9 mcum (8.59%). Firewood and charcoal accounted for as much as 91.5% (269.2 mcum) of the Indian Production (FAO, 1994). Although only less than 10% of the total wood production in the country is used for industrial purpopses, industrial demand has been rising sharply. Projected demands for forest products show a 22 to 183% increase from 1990 to 2000. By a long—term trend analysis of forest products in India, Rao (1992) showed that production of almost all products except pulpwood and particles and veneer sheets registered an increase in the 1980s. Industrial use of wood has been growing at the rate of 3.5 per cent per annum, according to him.

The decade from 1975–76 to 1985–86, saw Indian production of wood and wood products recording an increase of 22 to 135%. However, statistics on timber production is less revealing, perhaps as incomplete as its demand itself. Timber is normally obtained from government forests, community and private forests and farm lands. While the timber extracted from the national forests is reported in the official statistics, the timber harvested from the other sources goes unreported in the official statistics. Therefore, the epithet 'recorded production', a gross underestimate of total production is fashionable among foresters.

According to FSI, consumption of firewood exceeded recorded production by a staggering 195 mcum in 1987. All existing projections show that there is a big gap between demand and supply of industrial timber too. Total sustained yield increment of existing forests is stated to be 35 million m^3 With an additional 4–5 million m^3 from private sources, it sums up to a grand total of 40 million m^3 (Campbell, 1987). To meet the industrial needs alone (64.4 mcum in 2000 AD, according to NCA, 1976), an additional sustained yield increment of 24 mcum will be needed. Furthermore, all indicators suggest that this gap is going to grow. Presumably this wide gap between demand and sup[ply is being met from unrecorded sources like farm lands and agroforestry and other privately owned sources.

Given this huge deficit in industrial timber availability in the country, we may probably have two options. The first, is to enhance the area under plantation forests and to improve their productivity. However, given a conservative average productivity of 0.3 cum/ha for long rotation timber and roundwood species, and 3–5 cum/ha for short rotation pulp wood, this would then mean at least 30 million ha of new plantations for timber species and two million ha for pulpwood–a total for 32 million ha for industrial needs alone (Campbell, 1987). Considering the poor productivity of forest plantations and the general inhability to expand area under plantation forestry, it is impossible to achieve such gargantuan targets through the plantation forestry route.

India's wastelands

The reclamation of wastelands is not an easy task and warrants careful approach with a defined methodology. This, in turn, requires survey and mapping of such lands in their natural environment. Such maps showing the localities of different categories of wastelands with soil and site characteristics, climate, land form, erosion, land use, etc. hould be prepared, because all these factors individually or in combination influence the growth of wasteland. Otherwise, any planning for the reclamation of the wastelands, which does not take into account the geographical aspects, may not bring about the desired result.

The basic requirement for the development of wastelands is the creation of a suitable vegetative cover which not only prevents further degradation but improves the environment. On wastelands, if a green cover with grasses, legumes, shrubs and trees is established and maintained and cutting and grazing are prohibited, the land may slowly recover on its own and may eventually even become productive. The choice of plant species for reclamation and afforestation of any type of wasteland should be such that it should suit the local conditions and grow normally with least attention.

Some of the important tree species suitable for the reclamation of degraded and wastelands are Acacia auriculaeformis, A. catechu, A. nilotica, Albizia lebbeck, Anacardium occidentale, Anogeissus latifolia, Zadirachta indica, Bambusa arundicacea, Bauhinia racemosa, Butea monosperma, Cassia siamea, Casuarina equisetifolia, Eucalyptus spp., Populus spp., Prosopis juliflora, Salix alba, Sesbania grandiflora, Syzygium cuminii, Tamarindus indica, Tamarix aphylla, Tectona grandis, Terminalia arjuna and Ziziphus mauritiana.

Many perenial grasses survive under adverse conditions and help in preventing soil erosion. Grass species such as Cenchrus ciliaris, Chrysopogon fulvus, Eulaliopsis binata, Imperata cylindrica (I. arundinacea), Panicum maximum, Panicum repens, Pennisetum pedicillatum, Vetiveriazianioides can be employed for reclaiming degraded and wastelands. Apart from the above mentioned grass species, many other herb and shrub species such as Calotropis spp, Datura spp, Tephrosia purpurea are good soil—binders and are helpful in controlling erosion and degradation.

Agro—forestry and social forestry provide an excellent basis of tree planting to prevent and reclaim soil from degradation. Agroforestry integrates agriculture and forestry on the same unit of land so as to meet the local demands of fooder, fuelwood,l timber and foodgrains and thus, further destruction of forests is stopped and a suitable ecological balance is maintained. Similarly, social forestry programme aims at growing the trees by utilising the land lying unused to meet the demand for fuel, fooder and timber, to check soil erosion and protect the ecology and environment.

Saline and alkali soils along with the acidic soils are the major problematic soils, the former often referred to as salt—affected soils.

Reclamation of alkali soils, basically, requires replacing of excess sodium on the soil exchange complex by calcium through amendments (gypsum being the cheapest and abundantly available) and leaching out of the exchanged sodium form the rootzone. For any lasting reclamation, provision of adequate drainage is important. Growing crops tolerant to alkalinity of soils such as barley, wheat, sunflower, etc. may ensure reasonable returns during the initial phases od reclamation. Similarly, management of waterlogged saline soils basically involves lowering of water—table below the root zone of crop and leaching of excess salts with good quality water. Acidic soils could be corrected by adding amendments such as lime to the soil.

Afforestation of wastelands through proper financial assitance by various agencies would provide income and employment opportunities to the poor and improve the quality of the environment. The government can play a facilitating role by removing obstacles and simplifying procedures. The lack of ground-level data has affected the afforestation programme, the author feels. The afforestation of wastelands has now emerged as an important feature in the present socio-economic and political scenario in India, which aims at solving the problems of scarcity of timber, firewood, fodder and other forest produce as well as reclamation of wastelands and degraded forests. India has vast tracts of wastelands, and these lands are mostly owned by government and village Panchayats and are highly degraded. Tree plantation is the socially optimum and ecologically-sound use of such lands. It may not be economically desirable for a farmer to plant trees on good lands which have a very high opportunity cost in terms of value of agricultural production forgone. However, tree planting may be profitable for a farmer in region prone to recurring drought and having unproductive soil which is not fit for growing agricultural crops.

Although the practice of planting trees is as old as cultivation of other crops, the need for government intervation to promote afforestation was articulated by the National Commission on Agriculture (NCA) in 1976. The government of India accepted the NCA's recommendation and subsequently various afforestation programmes like farm forestry, rehabilitation/ reforestation of degraded lands, formation of community woodlots and strip plantation were started in some States in the late seventies. Recent evidences from various parts of the country indicate that the success of afforestation programmes has been remarkable. In India, there is still a vast scope for implementing afforestation programmes in regions which are not yet brought within the fold of tree plantation schemes and in which there is acute shortage of firewood, timber and other forest produce.

In conjunction with technical guidance and financing, availability of wastelands for afforestation is the other crucial component of the wastelands development and afforestation programmes determing their success. There are many constraints which are hampering the implementation of afforestation programmes in various parts of the country. The non-availability of wastelands for afforestation programmes is one of them. In the absence of a comprehensive survey of land use, several estimates have been made about the extent of wastelands in India. One of the estimates of wastelands indicate that about 175 million hectares of (m ha) land fall in this category. The other estimate by the Society for the Promotion of Wastelands Development (SPWD) puts it at 129 m ha-93 m ha in non-forest area and 36 m ha in forest area (SPWD, 1984). The National Wastelands Development Board (NWDB, 1989) estimates wastelands to the extent of 120 m ha with 40 m ha in forest lands and 80 m a in agricultural lands. According to Singh (1994), more than half of the geographical area of India consists of degraded lands. The estimates for wastelands range between 38.4 m ha (11.7% of total geographical area of the country, Directorate of Economics & Statistics, GOI, New Delhi 1978-79) to 175 m ha (53.2% of total geographical area of the country, Ministry of Agriculture & Co-operation, New Delhi, 1982). However, Bentley has estimated that 200 m ha of land in India are partially degraded in terms of short-term productivity. According to Khan, the wastelands which may ultimately be available for development would not be more than 80 m ha, bulk of which is degraded forests and marginal agriculatural lands. There are many other estimates of wastelands in India.

The information needed for assessing the potential of non-forest and cultivated lands, like ownership, extent and type of degradation, and present and future uses, has never been collected on a systematic basis for the entire country (Romm, 1981). Recently, some initiatives have been taken to improve the availability of grass roots level data for this purpose. The Government of India has already implemented a National Wastelands Identification Project to identify the extent and type of wastelands in 146 districts in 19 States.

Greening wasteland

One of the most serious problems threatening the country today is its population growth. Although the foodgrain production in the last few years has kept pace with the population increase, the daunting task of feeding each and everyone in the next century is the biggest challenge before us. In our attempts to meet such increasing demands, the improper and over—use of chemical inputs had deteriorated the agro—ecosystems to a considerable extent. Moreover, the pressure due to growing human and cattle population on the land has added to the deterioration of land status of the country. The increasing deterioration of land due to soil—erosion, injudicious use of chemical fertilizers, water logging, salinity/alkalinity, shifting cultivation, etc. necessitates a more scientific approach towards the utilisation of these lands, often termed as degraded or waste—lands. The growing awareness world over on the environment conservation and the emphasis on the concept of 'sustainability' has focussed on the area of 'wasteland utilization' as an important component of 'sustainable development.'

There are various aerial estimates of wastelands in the country varying from one—third to one half of the country's total area. The primary reason of the variation in such estimates could be ascribed to the fact that until recently, wastelands had neither been systematically defined nor identified. The first comprehensive attempt to map out such areas and categories them, was done by the National Commission on Agriculture, which estimated different types of wastelands and suggested guidelines for reclaiming and developing such land.

The Commission had estimated the extent of wastelands in the country to be 175 million hectares which is more than half the total geographical area in he country. However, this estimate was not based on scientific data. As per an estimate by the Society for Promotion of Wastelands Development, the area under wastelands is around 129 million hectares or about one—third of country's total geographical area.

According to the statistics presented, the state with the greatest expanse of wastelands in the country is Madhya Pradesh with 20.14 million ha very closely followed by Rajasthan with 19.93 million ha. The states with over 10 million ha of wastelands each are Andhra Pradesh and Maharashtra. Gujarat, Karnataka and Uttar Pradesh have each approximately 9 million ha of wastelands.

To a layman, wasteland is a piece of land which is lying uninhabited or uncultivated. These lands are also commonly perceived to produce much less than their potential. Despleted of the green cover and productivity, such lands are often in a critical condition. Boradly, wastelands may be defined as land where the production of biomass is less than its opotimum productivity. Wasteland also refers to lands which are economically unproductive, ecologically unstable and subject to environmental deterioration.

According to the Technical Task Group, constituted by the Planning Commisison and NWDB (National Wastelands Development Board), wasteland is defined as that land which is degraded and is presently lying unutilised except as current fallows due to different constraints.

Wastelands have been classified by NWDB into culturable and unculturable wastelands.

Land which is capable of or has the potential for the development of vegetative cover and is not being used due to different constraints of varying degree is termed as culturable wasteland. The culturable wastelands comprise the following categories:

— Gullied and/or ravinous land;

— Undulating upland with or without scrub;

— Surface–waterlogged lands and marsh;
— Salt–affected land;
— Shifting—cultivation area;
— Degraded forest—lands;
— Degraded pastures/grazing—lands;
— Degraded non forest—plantation land;
— Strip—land;
— Sands; and
— Mining/industrial wastelands.

Lands, which can not be developed for vegetative cover, are defined as unculturable wastelands. The unculturable wastelands comprise the following categories:

— Baren rocky/Stony wastes/Sheet–rock area;
— Steep–sloping area; and
— Snow–covered and/or glacial area.

Besides the above categories of wastelands, the following could also be included:

— Over cultivated soils leading to depletion of micro–nutrients;
— Acidic soils; and
— Land overgrown with aggressive weeds.

The major causes of land being rendered waste include—deforestation, overgrazing, faulty water management practices, extensive mining activities, etc. Deforestation and overgrazing distinctly hastens the process of soil erosion and land degradation. Faulty water managemnt practices lead to problems such as water logging, soil salinity/alkalinity, etc. Deforestation has often been described as the most primary reason of land degradation and the factors in deforestation are—conversion of forest land into agricultural land, the urban and industrial demand for forest products, indiscriminate quarrying for mineral resources, etc. Besides the above mentioned casuses, the environmental factors like slope, intensity of rainfall and the pedogenic characteristics of a particular area interact to increase the formation of wastelands.

An important feature of the SFP has been the raising of trees on the tank foreshore areas. The afforestation of the tank foreshores has been taken up with various objectives such as (a) to prevent the farmers adjacent to the tank-bed from encroaching; (b) to provide a source of income to the local government through sale of forest produce; (c) to provide a source of income to small farmers by giving a claim on forest produce raised on the tank foreshores; and (d) to reduce the pressure on the forest for firewood and small timber.

But our observation is that the scheme has failed not only to fulfil the above objectives but also has taken away several advantages hitherto enjoyed by the village community.

As the villagers do not possess any swimming pools and playgrounds, they were using the village tanks for playing when the tanks were empty and for swimming when the tanks were full of water. Such benefits have been taken away by planting the trees on the tank foreshores. Earlier, tanks were major component of the common property resources in many villages, which the villagers were using extensively for grazing of cattle during summer season. On several occasions, small and marginal farmers used to grow very profitable cash crops such as cucumber, watermelon and other vegetables. Because of plantation, they have lost a source of income.

Further, tanks were used as pathways for transporting manure to land and bringing the agricultural produce to the harvesting yards. The planting of trees has deprived the villagers of this infrastructural facility.

Afforestation on tank foreshores has badly affected fishing activity depriving the villagers of nutritous food in the form of fish. Besides, the raising of trees such as Acacia Nilotica on the tank foreshores has resulted in water pollution (on account of cumulative accumulation of leaves, flowers, thorns and pods on the tank-beds and their subsequent decomposition) making it difficult for the villagers to use iteither for drinking, bathing or washing purposes. One has to carefully examine these issues more scientifically.

Now we venture to make some suggestions to tackle the above mentioned problems relating to the Social Forestry Programme.

In order to make people participate actively in social forestry activities, efforts should be made to create proper awareness among them through door-to-door canvassing, training programmes, shows of documentaries, besides displaying eye-catching billboards at strategic places like local markets, shops, schools and so on. It is also important to make serious efforts to impress upon the people that common property resources belong to them and that it is their responsibility to maintain them for the collective good of the community.

VSFC should comprise such members as are enthusiastic and community-welfare oriented. Efforts shuld be made to convene meetings frequently to discuss issues concerning forestry Programme can also be given to selected VSFC members. Last but not least, a vast VSFC should be formed on an informal basis comprising villagers from different sectons of society, and not through election; for, elections may possibly politicize the functioning of VSFC.

Before selecting plots, the people should be consulted about the soil and environmental suitability of the sites. It will avoid any conflict which may arise between officials and local people at a later stage. Further, the plantation work should be carried out in phased manner as it would help the villagers graze their livestock in the implanted areas.

The fruit bearing and timber giving plants can be raised on common property resources. More incentives should be given to the private land owners who like to take up agro forestry on a large scale.

The success of social forestry activities depends on the co-operation of the people, but in the absence of social cohesiveness—due to excessive commercialization—the government and NGOs have an important role to play not only in the revival and management of common property resources but also to see that benefits of Social Forestry Programmes 'rickle down' to the common people as the social needs of the people for food, fooder, firewood and timber may not be met within the market framework.

While the government can take initiative in reviving and maintaining CPRs till such time as the process becomes community-based, NGOs can act as a catalyst in mobilizing people and creating awareness among them about CPRs.

It is also important that revival and maintenance of CPRs is viewed as a component of the overall development process through institutionalization of people's participation as it is well-known that there is a close relationship between forest, agriculture and 'sustainable development.'

India's indigenous communities

Degradation of forest land and denial of forest resources

due to rigid local forest laws have seriously affected the local indigenous communities. Limited substitution possibilities or alternative sources of livelihood have added to their improverishment. Better management of forest resources by redefining their access to forest resources and clarifying their roles and responsibilities is the need of the hour. Their deprived status can be improved, if not fully restored, by involving them in decision-making regarding regeneration of forest wealth. The subject of environment and development has become a critical topic especially in the context of the modern race towards industrialization. As more and more of industrialization is taking place leading to sizeable increase in national income, the costs in terms of permanent loss of limited environmental resources is also being realized in most quarters. Experts across the world are searching for models which would yield 'industrialized development' which at the same time is 'environment-friendly'. The search is still on but the 'trade offs' in terms of destruction of environment has become continuous phenomena.

In the current development literature, there are at least four schools of thought on environment and development. The conventional or old school of thought is the 'exploitative school' which is preoccupied with maximum gain in terms of the present generation and takes a narrow view of 'development' as that of creating material assets. It propounds the view that natural resources like any other resources exist for the purpose of development and maximum effort should be made to maximize use of such resources for obtaining higher returns. In recent decades, this school has fallen from grace and three other schools have emerged which are propounding the theory of sustainable development, where the development needs to be sustained much beyond that of the present generation. Such schools emphasize on the fragility of environmental resources, the critical life-support system which environment provides and the permanent damages inflicted to environment as a result of development activity.

One such school is conservationist school which argues that any development activity needs to consider the 'trade off' in terms of environment and any such damage done to environment needs to be adequately compensated. Another school is the preservationist school which believes in having standards set and areas and zones of nature preserved from development activities. The environment is not meant for development and there has to be rules, regulations and standards for preserving nature. Still another school is the extreme school of sustainable development which believes in maximum ecological preservation where human beings are to live in harmony with nature. Hence, sustainable development has different dimensions contours depending on the school propunding it.

One of the most urgent and crucial tasks was the identification of the primitive tribal groups. The VI Plan emphasized the identification of these groups and then taking up unique programmes for each group relevant to its ecosystem. The Working Group on tribal development for the Sixth Plan admitted that in planning for tribal development, the basic handicap was the lack of basic statistical data relating to the Scheduled Tribes.

The Dhebar Commission also mentioned that many tribals in order to circumvent the provisions of the Act related to land, changed their names and adopted non-tribal names. Mundas changed to Mahadeo Pal because Mahadeo Pal is not a Scheduled Tribe. This change of name resulted in the parting of lands by the tribals.

In Darjeeling areas, the Bhutias took advantage of the Alienation Act and got lands from poorer sections of the tribals, i.e. Lepchas, at very nominal prices. Article 350A of the Constitution lays down that adequate facilities for instruction in the mother tongue at the primary stage of education shall be endeavoured to be provided. To protect and promote tribal language and culture and to search out talent, tribal language must be promoted as medium of instruction at the primary level. The Central Institute of Indian Language, Mysore, NCERT, and State Tribal Research Institutes have been making their contributions in the preparation of textbooks and teaching aid and materials.

The Dhebar Commission also mentioned that the tribals and their leaders emphasized that the instruction in primary schools be imparted to them through their mother tongue. Teachers from amongst them, or tribal dialect-knowing teachers may be appointed. Boys and girls may be taught in their mother tongue up to the primary stage. In Sikkim, Lepcha language is being taught up to the primary stage.

A recent report of the Planning Commission also mentions that 'a policy decision had to be taken in regard to adoption of tribal language as medium of instruction at the primary stage', and suggested that the efforts of various agencies in this direction might be coordinated.

Another important aspect involving the improvement of life of the weaker tribe is education. While the overall situation in the field of tribal education improved as the literacy percentage went up from 11.3 in 1971 to 16.35 in 1981, and 23.03 in 1991, yet the general awareness of the tribal community to protect itself from economic and exploitative onslaught from outside has not improved much.

Formal and non-formal education, forest education, and vocational courses need to get due emphasis. Teacher should be recruited from amongst the tribals so as to engender confidence among the children and make the school functional, and minimize absenteeism among teachers. As the Christian missionaries have done for the spread of education in the north-eastern States, so should the voluntary organisations be encouraged to do among the tribal people.

A few years ago, the Ministry of Education at the Centre set up a committee consisting of social scientists, educationists and administrators et al to examine the relevance of educational curricula and contents to the tribal context and make appropriate recommendations. What happened to the Committee is not known. The committee should be revived to take up its work urgently.

The VII Plan emphasized that education in tribal areas be given highest priority; and scheduled Tribe boys in large number be placed on vocational courses; non-enrolment and drop-outs be reduced; low literacy areas and low literacy groups among Scheduled Tribes be identified; and residential schools be opened in such areas.

Surprisingly, an element of exploitation entered into the tribal areas through educational institutions permitted to be run by non-government outside agencies. Permission to such new schools to be opened may not be granted, no foreign funds be allowed to flow to educational institutions in these areas whether through foreign agencies or voluntary organizations within the country, unless a specific clearance had been obtained.

Hostel facilities at primary, middle and secondary levels both for boys and girls, sports facilities and encouragement to various aspects of tribal culture in the sphere of art, music, painting and dance be provided. Institutions like Lalit Kala Akademi, Sahitya Akademi, Sangeet Natak Akademi, besides, Tribal Research

Institutes should undertake to encourage these. There is no end to the debate on environment and development. However, instances of the preservationist approach is to be found in the local indigenous communities living in and around forests. In real life, such communities have been seriously affected as a result of both degradation of forest land and their reduced accessibility to forest resources on account of strict forest laws. Degradation of surrounding environment and rigid forestlaws have adversely affected food accessibility, livelihood options and quality of life of local indigenous communities. Such degradation has often caused periodic phases of hunger and malnutrition in the absence of supportive means of livelihood for acquiring basic essentials of life.

Forest plantations of eucalyptus and other species no longer provide the rich biodiversity available earlier in natural forests. Common property resources, in which groups of local people have co-equal use rights, such as community pastures, community forests, wastelands, village ponds, rivers, etc have declined at a rapid pace. Such phenomenon has led to a diminished role of local natural resources which have traditionally constituted invaluable asset-base for meeting basic needs and livelihood requirements of indigenous communities.

Such relatively undisturbed lands include forests, grasslands, wetlands, water bodies, etc which constitue habitat for indigenous communities, plants and animal species and thus contribute to maintenance of human and biological diversity. Such lands perform important environmental functions and also constitute essential means of livelihood. As far as fragility of such ecosystems is concerned, the indigenous communities have traditionally presented little threat to sensitive ecological zones, because their production systems have been sustainable, scattered over a large area, and they have traditionally kept encroachers, poachers and others out of the area.

The benefits provided by forests, trees and common property resources are basic to such communities and amongst direct benefits, the following are included:

— food such as nuts, wild fruits, vegetables, leaves, flowers, roots, stems honey, wild animals insects, etc;

— habitat and shelter;

— raw materials like bamboo, canes, fibres, oils, bhabbar grass, waxes, resins, gums, dyes and wood for furniture and capital equipment for agriculture, artisanship, etc;

— wood for building, fencing, tool making, etc;

— firewood;

— medicines and drugs;

— fodder such as grass, branches, twigs and leaves, grazing sites;

— means of livelihood, both seasonal and annual;

— shade;

— ornaments, religious items and cultural symbols; and

— drought relief.

Apart from direct benefits, forests, trees and common property resources also provide indirect benefits, such as preventing erosion, conserving moisture, conserving water, recycling nutrient, preventing drought or reducing its impact, providing leaf manure, fixing nitrogen by leguminous trees, regulating climate and rainfall, providing greenery and beauty and reducing pollution.

In short, forests, trees and common property resources provide safety nets to the local indigenous communities. In the presence of spiraling prices, reduced wages in real terms, unemployment, sickness, reduced productivity from land, and recurring shortages, forests, trees and common property resources act as a kind of safety net for local communities, protecting them from the harshness of market forces. They come to the rescue by providing a safety net against food and livelihood insecurity, drought attacks, pest attacks, illness, pollution, high prices, high rents, etc. They play a dominant role in providing alternative sources of livelihood and in offering coping strategies to local communities.

3

Crop Productivity and Agriculture

The second International Crop Science Congress, held in New Delhi from November 17 to 24, has displayed the International scientific community's will to solve the mankind's basic problem of hunger and to lay the foundation for a vibrant, yet ecologically sustainable, agriculture to meet future needs. The world's largest assembly of crop scientists, over 1500 from nearly 70 countries, emphasised that the modern biotechnology, coupled with traditional wisdom, can mould future to suit the interest of the human society. Though new challenges will keep cropping up, the science would perhaps not only be able to deal with them but might indeed convert them into opportunities for the good of humanity.

The optimism would, however, hold true only if it is matched by political will to raise farm productivity as also to distribute its gains equitably. New technology accompanied by appropriate marketing policies and international cooperation holds the key to ensuring foods security in the years to come.

Deliberations of the mega scientific event, organised jointly by the National Academy of Agricultural Sciences (NAAS) and the Indian Council of Agricultural research (ICAR), once again confirmed the widely held notion that while the scientists would be able to cope with humanity's needs they may become helpless to cope with its greed. The world renowned agricultural expert, Dr. M.S. Swaminathan, who chaired the Congress, did not mince words in passing on this message. He said: "Whether in agriculture or aquaculture, we must curb the greed revolution and promote an ever-green revolution capable of bringing about continuous advances in terrestrial and aquatic productivity without harm to the environmental capital stocks of land, water forests, biological diversity, oceans and climate upon which such advances depend."

The theme of the Congress, "Crop productivity and sustainability—shaping the future"—was highly appropriate and topical for several reasons. Despite phenomenal growth in food production, nearly one-fifth of the world population is still malnourished and hungry. The impact of the green revolution is waning and concerns of productivity decline in major crop production systems are being expressed globally, diminishing per capita availability of land and water resources, expanding biotic and abiotic stresses and natural resources, including land, forest and environment, are fast degrading. This calls for greater resolve to ensure synergism among productivity, profitability and sustainability of major cropping systems. Moreover, for safeguarding food and nutritional security at the household level, crop intensification and diversification are needed on an ecologically sustainable basis.

Agricultural development projects

The Agricultural Development Projects (ADPs) with the assitance from the World Bank are being implemented in the states of Bihar, Rajasthan and Tamil Nadu to enhance the long term sustainability in agricultural development and to create necessary infrastructure in the rural areas. Besides, three on-going ADPs, a project for Assam has been recently negotiated and three ADP proposals in respect of Andhra Pradesh, Maharashtra and Haryana are in the pipeline and under active consideration.

UNDP/FAO supported 'Farm Centred Agricultural Resource Management (FARM) Programme' has been started in 1994. Five on-going watersheds of NWDPRA have been selected as demonstration sites for the programme.

Danida aided projects

The Government of Denmark initially launched one Integrated Watershed Development Project in the State of Karnataka in 1990-91 to cover an area of 41,032 hectare at an outlay of Rs. 11.25 crore for five and a half years. Keeping in view the successful implementation of this project DANIDA agreed for a phase-II project which has appraised in February 1995. The second project i.e. Comprehensive Watershed Development Project, Tirunelveli, Tamil Nadu, to cover an area of 18,000 hectare with an outlay of Rs. 6.25 crore for three and a half years is in operation since 1990-91. Second Phase of this project has been negotiated and the project has become operational from 1994.

Another DANIDA assisted Comprehensive Watershed Development Project is in operation from 1992-93 in Koraput district of Orissa to cover an area of 43,000 hectare at a cost of Rs. 13.25 crore. The fourth project i.e. Comprehensive Watershed Development Project in Tamil Nadu-Ramanathpuram has also become operational from 1994 to cover an area of 11,000 hectare at a cost of Rs. 13.03 crore. Appraisal of a Comprehensive Watershed Development Project in Madhya Pradesh was completed. Appraisal report of this project has been received.

European economic community assisted projects

European Economic Community (EEC) assisted Integrated Watershed Management Project namely, Doon Valley Integrated Watershed Management Project is in operation in Uttar Pradesh since April 1993 with an area of 1,72,155 hectare at a cost of Rs. 808.5 million for nine years. The major components are social forestry, livestock, horticulture, minor irrigation, agriculture, soil consevation, energy conservation, community participation, management and administration. South Bhagirathi (Phase II) Integrated Watershed Management Project, has started in 1989 for a period of seven years with an outlay of Rs. 141.75 million to cover an area of 48,915 hectare. Bhimtal Integrated Watershed Managment Project, UP was implemented from 1991 for a period of seven years to area of 21,582 hectare at a cost of Rs. 115 million. the major components are forestry, agriculture, soil conservation horticulture, minor irrigation, animal husbandary, pilot and administration activities.

FHW Germany assisted projects

Two KFW Germany assisted watershed development projets, one in Maharashtra at a cost of Rs. 550.75 million and another in Karnataka at a cost of 12 million DM are being implemented. During 1995-96, under Maharashtra Integrated Watershed Development Project monitoring of the progress under on-going micro-watershed project and appraisal of new micro-watershed projects will be carried out. Under Watershed Organisation Trust (WOTR) Project training activity and identification of non-governmental organisations (NGOs) will be taken up. Under Karnataka Watershed Project field activities will be initiated.

Swiss development cooperation assisted project

The Project aims to develop five watershed in five districts of Karnataka (three agro-climatic zones of Karnataka state) in line of the ongoing Participatory Integrated Watershed Development Project (PIDOW). This project is to be taken up in the districts of Bidar, Gulbarga, Bijapur, Raichur and Chikmanglur of

Karnataka covering a project area of 30,000 hectare (74,968 hectare of geographical area). The Project aims to develop the watershed with the active participation of the farmers by developing Sanghas as Self Help Groups with the active collaboration of NGOs in each of the district. The estimated cost of the Project is Rs. 20.73 crore for 1995 to 1998.

Agricultural development

To have an overall idea about the extent of development in the field of agriculture in South Assam only a few indicators, namely creation and utilisation of irrigation potential, use of high yielding variety of seeds and consumption of fertilizer were taken into account for their analysis. It was found that upto 31st March, 1994 only 39,164 hectares of land were brought under irrigation in South Assam. There has been a very poor tendency of increase in the creation of irrigation potential for the last five years in this part of the state. Least irrigation potential has been created in the Hailakandi district. Karbi Anglong is the only fortunate district having both the minor and medium/majopr irrigational facilities. Surprisingly only 35.2% of the total irrigated area comes under the three plain districts as against 64.8% in the two hill districts.

As far as the utilisation of these potential is concerned there has been very poor response from the farmers in the area. A wide gap has been observed between the irrigation potential created and their utilisation. Excepting in Karbi Anglong, there has been more or less diminishing tendency in the utilisation of irrigation potential. This necessitates the importance of conducting an intensive study on the problem to identify the reasons and suggest the remedial measures. The study also reveals that the degree of utilisation of irrigation potential like its creation is found to be more in the hill districts than that of the plain districts,. Uniformly more weightage has been given to Kharif crops in the utilisation of irrigation potential in all the five districts. only a meagre 10% of the total irrigation potential has been utilised for the Rabi crops.

It is shocking to note that the area under high yielding variety (HYV)of paddy in South Assam has decreased from 1.4 lakh hectares in 1991—92 to 1.3 lakh hectares in 1993—94. This tendency is common to all the districts excepting hailakandi. More than 78% of the total area under HYV of paddy in this part of the state has been in the plain districts only. It is also observed that the farmers are using HYV seeds in three different seasons. Out of 1.3 lakh hectares of land brought under HYV, 73.4% and 24.7% of it have been devoted to winter and autumn paddy respectively and only a meagure of 1.9% to summer paddy and thus, keeping enough scope of utilising HYV seeds for producing summer paddy in these districts.

It is equally painful to note that consumption of fertiliser in agriculture is far from satisfactory. In 1993—94, more than 98% of the total fertiliser consumption was in the plain districts only. Moreover, there is an indication of insignificant increase in the consumption of fertiliser over the last five years. Besides, the use of fertiliser has been very poor in Rabi crops in comparison to Kharif crops.

In view of the above mentioned facts it is, thus felt necessary to state that there is a greater need on the part of the Government to take some bold steps to solve these chronic problems. There is an urgent need of increasing the literacy rate in South Assam and particularly in the Karbi Anglong district. Creation of more irrigational facilities is a must for the overall development of agriculture in south Assam in general and the plain districts in it in particular. There is a need to encourage the farmers to utilise the available irrigation potential to the maximum and paricularly steps be taken to see that rabi crops are not neglected in this regard. Since the area is very remote there is also a need for creating awareness among the farmers in the hill districts to use fertiliser and HYV seeds through some extension programmes.

High yielding variety programme

High Yielding Variety Programme was started in 1966-67 as a major plan of agriculture strategy for increasing production of foodgrains in the country. Cropwise details are shown in table 1. The programme is supported through a number of Centrally-sponsored schemes and thrust has been shifted from single crop to cropping system approach since 1994-95. Identifying potential areas, the country has been grouped in three major cereal based cropping systems viz., (i) Integrated Cereal Development Programme in Rice Based Cropping System Areas (ICDP-Rice); (ii) Integrated Cereal Development Programme in Wheat Based Cropping System Areas (ICDP-Wheat); and (iii) Integrated Cereal Development Programme in Coarse Cereal Based Cropping System Areas (ICDP-Coarse Cereal).

These thrust programmes are designed to increase the productivity and production of foodgrains through adoption of latest scientific production technology. Minikit demonstration programme aims at popularising newly released varietity and getting the newly released evolved varieties tested under field conditions. For this a large number of seed minikits containing 0.25 kg to 10 kg seed are distributed at a nominal cost to farmers. State level training programmes are being organised at agricultural universities and ICAR research institutes in collaboration with concerned state agriculture departments to disseminate the latest crop production technology to the district/block level extension officers.

Dryland/rainfed farming

About 990 lakh hecare area in the country is rainfed accounting for 70 per cent of the net sown area of 1,410.6 lakh hectare. Crops grown and cropping practices followed in these areas entirely depend on the rainfall which is often erratic and unpredictable. Bulk of the crops like rice, *jawar, bajara,* other millets, pulses, oilseeds and cotton are grown in this area under rainfed conditions. Farmers in these areas, particularly, small and marginal, are still practising subsistence farming and are in the vertex of vicious circle. Wide fluctuations in production occur in these areas year after year. Increasing and stabilising agricultural production in these areas is, therefore, of crucial importance.

Government has given high priority for the development of dryland areas and, therefore, several programmes and projects have been launched for utilisation of potential of these areas for: (i) realising the projected requirement of about 240 mt of annual food production by 2000 AD and to smoothen out fluctuation in annual production; (ii) reducing regional disparities between irrigated and vast rainfed areas; (iii) restoring ecological balance by greening rainfed areas through appropriate mixture of trees, shrubs and grasses; and (iv) generating employment for rural masses and reducing large-scale migration from rural areas to already congested cities and towns. Holistic approach for integrated farming system development on watershed basis in rainfed areas would be main pursuit of the development activities under the National Watershed Development Project for Rainfed Areas (NWDPRA) in the Eighth Plan.

Agricultural implements and machinery

The Governmental programmes have been oriented to promote the farm mechanisation and make the improved and modern agricultural machines available to the farmers throughout the country with a view to increasing the agricultural production and removing socio-economical disparity among the farmers. Farmers have been provided assistance for owning agricultural machinery including tractors. The infrastructure for human resource development on farm machinery has been expanded with a view to imparting training in the proper selection, operation, repair/maintenance and management of farm machinery. During these training programmes, emphasis has also been given on the energy conservation techniques in the use of agricultural machinery. Besides this, farm machines are tested with a view to evaluating their performance characteristics and upgrading their quality. However, despite a progressive increase in the use of agricultural machines, its sustainable benefits towards agricutural development have not been uniform in-as-much as only the improvement has mostly been in the northern states and in a few pockets/areas where irrigation facilities have been developed.

Although animal and human power continue to be the main power sources in agriculture, yet the power driven machines, namely tractors, power-tillers and combine harvestors continue to be in the frontline of farm machanisation. Fuel efficient tractors and better quality farm machines are now available in the country. Tractors are mostly sold in Haryana, Punjab, Uttar Pradesh and Madhya Pradesh and power tillers in Assam, West Bengal, Karnataka, Tamil Nadu, Kerala and Maharashtra.

During the Eighth Plan, thrust has been given to popularise the improved animal/power driven implements and small tractors with the objectives of promotion of mechanisation and to reduce the drudgrey associated with the farm operations. Water management has also been given specific attention and the water saving devices *viz.,* sprinkler and drip irrigation system have been promoted through oilseeds, pulses and horticulture development programmes. Industrial designs, prototypes, jigs and fixtures have also been developed * . These schemes would give a fillip to the promotion of agricultural mechanisation in the country.

Farm Machinery Training and Testing Institutes set up a Budni (Madhya Pradesh), Hissar (Haryana), Garladinne (Andhra Pradesh) and Biswanath Chariali (Assam) impart on-the-job training in selection, operation, maintenance and management of farm machinery. These institutes also undertake testing of farm machinery to ascertain their performance characteristics and suggest improvement in their quality. So far over 43,000 personnel were trained and 1,160 test reports on farm machinery released. Two more institutes are likely to be set up in Rajasthan and Tamil Nadu. To suplement the efforts of these institutes five state agricultural universities have been identified for undertaking training on farm machinery and two agricultural universities for testing activities.

State agro-industries cooperations

The Government of India and state government jointly established 17 state agro-industries corporations with the objective of streamlining input distribution and extending other agro-services to the farmers. These have significantly contributed to agricultral development, improvement of agro engineering services and promotion of agro-based industries during last two decades. Corporations in Gujarat, Haryana, Kerala, Maharashtra, Punjab and Madhya Pradesh earned estimated profits totalling Rs. 1,192.61 lakh during 1993-94. The National Productivity Performance Award for 1991-92 in the agro-industries sector was won by Punjab Agro-Industries

Corporation Limited and Certificate of Merit for sustained productivity efforts was won by the Gujarat Agro-Industries Corporation Limited.

Dangerous machines act, 1983

The Dangerous Machines (Regulation) Act, 1983 provides for the regulation of trade and commerce in production, supply, distribution and use of the products of any industry producing dangerous machines with a view to securing the welfare of labourers operating such machines, and for payment of compersation for the death or bodily injury suffered by any farmer/labourer while operating any such machines. The scope of the Act extends to the 'Dangerous Machines' intended to be used in agriculture and rural sectors. However, presently, only power thresher used in the agricultural production process has been brought under the purview of the Act.

The Government of India has adopted Integrated Pest Management (IPM) as a major thrust area and main plan of crop protection programme during Eighth plan. IPM approach is eco-friendly which aims at minimal use of hazardous chemical pesticides by employing all available alternate pest control methods and techniques such as cultural, mechanical and biological and bio-pesticides.

Plant protection

The Government of India has set up IPM Farmers Field Schools (FFS) for rice, cotton, sugarcane, vegetables, oilseeds and pulses etc., to impart training to farmers and extension workers. During, 1994-95, 844 farmers field schools were organised wherein 3,934 extension officers and 25,161 farmers have been trained. Besided 585 agricultural extension officers have been trained through season long training programme organised in rice, cotton and vegetables in various states.

The surveillance for pests and diseases on economically important crops was carried out by sample roving survey on an area of 5.55 lakh hectare and about 1,464 million parasites and predators were released for controlling identified pests on important crops during 1994. All the strategic areas in Thar desert were kept under continuous watch from April to October 1994 by conducting regular surveys and a few small concentration of locust hopper/adults of two grasshoppers species were detected and controlled over a total area of 327 hectare in Jaisalmer, Barmer and Jodhpur areas. As a result of timely operation swarm formation of locust has been effectively checked. To upgrade the skills of farmers and locust staff, two field training on locust control, one each at Bikaner and Palanpur were organised during November 1994.

The current legislation governing the plant quarantine rules entitled, 'The Plants, Fruits and Seeds (Regulation of Import into India) Order, 1989 (PFS Order 1989) came into force replacing the PFS Order 1984 in the wake of New Policy on Seed Development (NPSD) effective from 1 October 1988. The inspection procedure has been simplified in order to boost the export of floriculture and other agricultural commodities under NPSD.

The National Plant Protection Training Institute, Hyderabad continued to organise training programmes on various aspects of plant protection with special emphasis on IPM. It organised 30 training courses for master trainers in which 375 persons were trained. Beside special training course has been organised for technical personnel of fertilizer industry in Integrated Pest Management technology.

The Registration Committee constituted under the Section (5) of the Insecticides Act, 1968 received a total of 3,206 applications out of which 2193 registration certificates have been granted under various sections/ subsections of the Act. With a view to promote safer and non-chemical pesticides in IPM, biocides and plant origin pesticides like *Bacillus thuringiensis* and *Bacillus sphaericus* and need based pesticides have been provisionally registered and allowed commercialisation.

Property rights and Indian agriculture

There is massive evidence to support the fact that appropriate legal protection acts as an incentive for productive research. The Uruguay Round, which was concluded in 1994, marked the beginning of a significant transformation in the global economic and trade environment. Annex 1c of the final Act deals with the agreement on Trade-Related Aspects of Intellectual Property Rights (TRIPs). Section 5 (Part II) of the annex pertains to "Patents" under article 27. With reference to agriculture, the text states, "Members shall provide for the protection of Plant Varieties by Patents or by an effective sui generis system or by any combination thereof'. Since the Indian Patents Act (1970) excluded to put into place a sui generis system by evolving a legislation on plant variety protection (PVP) by the year AD 2000.

The 1970 Act was also inadequate in terms of covering processes but not the product patents in food, medicine, drugs and substances provided by chemical processes. It now stands amended through a presidential ordinance (31/12/94), thus ushering in a new patents regime.

The TRIPs agreement has introduced profound changes which will influence competitiveness, generation and diffusion of technological innovations and ultimately the technological development prospects of developing countries (DCs) The impact of the changes can thus be far-reaching, though at this early stage it is difficult to assess the full implications of the agreement. An attempt is made here to consider, in a preliminary manner, some possible implications of the new regimes. IPRs constitute an important element of trade negotiations. The GATT accord on TRIPs has raised a whole lot of apprehensions and engaged the attention of intellectuals, politicians, farmers and media for quite sometime now. The legal dimensions of TRIPs make it difficult to understand, and vulnerable to a host of misgivings. Some discernible patterns can be identified in areas relating to limited duration, PBR and exclusions. By and large, the low income and lower-middle income countries do not accord PBR and have shorter protection periods. Pharmaceuticals and foodstuffs are the most commonly excluded products.

Myth and reality

The debate on the implications of TRIPs began with reference to pharmaceuticals. Subsequently, myriad views have been expressed regarding the possible impact of TRIPs accord on Indian Agriculture.

Issues relating to germplasm and biotechnology are substantial and valid, but these are best pursued independently of the PBR debate. PBR is not a panacea, but can serve the farmers by increasing their access to improved seeds at reasonable prices by augmenting the efforts of public systems through private seed firms.

Educating the farmers

Research studies have pointed out a two—way relationship between education and other investments to improve agricultural productivity. Education—in the wide sense of the term primary education, literacy as well as extensional deucation and training—is a prerequisite qqqfor introducing modern methods of farming relying on fertilizers and new varieties of seeds.

Four basic stages of agricultural technology have been identified by Maureen Woodhall in a book on Education and Development and they are: (a) traditional farming depending on father to son tradition; (b) use of a single modern input like fertilizer, seed; (c) Several complementary inputs simultaneously; and (d) full irrigation—based farming. Each stage calls for different levels of education to farmers commencing from literacy, maintenance skills, rudimentary knowledge of chemistry and biology and ability to calculate the effects of changes in crops, climate and so on.

It is through adequately qeqducated farmers who constitute local resources and by making available such local resources for improving agricultural productivity that the Ninth Plan target of 4.5 per cent rate of growth in agriculture can be achieved. In such an approach, requirements for improving agricultural productivity and rural development converge and it is this model of rural development through local resource mobilizaton which is the crying need of the hour. With the present level of educational backwardness, it may be difficult to achieve the agricultural growth target. But with adequate human resource development, it will be possible to achieve to goal.

Education appears to be a prerequisite to increase the yield from other types of agricultural investment, Formal education of farmers also improves the effectiveness of agricultural productivity. The extension services will become more effective if farmers have a basic level of education. This raises the question of whether the formal and non—formal education including agricultural extension are substitutes for each other.

Tamil Nadu experience: In this connnection, it is worth referring to Tamil Nadu's effort to raise productivty through investment in human resources. In

1994—95, a sum of Rs. 76 crore was allotted for human resource development to upgrade the knowledge and skill of the persons engaged in the development of agriculture, fisheries, agricultural engineering, forestry, etc. For agricultural productivity improvement through broad—based extension activities, Rs. 41.81 crore was set apart in the State budget.

There can be productivity and social change simultaneously in the rural sector. For gaining an insight into this aspect one can look at theories of social and institutional transformation as an integrated process of economic development as Schumpeter, Adam Smith, Veblen,Max Weber have advocated. Farmer education should be regarded as one link in an integrated system of generating and transferring knowledge. Other links are research and the production system like industry, services, etc. A good system of communication will serve as an intemediary.

For quite some time now Tamil Nadu has been following though not explicitly the above model. It has been called knowledge, attitude, performance and practice (KAPP) model resulting in considerable improvement in productivity in al crops (e.g. rice productivity improved from 1,306 Kg in the fifties to 3,116 Kg in the nineties).

The local needs can be carefully identified and resources can be mobilized both locally and from various sources. On the basis of the local needs a plan will have to be carefully drawn up for this purpose. There are income generating shcemes through self—employment and wage—employment and both of them should take note of the local resource endowment and the over all development strategy. At present, it is not done adequately because of the absence of local planning. Efforts should be made to get the best out of such schemes through the development of human resources and better linkage with all development schemes.

Evergreen revelution

In agriculture, an Evergreen Revolution is called for, signifying the sustainable use of natural resources.As the eminent scientist Dr M.S. Swaminathan says the time has come to lay emphasis on knowledge-based inputs rather than on the physical inputs only (such as fertilizers and seeds) to derive the best from the land without depletng its inner strngth. A learning revolution is to be brought about. Fortunatley, icon–based computer technoloy shows that literacy need not be a barrier in bringing about a better awareness of theecofriendly methodsof cultivation. *It would beachallenge for the plannersto decentralize the knowledge based on agriculture to cover villages using computers and telecommunication links.* Modern ecofriendly practices such as biologicalpest control and post–harvest technologies) should find high priority on the S & T agenda.

It is heartening to note that the Ninth Plan approach has emphasized the importance of biocontrol agents and biogenic fertilizers.

The TRIPs agreement would require substantial changes in the patents regime of our country. Most developed countries, as they are members of the UPOV Conventions, accord protection to plant varieties. By contrast, only a handful of DCs have sui generis protection systems (e.g. Argentina, Chile, Kenya, the Republic of Korea, Uruguay and Zimbabwe). The PVP legislation proposed to be enacted is modelled on the basis of the International Union for the Protection of new Varieties of Plants (UPOV) guidelines. UPOV 1978 version allowed for the rights of plant breeders and farmers, whereas UPOV 1991 is more stringent in the sense that it disallows both. There is general consensus that we opt for UPOV 1978 and this option is available only till the UPOV 1991 is ratified by at least five member countries. But the...fourth International Conference on Plant Genetic Resources, at Leipzig (Germany), has vindicated the state of the DCs. It succeeded in getting a global endorsement for farmers rights, paving the way for the member countries to enact PVP legislation in ways that best serve their respective national interests. The "World Intellectual Property Organization WIPO) model law for developing countries on inventions" can serve as a general outline for the proposed law on PVP.

Although, patent laws are inherently a national issue, it is time we join (albeit, selectively) various international conventions/treaties, so that cost of obtaining patents and international search reports can be reduced substantially. Also, keeping in view the distinct variations in cost of patenting across nations, there is a case for differential slabs of application fees for foreign applicants seeking patents in our country. Judicious provisions for compulsory licensing and non-voluntary license should be the feature of the proposed legislation to curb possible patent abuses. The proposed PVP has adequate safeguards to take care of farmers, researchers and environmental concerns. It is high time that the proposed legislation is enacted so that this unnecessary irritant in our trade relations, particularly with the DMEs is removed.

The TRIPs agreement aims at a certain minimum standard of IPR protection. Successful implementation of the TRIPs agreement has a number of prerequisites, the important ones being legal, administrative and institutional reforms, appropriate research investments, and first rate science and technology capability. Provided the IPR protection is adequate and effective (worldwide), the TRIPs accord can promote innovations, transfer of technology, foreign direct investment, use of genetic resources and environmental protection. The returns from the economic value of protection system far outweighs its costs. However, while legal protection may be a necessary condition for innovative activities and technology transfer, it is by no means a sufficient condition, given the importance of a host of other factors affecting research investment and the transfer and diffusion of technology in DCs and its ability to internalize benefits from the new rules of the game. The nation's capacity to move from technology importer to technology exporter will be the major determinant of its position in international hierarchy. Foresight demands towards quality and frontier areas.

Creation of a patent cell in the ICAR, is a step in the right direction. Having a clear-cut intellectual property policy and promoting patent literacy (similar to CSIR) among its scientists, must be the next logical step. A massive awareness programme needs to be undertaken to clear doubts regarding the process of patent application and registration, patent information services, inspection of files, determination of national need and the whole gamut of related issues.

To maximize opportunities, DCs must foster and reward entrepreneurship and evolve a regulatory environment conductive to technological innovation. An effective IP regime will provide the synergy between the private and public sector research institutions. This will then provide a basis for future growth and development, particularly in the case of India which has a large pool of scientific manpower.

Allied sectors

Apropos the sectors allied to agriculture, the strategies are as follows:

Attention is to be paid towards proper blending of technology, credit, scientific management, post—harvest infrastructure and marketing for higher growth. Steps will be taken to increase productivity of perennial fruits and spices, reduce losses at different stages of storage, grading, packing, etc (which amount to 20%—40%) by developing a sound post—harvest infrastructure.

Steps will be taken to increase productivity, accelerate replanting activities, expand this sector in non—traditional areas, improve packaging and enhance quality standards.

R & D activities for production of quality fish seeds and feed are to be intensified. to increase fish production and productivity, indiscriminate growth of brackish water farms is to be checked, overexploitation of coastal fisheries will be prevented, and the marketing infrastructure is to be developed.

This subsector will get greater attention in the Ninth Plan, for it has substantial employment generating avenues, particularly in the rainfed and drought—prone areas. Effective control of animal diseases, declaration of disease—free zones, scientific management of genetic stock resources, extension services, increasing production, productivity and profitability of livestock enterprises, etc will be areas of concern in this Plan. Priority will be given to improvement of breeding services, upgradation of health care services, fooder and feed activities, strengthening of training and research facilities, provision of adequate credit and marketing support, extension of processing facilities and measures for involving entrepreneurs, co–operative institutions and voluntary agencies.

Agro—exports are soght to be given fillip, in recognition of the valuable foreign exchange they bring, besides opening up new employment avenues. The strategies in this sphere are: development of markets and products, branch names and dissemination of information among exporters, improvement in quality and packaging, encouragement to export—oriented units and enhancing backward linkages with growers.

The role of co—operatives is to be enhanced—they are to be made more efficient, viable and competritive, through greater professionalism, diversification of activities, evolving effective recovery systems, technology upgradation, quality improvement, human resource development, etc.

Plantation crops

Tea

Tea is India's traditional item of export besides being the most commonly consumed beverage. The domestic demand for tea has been rising faster than the expansion in its production, thus generating pressure on exportable surplus. Tea is a foreign exchange earner with negligible import content, besides being an important source of revenue to the Government. More than a million workers find employment in the tea industry. In 1995-96, 762.35 million Kgs. of tea was produced which was 34 per cent higher than preceding year's output of 737.4 million Kgs. Export of tea rose to 163.65 million Kgs. valued at Rs. 1191.19 crore in 1994-95. For 1996-97, a production target of 790 million Kgs. and an export target of 180 million Kgs. has been fixed.

Coffee

Karnataka state dominated with 53 per cent of country's are under coffee. Arabica and Robusta are the two main varieties grown accounting for 49 per cent and 51 per cent of area respectively under coffee. In 1995-96, coffee output was 2.23 lakh tonnes, bulk of which (76 per cent) was exported. Apparently, coffee has emerged as an export oriented product. Coffee export during 1995-96 was 1.70 lakh tonnes valued at Rs. 1524 crore. In September, 1996, trade in coffee was totally deregulated. Growers are now free to sell their entire production in the domestic or export market without any quantitative restriction or compulsory routing through Coffee Board. Goverment also put decaffeinated/roasted coffee on OGL which allows free import in case of domestic scarcity. Country's demand for natural rubber is largely met by indigenous production, with only a small proportion (less than 5 per cent) met through imports. Production of natural rubber has increased from a modest 15,830 tonnes in 1995-51 to 3.3 lakh tonnes in 1990-91 and 5.07 lakh tonnes i 1995-96. Area under rubber has also gone up from 4.75 lakh hectares in 1990-91 to an estimated 5.22 lakh hectares in 1995-96. Kerala is the major rubber producing state and, together with Tamil Nadu, accounts for 86 per cent of the total area under rubber contributing over three fourth of total rubber production. Rest of the 14 per cent of area is located in Maharashtra, Tripura, Meghalaya, Mizoram, Manipur, Assam, Nagaland, Andaman and Nicobar Islands, Goa, Orissa etc. Most rubber plantations are small and the average size of holding is 0.5 hectare only. As against production and consumption during 1996-97 is 5.42 lakh tonnes and 5.56 lakh tonnes respectively. Import of natural rubber from time to time is necessary to bridge the gap between demand and supply. Yield per hectare has increased from 284 kg. in 1950-51 to 1130 kg. in 1991-92 and to 1422 kg. in 1995-96.

Holticulture and folticulture

Immense agro-climatic diversity enables India to grow a large variety of horticulture crops which include fruits, vegetables, flowers, spices and plantation crops. Frcm organised upland tea and coffee plantations to extensive and often dense coastal strips of coconut trees as also the subterranian tuber and root crops characterise the variegated nature ofthe potential in the country. The country holds the first position in global production of bananas, mangoes, coconut and cashew and is amongst the first ten in citrus, pineapple and apple production. India holds first position in global production of cauliflower and is amongst top ten in production of potato, tomato, onion and gree peas. Horticulture products-fruits, vegetables, flowers, cashew, spices etc. account for nearly 25 per cent of total agricultural exports. Floriculture—the production of flowers-has emerged as a promising area of high growth in recent years, particularly for its potential of export of cut flowers. In 1994-95 export of flowers was estimated at Rs. 30 crore. More than 200 export oriented units have been identified for accelerating export growth in this area.

Investment of Rs. 250 crore was allocated in the Eighth Plan period (1992-97) for encouraging the use of green houses, plastic mulches and drip irrigation, with Rs. 200 crore having been earmarked for drip irrigation alone. The earlier restriction of permitting assistance for 1 hectare per beneficiary for drip irrigation was removed during 1995-96 and assistance is now provided for the entire holding of the beneficiary for growing horticulture crops. During 1996-97, subsidy has been enhanced to 90 per cent of the total cost or Rs. 25000 per hectare, whichever is less for small and marginal farmers, SC/ST and women farmers, and 70 per cent of the total cost or Rs. 25000 per hectare whichever is less for other farmers. Low cost green houses are being encouraged not only for export oriented floriculture projects but also in cold arid regions like Ladakh for growing vegetables during the off season.

Post-harvest technology

Due to lack of technology and poor ifrastructural support for handling, packing processing and preservation, substantial post harvest losses of fruits and vegetables still characterises the horticulture sector. Traditional mode of marketing fruits and vegetables currently results in an estimated loss of Rs. 3000 crore annually. National Horticulture Board (NHB) was provided Rs. 200 crore for implementing appropriate schemes (during Eighth Plan, 1992-97) for providing infrastructural support. The budgetary provision for 1996-97 is Rs. 41 crore.

Farming in the hills

In the hilly terrain of nagaland farmers have tilled land by constructing terraces. Traditionally terrace cultivation is termed as panikheti forests protect soil, they also regulate the rain water. the fertility of panikheti directly depends on the amount of land people can manage to keep under forests.

During the monsoons the fields are flooded. Rain water is used for irrigation, channelized through indigenous bamboo conduits. Young rice plants are transplanted to the panikhetis from the nurseries.

Through the months of August and September the paddy grows. During this time the paddy plants are bunched together and tied. This prevents them from being damaged by wind and reduces grain loss during harvest.

The Department of Agriculture in Nagaland has identified experts who in turn have guided farmers in other parts of the state in constructing panikhetis.

Traditional technologies

Erus provide an example of a traditional water management system still prevalent in Tamil Nadu. An ery is a reservoir of water formed by earthen embankments on three sides, with the fourth side open to the catchment to collect runoff water. Water distribution from each ery is managed by a water-users association, of which all cultivators of the area are members. To combat the problem of water shortage, people of Rajasthan and of north-east India use traditional techniques based on low-cost technology and locally available resources. A wide range of such technologies are practices even today. The rain water harvesting tank of Ranisar in Jodhpur built by Maharani Jodha in AD 1500, and a wide range of kundis in the thar desert are some marvellous examples of traditional sustainable technologies.

The people of Ladakh, inhabitting the edge of the trans-Himalayan Tibetan plateau at an elevation of 4,000 m, trap the streams coming down from glaciers with the help of small channels. The water thus diverted from the streams, towards evening, is taken into small tanks locally known as zing. The stored glacier water is then used next day in the fields. Each village has a vast network of canals and zings.

Clearing Ganga

The waters of the river Ganga sustan 37 per cent of the Indian population. Along its banks are pilgrim centres, industrial nuclei and large human settlements. As a consequence, the river is grossly polluted especially near the towns situated on its banks. The major sources of pollution are urban wasters, industrial effluents, surface runoff from waste dumps. To address these problems the Ganga Action Plan was formulated by the Government of India. A total of 261 schemes covering interception and diversion, sewage treatment plants, low-cost sanitation, river-front facilities etc. have been undertaken.

Paticipatory forest management

Van Panchayat is a democratically elected village level institution set up in Uttar Pradesh for the management of forests. It is responsible for the management of grazing, collection of fuelwood, fodder and timber, and protection of community forests. A Van Panchayat can be formed if one-third of the inhabitants of a village resolve to form one. At the village level, it is the sole arbitrator for the management of the Van Panchayat forests. It has linkages with the Forest Department of technical assistance and for the preparation of developmental plans.

Water mission

To tackle the problems of providing rural areas with safe drinking water, the Government of India set up the National Drinking Water Mission in 1986. The objectives of the Mission are identification of new sources where there are none, better management of existing water resources using cost-effective and practical technologies, development of such technologies through existing scientific know-how, and ensuring sustained supply of safe drinking water to the community.

The Ministry of Agriculture is collaborating with the council of Scientific and Industrial Research, the Ministries of Science and Technology, Health and Family Welfare, Water Resources, and Environment and Forests, Defence R&D, Departments of Space and Atomic Energy and the state governments towards achieving this end. The Mission is focusing on conservation of water and recharging of aquifers, eradiction of guineaworm, control of fluorosis, desalination of water where it is brackish, and removal of excess iron. The Mission is also coordinating with various voluntary organizations to brig about people's participation of the government schemes.

In 1976 Anna Hazare, a retired army officer, returned to his village Ralegan siddhi in Maharashtra. A victim of recurring drought, the village was a picture of economic stagnation. Hazare resolved to change things. He felt water was the key and so studied the topography of the village and initiated steps to conserve rain water. Next, soil conservation was taken up under the state government's Comprehensive Wasteland Development

Programme. Massive tree plantation was taken up, with a survival rate of 90 per cent as compared to 50-60 per cent in official programmes. Biogas plants and smokeless chulhas were installed. Today the village has proved its capability to withstand drought and has been selected by the Government as an Urja Gram (Energy Village) and is entitled to technical and financial assistance.

Forest conservation and policy

The Forest Conservation Act of 1980 is a unique piece of legislation to ensure the examination in depth of the diversion of forest land for non forest uses. It has been instrumental in slowing down such diversion while ensuring that developmental needs are married with environmental considerations.

The Forest Policy of 1988 is another landmark, wide ranging in its coverage and focusing on conservation efforts in Indian forestry coupled with sustainable utilization and people's participation.

Fodder in desert

In the thar desert rainfall levels fluctuate drastically from year to year. People therefore rely heavily on animal husbandry for survival. This in turn demands wise management of fodder resources.

The Thar desert has three excellent sources of fodder-a grass called sewan (Lesirius— Sindicus), a bush called jharberi (Zizyphus mummularia) and a tree called khejdi (Prosopis cineraria).

Sewan is an extremely nutritious grass which grows in clumps. It can grow fast even with little rainfall.

The *jharberi* and the *khejdi* provide excellent fodder during the dry months when no fodder is available. When the rains are inadequate and crops wither, with farmers are still assured fodder from these grasses and bushes. Similarly, farmers do not cut the khejdi tree. Though rarely planted, the tree grows through natural regeneration. the density of the khejdi tree in the 300 mm to 500 mm rainfall zone of the Thar desert is about 40 to 100 trees per hectare, and this gives agricultural fields the appearance of an open woodland.

In the 1970s Sukhomajri near the Shivalik hills was like most Indian villages—impoverished. It came into prominence when 70 per cent of the Sukhna lake at Chandigarh was found filled up with silt from the denuded Shivalik hills. Soil conservationists initially attempted to deal with the denudation problem through technical soil conservation measures. However, it soon became evident that the problem lay in the poverty of the villagers and not in the hills. Initiating a dialogue with the villagers resulted in an earthen water— harvesting dam being built in the hills for irrigation of fields. A system of equitable distribution of water through the villagers' own organization, Hill resource Management Society, was instituted. With the resulting three-fold increase in crop production, the villagers could stop grazing their cattle in the hills. 'Social fencing' resulted in dramatic regeneration in the hills, providing increaed fodder and fibre grasses to the villagers through hand harvesting. Sukhomajri is now capable of withstanding the severest drought.

Wasteland development

Unprotected land or land degraded due to extensive soil erosion, salinity, desertification etc. is termed as wastland. The Government on India set up the National Wastelands Development Board (NWDB) with the principal aim of reclaiming wastelands in the country through a massive programme of afforestation and other appropriate measures. While doing so it is expected to restore the disturbed ecological balance and provide employment opportunities in rural areas. The thrust in the Board's methodology is to secure people's active involvement in afforesting government as well as private wastelands.

Non-convensional energy sources

To mitigate the energy crisis by developing technologies to harness non-conventional sources, the Department of Non-Conventional Energy Sources was set up in 1982. New and renewable sources of energy are being explored. In this effort entrepreneurial activity and industrial production are based entirely on indigenously developed technology. In the fields of biogas, improved chulhas and solar energy, India is leading in technology development and application. Over 1.2 million biogas plants have been installed all over the country. These plants are capable of producing 1,488 million cubic metres of gas, the fuel value of which is equivalent to 4.38 million tonnes of firewood. In addition, these plants produce high quality enriched manure.

The forest wealth in many partsof India has undergone a serious degeneration due to continuous jhum or shifting cultivation, heavy exploitation and maltreatment by burning and lumbering and ths has made a large area of land degradable. As shifting cultivation is generally practised as a food production system, we must think of a sustainable livelihood to the concerned people while suggesting alternatives to shifting cultivaton. As a mixed land—use system, agri—horti—silvipastoral system of land–use has often been suggested. The system comprises agricultural land use towards the foothills, horticulture in the mid portion of the hill slope and silvipastoral land use, towards the top of the hill. Contour bunding and bench terracing are the common conservation measures required for treatment of such lands. Subsidiary sources of income such as fish—production units should be promoted.

Other degraded lands having special disabilities also can be reclaimed by appropriate available technologies, so that these could be made suitable for bio—mass production. For example, aerial seeding techniques could be employed for regenerating/revegetating difficult and inaccessible areas like ravines, hills/mountains, desert areas, etc.

Realising the central importance of the utilisation of wastelands and an imminent ecological and socio—economic crisis due to continuing deforestation, the Government established the National Wastelands Development Board (NWDB) in May, 1985 with the principle aim of bringing the wastelands under productive use through a massive programme of afforestation and tree planting. The NWDB has taken up a number of schemes and activities since then and perceptions of wastelands as a problem and various strategies needed to develop them have evolved, as a result of better diagnosis. Various voluntary agencies/ NGOs have also lent their helping hands in the field of aforestation and wastelands development. The NWDB has also been working in close collaboration with Indian Council of Agricultural Research (ICAR), Council of Scientific and Industrial Research (CSIR) and specialised research institutions for the development of suitable technologies for development and utilisation of wastelands.

Land in the country available for productive use in limited and with the ever increasing population, the per capita cultivated land has dwindled further. As is mentioned earlier, a large area of the country (one third to one—half as per different estimates) is considered degraded in some form or the other. It is estimated that by the year 2000, the requirement of foodgrains would be around 240 million tonnes to feed about a bilion population. In addition, the large population of livestock will also add to the deterioration of lands. In such a situation, it has become imperative not only to halt any further deterioration of land but also to reclaim, properly develop and utilise the already degraded land for sunstainable development. This would also improve the environment and restore ecological balance.

Conserving our biodiversity

India is recognized as a country uniquely rich in all aspects of biodiversity—ecosystem, species and genetic. For any one country in the world, it has perhaps the largest array of environmental situations by virtue of its tropical location, vaired physical features and climatic types. India has the widest variety of biomes, and attribute further enhanced by the meeting of three major biogeographic realms, namely Indo—Malayan (the richest in the world), the Eurasian and the Afro-tropical. India owes its unique biodiversity to this unmatched interspersion of biogeographic and environmental values. It is estimated that over 75,000 species of fauna and 45,000 of flora are found in India.

Over the centuries people in India have had a fascination and respect for this natural heritage. These sentiments were expressed in the Ishopanishad which dates back to over 2000 years.

(All in this manifested world, consisting of moving and non-moving, area covered by the Lord. Use its resources with restraint. Do not grab the property of others—distant and yet to come.)

It is seldom realized that the world's first recorded conservation measures, especially for wildlife, were enacted in India during the third century BC. Emperor Ashoka's benevolence extended to all living beings he set up hospitals and reserves for wild animals and birds, and extended his protection to many species. Some of his decres engraved in stone have survived to this day. But it was not only the rulers of India who protected and preserved this heritage. Common people were as involved. An example is that of the Bishnoi faith, founded by a saint towards the end of the fifteenth century. Bishnois emphasize non-violence and respect for all living things. They actively protect wildlife and do not permit hunting or felling of trees in their areas. In 1730 the Maharaja of Jodhpur ordered his men to fetch timber from a Bishnoi area. The Bishnois hugged the trees to save them from the axemen, and over 360 of them, mostly women and children, were hacked to death before the kings men gave up. Even today the Bishnoi lands stand apart as oases in the vastness of the desert of Rajasthan.

The tradition continues. The Chipko movement, active since 1973 was one of the most successful examples of people-oriented environmental restoration. The brave method of hugging trees to save them was adopted. This movement, in which women played a key role, led to the cancellation of tree-felling programmes in parts of the Himalaya. Today the Chipko movement is not confined to tree protection or plantation but concerns itself with the safety and preservation of the environment, as also with achieving social justice and equality. Such restoration is now being carried out in many parts of India, where local people have fully participated in its planning and implementation. Like the Chipko movement, the Appiko movement was launched to save the tropical forests of the Western Ghats. This simple, non-violent action became popular and people have joined this movement spontaneously.

Sacred groves are another unique tradition which have been responsible for preserving pockets of biodiversity in various parts of the country. Usually a part of temple land, sacred groves are areas which are important as they represent the original flora of the locality, preserved in its natural form without outside disturbance. These patches of vegetation, and sometimes the fauna within, for example snakes and monkeys, are considered sacred and are worshipped by people. Such groves occur mainly in the Western Ghats and north-eastern India.

According to a recent clasification done by the Wildlife Institute of India, the country has 10 biogeographic zones :

— Trans-Himalayan

— Himalayan

— Indian Desert

— Semi-arid

— Western Ghats

— Deccan Peninsula

— Gangetic Plain

— North-east India

— Islands

— Coastal India

The Trans-Himalayan region with its sparse vegetation has the richest wild sheep and goat community in the world. The Snow Leopard (Panthera Uncia) is found here, as is the migratory Blacknecked Crane (Grus nigricollis). The Himalaya, the highest mountain range in the world, is located at the boundary of many boigeographical regions and is therefore one of the richest areas of India in terms of habitat and species diversity.

In the north west is the desert region with extensive grasslands. The Great Indian Bustard (Ardeotis nigriceps), a highly endangered bird, is found here. Adjoining the desert is the semi-arid region, a transitional zone between the desert and the denser forests of the Western Ghats. Beyond the ghats is the Deccan plateau, which is also a semi-arid region lying in the rain shadow of the Western Ghata.

In the north is the Gangetic plain extending up to the Himalayan foothills.

North-east India is one of the richest regions of biodiversity in the country. It has several species of orchids, bamboos, ferns and other plants. This region is also one of the early centres of domestication of cultivated plants such as banana, mango, citrus and jute.

India has two major groups of islands, Lakshadweep in the Arabian Sea, and Andaman and Nicobar Islands in the Bay of Bengal. The Andaman and Nicobar Island have some of the best preserved evergreen forests of India. Several species of plants and animals are endemic to these islands. India has a very long coastline extending over 5,500 kms. mangrove vegetation is characteristic of the estuarine tracts along the coast.

All the ecosystems are under pressure. Agriculture has largely replaced natural vegetation in most of the Gangetic plain and in extensive parts of the Deccan. Over the past century, tea and coffee plantations have come up in large tracts of what used to be the most forested regions of the Western Ghats, and in the north-east. the ever-shortening rotational cycles of shifting cultivation have also been a major cause of forest loss in the north-east.

Besides agriculture, industries and large-scale felling for wood, forests have been under pressure from river-valley projects, irrigation and mining. This pressure is particularly high as most mineral wealth and some of the best sites for water impoundment lie in areas which have high biodiversity. Replacement of natural forests by plantations of teak, eucalyptus, Prosopis juliflora etc., have done nothing to stem this loss of biodiversity. In the desert and semi-arid areas where vegetation is relatively sparse, requirements of fodder and of fuelwood have led to loss of vegetation. While there is pressure on all ecosystems, the more fragile ones such as mangroves, wetlands and coral reefs are particularly vulnerable to human activity.

The creation of protected areas in recent times started with the establishment of the Corbett National Park in 1936 in the foothills of the Himalaya. With the setting up of the Indian Board of Wildlife in 1952, growing consciousness about wildlife preservation and the enactment of the Wildlife Protection Act in 1972 the number of national parks and wildlife sanctuaries grew rapidly. As of 1992 there are 75 national parks and 419 sanctuaries covering about 138,000 sq kms or about 4 per cent of India's land area. These protected areas, from marine national parks to desert parks, cover a wide range of ecosystems—from wetland areas to mountain ecosystems.

It is also widely recognized today that preservation of habitats must extend beyond protectd areas. The biosphere reserve concept which is being developed in 14 potential sites extends the conservation initiatives beyond national parks and sanctuaries through developing an overall planning strategy for the area.

National parks and sanctuaries are managed by the forest departments of the state governments. However, the initiative for the creation of protected areas has not been confined to the Forest Department but has also been taken by individuals and NGOs. The declaration of Silent Valley in Kerala as a national park is an example of people's action leading to the declaration of an areas as protected. Similarly the World Wide Found for Nature (WWF) played an important catalytic role in the establishment of 'Project Tiger' an effort which not only aimed at saving the tiger but doing so through protecting entire ecosystems which form its habitat.

There is now widespread acceptance that our management strategies for protected areas should actively elicit the participation of local people for the sustainable utilization of natural resources and the effective conservation of biodiversity. Buffer—zone development programmes which balance the conservation requirement with the resource needs of the people are being initiated by forest departments as well as NGOs. In addition, public awareness programmes for people in the buffer zones, and interpretation programmes for visitors have also been initiated.

Species diversity

The Zoological Survey of India, the Botanical Survey of India and the Forest Survey of India have been studying and documenting the plant and animal diversity of the country. Of the estimated 45,000 plants species, about 15,000 species of flowering plants have been described. Estimates of other plant taxa include 5,000 species of algae, 1,600 lichens, 20,000 fungi, 2,700 bryophytes and 600 pteridophytes. there are about 75,000 species of animals including 50,000 insects, 4,000 molluscs, 2,000 fishes, 140 amphibians, 420 reptiles, 1,200 birds and 340 mammals, and other invertebrates.

A very large number of the species described are endemic to India. Among the larger animals 79 species of mammals, 44 of birds, 15 or reptiles, and three of amphibians are threatened. Nearly 1,500 plant species are considered endangered. The main strategy for the conservation of species is the protection of viable habitats in representative ecosystems. In addition, specific measures have been taken to prevent poaching and trade in wildlife products. Special steps to check illegal trade in ivory, rhino horns, furs, skins, musk and peacock feathers have also been taken. India is also a signatory to the Convention on International Trade in Endangered Species of wild fauna and flora (CITES).

Certain species have been identified as needing a concerted and specfically directed protection effort. Projects such as Project Tiger, 'Save the Barasingha' campaign, and more recently a project on the Asiatic Elephant, have been initiated. A citrus sanctuary has been set up in Meghalaya. These programmes, though focused on single species, have a wider impact as they conserve habitats and a variety of other species.

Ex situ conservation is another thrust in conservation efforts. The Indian Botanical Garden in Howrah (West Bengal) is over 200 years old. Other important botanical gardens include those in Bangalore and Lucknow. Whereas zoological parks have been looked upon essentially as centres for education and recreation, they have also played an important role in the conservation of species such as the Manipur Thamin Deer (Cervus eldi eldi) and the Whitewinged Wood Duck (Cairina scutlata). Notable examples of successful captive breeding are those of the Gangetic Gharial (Gavialis gangeticus), turtles and the white tiger.

Genetic diversity

A great deal of research needs to be done on the conservation of genetic diversity in India. Sanctuaries and national parks have isolated populations of wild animals thereby decreasing chances of one group breeding with another. Experiments are under way in creating corridors between parks and integrating different parks into larger protected zones in order to broaden the genetic base.

India has a long tradition of breeding domestic animals for specific qualities. These include cattle, goats, pigs and sheep, as well as horses and pigeons for sport. With the focus on increasing milk yields through cross-breeding, some of the original cattle breeds are in danger of becoming extinct. efforts for the maintenance of pure breeds of native animals need to be considerably strengthened.

A good deal of attention has been paid to the genetic conservation of domesticated plants. Both in situ and ex situ conservation methods have been put into practice. However, as in the case of cattle, hybrid varieties of crops are rapidly replacing the land races. Out of an estimated 50,000 varieties of rice in India, the country may be dependent on just 300 in the next decade.

Numerous locally adapted varieties which performed well under low or no input conditions are being replaced by a few high yielding strains dependent on large quantities of inputs. Such replacement, in large contiguous areas, presents the danger of the spread of serious diseases capable of wiping out entire crops.

Ex situ collection and preservation of genetic resources is done through the National Bureau of Plant Genetic Resources (NBPGR), New Delhi, for wild relatives of crop plants, the National Bureau of Animal Genetic Resources at Karnal in Haryana, for domesticated animals, and the National Bureau of Fish Genetic Resources, Lucknow. The NBPGE is the nodal agency for providing germplasm on request to scientific and research institutions both within and outside India. The Department of Biotechnology, established by the Government of India in 1986, aims to guide, supervise and develop biotechnology programes in the country and to establish infrastructural support for them.

Genetic resources

The Government of India established the National Bureau of Plant Genetic Resources (NBPGR) to act as the nodal agency for the collection, introduction, evaluation, documentation, conservation and exchange of the genetic wealth of crop plants and their wild relatives, NBPGR has its head office in New Delhi and field centres all over the country. The bureau is also a repository for in vitro cultures of agricultural crops. The NBPGR works through regional stations and base centres, and has linkages with crop institutes and projects in India and 40 other countries.

The National Bureau of animal Genetic Resources and the national Institute of Animal Genetics at Karnal (Haryana), are the main national agencies for conserving the genetic resources of indigenous livestock and poultry. They maintain a data bank on indigenous breeds of cattle and poultry. the institute has initiated measures to conserve local breeds which are facing extinction in the near future.

The National Research Centre on Equines is the premier institute for conserving the native heritage of hcrses and donkeys. The centre conducts basic research on equine health and undertakes outreach programmes for effective transfer of technology.

The Ministry of Environment & Forest has the mandate for the conservation of ecologically fragile regions and biological diversity in India. The Ministry implements the following schemes/programmes on this:

— Biosphere Reserves.

— Integrated Action Oriented Research Demonstration and Projects for Himalayan Regions.

— Association of Scheduled Tribes and Rural Poor in the Region of degraded Forest.

— Modern Forest Fire Control Methods.

— Development of National Parks and Sanctuaries.

— Project Tiger.

— Beneficiaries Oriented Scheme for Tribal Villages of Project Areas, National Parks and Wildlife Sanctuaries.

— Eco-Development around National Parks including Tiger reserves.

— Project Elephant.

— National Afforestation & Eco-Development Board NAEB.

There are many schemes in NAEB with the mandate of conservation of ecologically fragile areas. They are :

— Integrated Afforestation and Eco-Development Project.

— Fuelwood and Fooder Project.

— Aerial Seedling.

— Non-Timber Forest Produce, including medicinal plants.

All the above schemes are supposed to address basic issues of conservation of degraded forest areas.

The State Governments have also many programmes which help conservation of ecologically fragile region. Some of the important schemes of State Plan are:

(a) Afforestation and regeneration of degraded forests.

(b) Greening of rural and urban areas.

(c) Social forestry.

(d) Development and conservation of minor forest produce

(e) Development of National Parks and Sanctuaries.

(f) Regeneration of Sal and Oak forest.

(g) Rehabilitation of common lands in Aravalli hills.

(h) Western Ghat forestry project.

Agroforestry and private forestry (industrial and non–industrial) constitute the second option in this regard. There exists a vast potential for using agriculturtal lands as sources of timber and for meeting the wood requirements of the society. Agricultural lands (net area sown) make up as much as 43.5% of the total geopraphical area of the country, while forests (including degraded) occupy only about 20%. Moreover, many of our traditional land use practices are examples of integrated, intensive farming systems/practices that blend trees with various other life forms. Trees including perennial horticultural crops have traditionally formed an integral component of our agricultural landscape. Growing trees of various kinds is part of the tradition in India. Most people also perceive the economic, social and cultural benefits of trees as a source of fruits, fuelwood, fooder and timber. The Kerala homegardens form a spectacular example in this regard. Homegardens create a forest-like multi–storey canopy structure and is also a source of tremndous agrobiodiversity.

Plantation agriculture, is another important land use activity in many parts of the country. Examples include palms, rubber and many fruit trees. Other salient traditonal agroforestry systems include, growing multipurpose trees (trees that yield fruits, vegetables, fooder, fuelwood, timber etc.) either on the farm boundaries or as scattered trees on the farm fields, growing commercial crops (tea, coffee, pepper etc.) under planted shade trees and/or trained on to them, growing commercial crops (nutmeg, clove, cacao etc.) under the shade of planted commerical tree crops (coconut, arecanut etc.) growing commerical crops (cardamom) under the shade of trees in natural forests, commercial woodlots, live fences, silvopastoralism, grazing in natural forests and shelterbelts.

A wide spectrum of trees and shrubs is often encountered in all these land use systems. The floristic elements, however, vary from region to region and depending on size of holdings, socio—economic factors and the socio-cultural background of farmers. Wood productivity in agroforestry is also correspondingly diverse. Predise macro-level data are, however, not available concerning availability and/or standing stock of wood from agricultural lands. Available microlevel studies, although limited, indicate that standing stock of commercial timber from the Kerala homesteads, is between 6.6 and 50.8 m^3 ha^{-1} (Kumar et al 1994). In another study Krishnankutty (1990)assessed the wood harvested from rubber plantatons of Kerala in 1987 at 0.999 mcum. To enhance timber productivity from the traditional land use systems, therefore, concerted efforts are necessary with respect to selection of better genotypes/provenances/clones of multipurpose trees, making available quality planting stock and evolving appropriate technological packages on tree management.

Private industrial forestry, nevertheless, is a recent phenomenon. It involves growing high value timber species such as teak and other fast growing tree species (e.g. teak, eucalyptus, popular, mangium and many soft wood species) under short rotation intensive cultural systems (SRIC) on private lands. Nonetheless, such practices are in vogue in many developed and less developed nation-states including China New Zealand etc. In the Indian context also, there are many examples where the farmers' initiative has been effectively harnessed by the wood based industries for raw material production. Examples include tree planting programmes sponsored by industrial houses such as South India Viscose Ltd., ITC Bhadrachalam Paper Boards Ltd. and WIMCO. Such industrial establishments in general supply planting stock and technology packages to the farmers besides, reaching 'buy back' agreements with them on purchase of produce. Private forestry assumes significance in view of the shrinking forest resource base and its ability to ese pressure on shrinking forest resource base. Perhaps with little over 2% of the total geographical area of the world and about 15% of its human and livestock population, India already expereinces a critical imbalance in its natural resource base. The National FOrest Policy 1988 also highlights the importance of the wood based industries producing their own raw materials.

There are, however, institutional, technological and socio—economic factors acting either separately or in unison, which constrain or obstruct the spread and diffusion on tree farming in India. Restrictions on tree felling, non–availability of quality planting stock, lack of appropriate technology packages especially for polycultural systems and the absence of public policy support hamper adoption of tree farming by private entrepreneurs. For fear of interspecific competition, many small farmers are also reluctant to grow timber and fuel wood species in association with woody perennial plantation agricultural species. Furthermore, as agroforestry extension and communication networks are choked, credit and other facilities are limited.

Agroforestry has tremendous potential to convert India into the 'wood basket' of world. Implicit in agroforestry and tree farming are two fundamental themes: ecological security and generation of income and employment. Quite apart the indirect ecological benefits, tree farming is an economically viable land use option.

Demand for timber land other forest products is expanding at a very rapid rate. Incokrporation of tree growing as part of the farm system technology can make significant contribution to the supply of wood based products. However, a paradigm shift in our planning and development thinking is imperative to make it operational. Evolving appropriate technology packages for tree farming (SRIC systems) and provision of inputs are central to this.

Lack of an apropriate public policy support and absence of technological packages too are critical constraints in this regard. Agroforestry extension is particularly weak. At present, enither the Forest Department nor the Agriculture Department considers integrated land use systems such as agroforestry important. Presumably they act as water-tight compartments, although agroforestry is a mixture of agriculture and forestry. Suitable corrective mechanisms are indispensable in this regard. This includes amendment to the restrictive provisions of laws, providing public policy and credit support to the tree farming enterprises, evolving improved post harvest processing techniques, removal of hidden subsidies to the wood based industries, strengthening agroforestry extension and encouraging farmers' initiative in rural afforestation and raw material production for wood based industries.

Social forestry programme

Analysing the performance of the Social Forestry scheme in Karnataka vis-a-vis the objectives set, the authors suggest some effective steps tomake the programme a success. Inclusionof politician in thevillage Social Forestry Committes, belated formation of the committees, the indifferent attitude of the members and the lack of awareness among the people have affected the effective management of the scheme. Serious effort are to be made to impress upon the people that the common property resources belong to them and that it is their responsibility to maintain them for the collective good. Forests are significant segment in a country's economy. In fact, they acan be considered as the very 'lifeline' of the economy, for apart from meeting the basic social needs of the people such as fodder, firewood and small timber, they also play an important role in earning foreign exchange. Indirectly also, their role is significant in retaining soil moisture, preventing soil erosion, building soil fertility and keeping the environment clean.

Of late, the tremendous increase in human and animal population, concomitant rise in the number of landless labourers and small landholders, and growing instances of enroachment of forests and other common property resources (CPRs) have led to unviable agriculture. This disturbing situation is reflected in the fact that while the cultivated land in India is more than half of its geographical area, in other developing countries like Pakistan, Sri Lanka, and the Philippines, the ratio is much lower. Besides, the cost per unit of output has increased substantially in recent years indicating strains on sustainability of agriculture.

Depletion of forest cover

A recent estimate by the satellite shows that only about 19 per cent of the land is covered by forests; it means that per capita availability of forest area is now barely 0.1 hectare as against the international average of 1.1 ha. The situation in Karnataka is no different either. The area under forest was about 18.82 per cent of the total geographical area in 1973; this proportion rose to 20 per cent during 1993-94 (according to the Forest Department data). However, the recent satellite imagery data (estimates) show that the actual forest area in the State accounts for just about 14 per cent of the total geographical area which means the per below the availablity of forest area is 0.08 ha much below the international (1.1 ha) and the national (0.1 ha) levels. Ironically, due to excessive biotic interference, even the surviving forests are getting increasingly denuded, thereby accentuating the fears about the greenhouse effect, floods, frequent droughts and loss of top soils.

New scheme to revive forests: Realizing the importance of forests, steps were taken in recent years for controlling the denudation and reviving forests. One such measures was the introduction of the Social Forestry Programme (SFP) in different States.

In Karnataka, this scheme was launched in 1983-84 with the financial assistance from the World Bank and Overseas Development Administration of Britain. A total outlay of Rs 55.23 crore was earmarked for the purpose. Of which, 47.7 per cent were provided by the World Bank, 46.6 per cent by Overseas Development Administration and the remaining 11.7 per cent were met by both the Central and State governments. This scheme came to an end in 1991-92. However, the State government continued the programme as a part of Zilla Parishads (now known as Zilla Panchayats).

The basic idea of the scheme was to convert the wasteland around the villages into economically productive lands or plantations, with the specific objective of providing basic needs like firewood, small timber, food and fodder to the rural people, bamboos for cottage industries and seedlings free of cost to farmers for raising plantations on private holdings.

4

Agroforestry's Potential for Meeting Industrial Wood Requirements

Agroforestry connotes land use systems where woody perennials (trees and shrubs) are deliberately grown with field crops and/or livestock, either simultaneously or sequentially, on the same land management unit. It implies a combination of agriculture and forestry aiming at diversified and sustainable production. Agroforestry practices frequently include tree/pasture systems, tree/speciality crop systems, alley cropping, windbreaks, living fences, etc. riparian buffers, stream band bioengineering, wildlife habitat and some other vegetation management systems also have been lately included under it. Such diverse land use systems encompassed by the generic concept of 'agroforestry', broadly falls under agrisilviculture, silvopasture, agrisilvipasture and other (miscellaneous) systems.

The basic philosophy of all agroforestry, however, is two-fold: (1) to optimise the combined production of woody perennials and agricultural crops and (2) to conserve and improve the site. Agroforestry, thus aims at ecological security, increased productivity and above all, sustainability. It is a prominent example of the traditional ecotechnological aproaches adapted by tropical farmers ('Ecotechnology' denotes technology rooted in the principles of ecology, economics and equity). Multiplicity of goods and services is a unique feature of agroforestry. Agroforestry systems in general, are capable of producing timber, fuel, fooder and green leaf manure besides, performing various ecological functions such as reducing wind speed, checking soil erosion and causing microclimatic modifications. Production of wood, however, is a dominant function of agroforestry. This is further exemplified by the fact that homesteads, a prominent agroforestry system in Kerala, contribute as much as 74.4 to 83.6% of its effective wood demand (14.645 mcum in 1987-88) and about 67.2–75% of its firewood requirement.

Estimates on timber requirements vary widely in the Indian context. Different agencies voice digressing figures. Statistics on wood requirements and availability, therefore, presents a hazy picture. Precise studies have not been conducted to assess the timber requirement in our country. Furthermore, demand for timber in the unorganised sector has been grossly ignored. The 1988 National Forest Policy also laments about the poor data environment in this regard. It states succinctly, "inadequacy of data regarding forest resources is a matter of great concern...."

Regarding India's industrial timber requirement at the turn of the century, the oft cited National Commission on Agriculture Report (NCA, 1976) indicates a ranges of 47.1 to 64.4 million cubic metres (mcum), depending on production, growth and economic development. Wood requirement of any society, is presumably a function of the size of populaltion, level of development, availability, price ad the like. The higher estimate of NCA pre–supposes a high growth rate and consumption. Of the 64.4 mcum of wood required by India in the year 2000 AD, approximately 30 million for pulp and paper and 13 million for round wood (NCA, 1976). Inventories made by Forest Survey (FSI, 1987) on demand for woood (other than firewood), however, puts India's total industrial wood requirement at 27.58 mcum and supply at 12 mcum. The Interministerial Group on Wood Substitution, estimate it as 24.88 millions. Demand projections of industrial round wood by Rai et al using a compound growth rate equation and transcendental production function had given figures such as 30 mcum and 11 mcum respectively for the year 1995. In another study, Kalla, estimated that demand for industrial roundwood in Indian in 1990 would be 24.07 mcum.

To generate knowledge of the extent and distribution of different soils for planning rational land use, National Bureau of Soil Survey and Land Use Planning (NBSS and LUP) and state soil survey units have taken up Soil Map of India Project. The soil resources and land-use maps of West Bengal, Haryana, Pondicherry, Punjab, Bihar, Orissa, Tamil Nadu and Gujarat have been prepared in 1:250,000 scale and released for users and planners. Training courses are being conducted by the Bureau to train state and agricultural university officials in the area of soil survey, soil correlation and land-use planning.

Intensive and high-yielding cropping systems suitable for irrigated areas and involving major crops have been indentified for different agroecological zones. These systems are capable of producing over 10 tonnes of grain per hectare. Cropping systems for rainfed and problem areas such as Wastel land and diara land etc., have also been evolved and watershed programmes are being advocated for sustained productivity. A number of seedling machines have been fabricated for uniform and timely saving. For effective utilisation of soil and other natural resources suitable agroforestry systems have been developed for marginal and non-forest areas.

Technologies have been generated to control soil erosion from different soils and agro-ecological regions by using biological and mechanical measures. Attempts have also been made to stabilize the areas prone to landslides and restore and revegetate the degraded areas. Alternate permanent agricultural systems have been developed to wean away the farmers from shifting cultivation (jhumming) in the north-east region. Technologies are availabe for arresting the sand movement in the desert areas by planting shelter belts and stabilising the shifting sand dunes with the help of vegetation. Improving productivity of the sandy soil through arid horticulture and introduction of multi-purpose tree species and grasses have been highly remunerative to farmers. The Central Soil and Water Conservation Research and Training Institute (CS and WCR and TI), Dehradun runs a five and a half month training course on soil conservation and watershed planning for state officials.

The use of micro-nutrients has helped to increase the production in specific nutrient-deficient situations and it maintains the soil health. Water management programmes aim at developing technologies for efficient use of available water with minimum degradation of soil. The methods and frequency of water application have been worked out for major cropping systems to increase the water-use efficiency and improve the productivity on the one hand and saving large quantities of water on the other. For judicious use of water, adoption of sprinkler/drip irrigation is being advocated.

The contribution of research in the field of agricultural engineering since Indpendence can be gauged from the fact that India is presently self-sufficient in production of improved farm machinery used by the farmers. All this has been possible because of the sustained research and extension work carried out by the

ICAR's Central Institute of Agricultural Engineering, Bhopal, agricultural universities under ICAR research system and commercial production of machines undertaken by Indian farm industries.

Efforts have been continued to develop improved agricultural implements for ensuring timeliness of operation with available power sources. An improved animal drawn blade harrow, high ground clearance self-propelled sprayer, improved multicrop thresher, groundnut pod stripper and yarn testing device have been developed. Studies have indicated possibility of adoption of self-propelled vertical conveyer reaper in the State of Kerala.

A small capacity boiler for treating sunflower seed with steam at rural level, scaled-up of cassava peeling knife, grain flour separator, technology for production of protein hydrolysate from soyabean meal using Bacilus subtillis cells, preparation of citric acid from soywheg have been developed. Blends of solution of lac shellac and poly (vinyl acetol)/vinylacetale) has been found to possess higher tracking index valves and resistance towards humadity. A pigmented (red-coloured) lack shellac-based insulating varnish has been developed with superior quality than imported varnish used in railway traction motors. A substituted cournerin derivative compound usable in perfumery and artificial flavouring has been developed from jailoric acid (major constituent acid from lac resin) which possess antibacterial and antifungal properties. Laminated and non-laminated corrugated boxes for packaging of fruits have been prepared using kraft paper made out of cotton plant stalk. Technology for production of particle board from cotton, plant stalk has been transferred for commercial exploitation. A noval fancy yarn has been developed out of jute yarn and viscous multifilament yarn and has potential for use as weft in handloom industry for weaving of decorative fabircs. Adhesive bonded jute and jute-polypropylene blended non-woven prepared with phosphate-based fire retardent chemicals have shown significant fire retardency. Several end products viz., geo-textiles, filter-media, floor covering reinforced plastics were developed by cross-laid, needle-punched non-wovens prepared out of jute and its blends.

In the energy sector, a rice husk gasifier, improved animal yoke, assessment of draftability of donkey for field operations have been developed/undertaken.

Application of sub-surface drainage technology in Andhra Pradesh have resulted in maximum leaching of 648 kg of salt per hectare-centimeter of water drained from crop root zone for rice cultivation. This improved the paddy yield between 16-36 per cent and betal vine crop by 28 per ent in farmer's field.

The Indian Council of Agricultural Research discharges the frontline extension education responsibilities through a network of 261 Krishi Vigyan Kendras (Farm Science Centres) in the country. The KVK functions on the principles of collaborative participation of scientists, subject matte specialists, extension workers and farmers. The KVKs are implemented through state agricultural universities, ICAR institutes, registered reputed NGOs having experience in agriculture and rural development and state governments. The mandate of the Krishi Vigyan Kendras are; (i) collaborate with the subject-matter specialists of the state agricultural universities/scientists of the Regional Research Station, NAEP and the State Extension Personnel in 'On farm testing', refining and documenting technologies for developing region-specific sustainable land use system; (ii) organise training to update the Extension Personnel within the area of operation with emerging advances in agricultural research on regular basis; (iii) organise long-term vocational training course in agriculture and allied vocations for the rural youths with emphasis on 'learning by doing' for generating self-employment through institutional financing; and (iv) organise front-line demonstrations in various crops to generate production data and feedback information. Based on the mandates, four major functions viz., on farm research, inservice training, vocational training for farmers, farm-women and rural youth ad frontline demonstrations have been identified for the KVKs. Under 'on farm research' adaptive trials are conducted on farmers' fields on technologies ranging from new varieties to new agronomic practices and plant protection measures. These trails conducted by the farmers with the support from scientists/subject matter specialists. These trials are conducted to generate scientific data on the performance of new technologies and provide feed-back to the research system. In-service training of grass-root level extension workers is conducted to up-date the knowledge of these functionaries. These trainings are arranged in collaboration with the State Department of Agriculture, Horticulture, Fisheries etc. Vocational training for farmers, farm-women, rural youth and school drop-outs are conducted so that the training results in self-employment income generating enterprises. Frontline demonstratins are organised to aim at demonstrating the production potentialities of newly released and pre-released production technologies of cereals, pulses and oilseeds on farmers' fields.

The KVK network gest technical support from regional research stations of the state agricultural universities and ICAR research institutes located in the country. The eight trainers' training centres established in eight specialised areas of agriculture give a back-up support to these KVKs. The monitoring and evaluation of KVK activities are done at three levels viz., KVK level, zonal level and central level. Strong monitoring and evaluation mechanism have been developed for this purpose including performance evaluation by Quin-quinniel Review Teams (QRT). Periodic workshops and training programmes are organised at state level and at zonal level.The eight zonal coordiantors located in eight zones monitor the activities of KVKs. Thus the KVK is one of the potential first-line transfer of technology institution at the district level which has to act as a light house of knowledge in the district.

Keeping in view the importance of women in agriculture, a National Research Centre for women in agriculture has been established at Bhubaneswar in Orissa. This Centre will be responsible to generate women's specific technical information and refine the same in order to make them appropriate for the women in various parts of the country.

One of the objectives ICAR is to act as a clearing house of research and general information relating to agriculture, animal husbandry, home science and allied sicences and fisheries matters through its publications and information system. The publications and information division publishes nine journals and a range of publications in Engligh and Hindi for the benefit of scientists, policy makers, scholars and the public. The publications in English comprise four research journals. In additions to these journals, the Division brings out scientific bulletins, reports, directories and other miscellaneous publications. The science popularisation unit releases features to the print and broadcast media.

The ICAR also operates an Agricultural Research Information Centre (ARIC) which is an integral part and a constituent unit of the publications and information division. ARIC brings out directories of agricultural personnel, research workers in India, research schemes, etc. Besides these, exhibitions and film shows are organised for disseminating agricultural technologies to the farmers.

Cottage and agro industries

The meaning attached to the term "Cottage Industries" has undergone changes with the progress in technology and its definition no longer restricts it to industries using manual labour and simple tools only. The use of power and machines has been admitted in the definition of the term. The basic implications which differentiate the cottage industries from large scale and heavy industries are: (1) the small scale of production, and (2) usually the worker works on his own, although the employment of wage-paid labour is not ruled out. Attempts to define the term very precisely have not been quite successful. With technological progress the concept behind cottage industries has been undergoing modifications. However, the sense in which the term is employed is commonly well understood. (Some of the definitions are given in an Appendix to this chapter).

Cottage industries may be divided into four broad classes, viz., handicrafts, home industries, small-scale industries and village industries. The dexterity of human hands and mainly their use in making the final product are the characteristics of handicrafts. Handicrafts, as the name indicates, always represent the best type of art for the art produced by hand can hardly be excelled.

In home industries, hand or power driven machinery may be used. But the chief characteristics of home industries is that raw materials are procurable locally and labour consists normally of family members. If there are any outsiders they are employed only as apprentices. The industry thus gets the most careful attention of the master.

Small industries are distinguishable by the place of work, the amount of capital invested and equipment used. They are carried on either in the house of the artisan or in a small workshop run by the entrepreneur. The capital invested may be theoretically large as is the case with ivory carving. But generally the capital is limited and this places restrictions on the employment of labour, the use of machinery, etc.

Hired labour may be employed both in the small-scale and village industries; but the village industries have necessarily to be located in the villages, while the small industries may even be located in the urban or semi-urban areas. The number or employees in the small industries should also not be large and may not exceed nine persons.

The importance of village and cottage industries is emphasised by the fact that India, in spite of considerable progress towards urbanisation in the recent past, still lives in villages and her national economy is predominantly agricultural. Her agriculture, even when the required degree of intensity of cultivation is achieved through the development of irrigation, use of fertilizers and above all with the assistance of an all-pervading extension service, by its very seasonal nature and overcrowding in it, would not be able to free itself from the disguised unemployment and underemployment.

The industrial development, with its concentration in towns, is no solution to the problem of unemployment in villages. The small enterprises employed about 20 million workers as against about five million workers in the factory establishments in 1966. There has been a great rise in building and other construction activities and people have found new employment opportunities in them. But this is so only during the transitional stage of economic development and the tempo of construction programmes may slow down. Therefore a more stable source of employment has to be looked for. Rural industries provide great promise in this respect.

The greatest advantage of small and cottage industries is that employment is provided in the natural setting of the workers' own place with numerous physical, moral and other benefits that go with such employment. It helps them to develop inherent talents and aptitudes in occupations congenial to them. Another important reason for employment to be found in the villages and not outside is that agriculture may not provide full employment, yet a larger labour force has to remain in villages at certain periods to provide the needed labour for cultivation, weeding, harvesting and other operations. Mechanised agriculture, to any appreciable extent, does not seem to be a practical proposition for many years to come. The introduction and encouragement of well-chosen village industries in each region of India, on grounds of availability of raw material, local talent, the ability of the industry to fit in with and adjust within a limit with the peak labour demand in agriculture, should add to rural welfare in many ways.

— It will reduce considerably unemployment and underemployment in many regions.

— It will provide useful outlet for many of the raw materials and waste material of agriculture, the transport of which, for reasons of their bulk and low value, is not economical over long distances. Such raw material will be converted into national wealth.

— The farmer and his family members will get an additional source of income which is so needed to raise their standard of living and help them tide over difficulties caused by the failure of crops.

— The country is facing an extreme shortage of foreign exchange. The restrictions on imports does not help very much to ease the problem. An all-out effort required to encourage exports. The produce of cottage industries hae fairly reasonable prospects of commanding foreign markets where there is great demand for them. The opening of cottage industries emporia in some of the European countries has already brought to light the potentialities of these products as earners of foreign exchange.

— Phulkaris of Punjab, shawls, wood work and art pieces of Kashmir, are but a few items, which are much in demand in other countries and promise to fetch prices commensurate with the labour put in the production of these commodities.

— The products of small industries which employ local raw materials and talent do not call for any heavy capital investment. This suits our austere economy.

— There need not be any clash between the large and small industries. If properly organised, small industries will provide employment opportunities to enable India to achieve her cherished goal of full employment, but also act as feeders to large industries.

— A developing economy depending upon deficit financing has to face a time lag between the commencement and completion of big projects particularly when the country lacks technical know-how and equipment. During this period, the available consumption goods cannot keep pace with the rise in the purchasing power. Products of cottage and small-scale industries would come in very handy under these circumstances. In addition to making available a variety of consumer goods, they will to a great extent be free from the distribution problem. Transportation over long distances would not be necessary and a major portion of the products would be consumed near the producing centres. These readily available goods will help to mop up the newly released purchasing power and fill the necessary gap, till the investment on capital good strats producing consumer goods.

— India is wedded to a democratic form of government and is committed to a socialistic pattern of society. Like peasant farming in agriculture, cottage and small industries in the industrial sector strengthen the foundation of democracy and socialist structure of society. For this reason also, cottage and small industries have to get a place in the national economy to usher in economic democracy and the desired social order.

In view of the benefits conferred on the national economy and increase in rural welfare, cottage and small scale industries have a very strong case for rehabilitation and development. The power projects completed and nearing completion under the Five Year Plans are adding to the supply of total electricity in the country at reasonable costs. The Government have already taken up the programmes of rural electrification. This should give further impetus to development of small industries in villages. This favourable development in the availability of cheap power in rural areas can greatly help to remove the stigma attached to cottage industries of being sweated ones with low returns. As technological progress in the form of the steam engine gave a staggering blow to the small scale production in the 19th century, the change from steam power to electric power, particularly in countries where the electric power can be produced cheaply, can help in reversing the process from large scale to small scale production in the case of a number of products on economic grounds, considerations of rural welfare and decentraliisation of economy in the interest of a democratic socialistic set up. It is just not a theoretical deducation but is in actual practice in countries like Japan and Switzerland. The various forms of help needed by the small scale industries are described below:

— An organised extension service of technical guidance to the cottage workers in designing, use of tools and machines and production of quality goods or goods according to demand.

— The extension service has to be supported with appropriate research institutions at central, regional and state levels.

— Development of industrial cooperatives for supplies, services, finance, and marketing of products and in some instances even for production. If farming can be run on cooperative lines, there appears no reason why it cannot be done in the production of goods in certain cottage or village industries as well. For an understanding of the causes of failure of cooperative societies in the past, the findings of Sri Vishwanathan Vekumalla who surveyed some of the representative industrial cooperatives in Andhra would be of interest. These are:

— Lack of adequate capital. Societies do not have enough capital either to give full time work to members or to enable them to manage until the products are sold. Consequently the members are obliged to produce for the local market or for the local sahukar.

— Lack of good faith among the members. The limited benefits conferred by the societies make the members disloyal. The artisans distrust one another.

— Personal interest of office-bearers. Some influential members as office beares utilise the societies' funds to further their own personal ends.

— Low purchasing capacity. The consumer, majority of whom have low incomes, care more for cheap goods rather than for quality. The member artisans face keen competition from non-members who under-sell by producing inferior stuff for the market.

— Lack of cooperation among departmental and non-official staff. Instead of obtaining the cooperation of the supervising officials, the office bearers of some societies actually betray their own cause by hoodwinking them.

With cooperative education, proper training and supervision, these difficulties can be overcome but it must be clearly realised that efforts on a cooperative basis in all possible directions are necessary for the development of handicrafts and cottage industries. It is only through cooperation that these industries can reduce their costs of production and marketing.

— There should be adequate and institutional credit made available to the cottage workers for meeting the financial needs of their business.

— The State should help develop home and foreign markets for cottage goods.

— A system of quality control must be imposed on the cottage products.

— Government should give preference to cottage products in buying their requirements.

Nobody quite knows who first propounded the thesis that India could stamp out poverty by setting up agro-industries in a big way. The term came into vogue no more than a decade ago. But since then it has become highly fashionable. Almost everything ranging from a giant nuclear power reactor to cellophane packing is now sought to be justified on the ground that it is necessary to promote agro-industries. Most of the big business houses have already diversified into the field and others want to do so.

For the new entrepreneurs it is not merely a matter of keeping up with the established industrial Joneses. The opportunities are vast and highly attractive, considering the governmental incentives on offer. The authorities in their anxiety to industrialise the countryside have decided to extend the benefits to a large number of industries whose link agriculture is remote if at all one exists. The 155-point list of "agro-industries" issued by the Commissioner of Small-Scale Industries, for instance, includes refrigeration plants for milk and factories for the canning of fish.

The Planning Commission goes even further. It says that any enterprise which processes farm produce, supplies chemical inputs to agriculture (fertilizers, insecticides, etc.), manufactures improved agricultural equipment (hoes, bullock cart tyres, tractors, etc.), or helps raise farm output is an agro-industry. This means that the term not only covers the nation's biggest industry—cotton textiles—but also the whole range of plantations like tea, coffee and cashewnut and of course, jute.

Going only by statistics the result is somewhat ironical. They show that a much bigger segment of the Indian industry was agro-based at the time of Independence than has been the case in recent years. In 1951 agro-industries accounted for 75 per cent of the total productive capital employed and 78 per cent of all value added by manufacturing in the organised sector. By 1963, however, these percentage had fallen respectively to 34 and 53. The steep decline in these figures does not mean that agro-industries are on their way out. But it does indicate that their growth has been slow in comparison with the phenomenal expansion of other industries like steel, oil refining or electronics.

The word "agro-industries" broadly means industries manufacturing "input" for agriculture, or processing agricultural "output." Agencies supporting agriculture by designing and manufacturing inputs are termed as "agro-industrials" and those supported by agricultural products are classed as "agro-based industries."

Generally most of the industries use agricultural output as basic raw material. But the concept of agro-based industries leave out of account "industrial product". It is confined to those industries that are engaged in processing the agricultural produce either for consumption or for the use of industry. They include wheat milling, rice milling, dal-making, oil crushing, cotton ginning, khandsari, fruit beverages, and so on. Thus, the agro-industries serve at both the ends of farming.

In the first instance agro-industrials provide the essential input and in the second phase agro-based industries function as an outlet for agricultural output. The purpose of helping these industries is to make farming a profitable and commercially viable proposition; since agro-industrials directly influence the cost structure of farming and agro-based industries, they have their impact on the receipts of the farmer. Agro-industries also serve as a means for providing better employment opportunities to the labour during off season.

The concept of agro-industrial is not new. Formerly the village smith, the carpenter and cobbler used to prepare and repair the various traditional types of agricultural tools and implements. These industries were, and in some regions still are, the part and parcel of rural life. The agricultural implements are exchanged for a share in the harvest.

Likewise in its refined form modern agro-industrial manufacture, process and supply agriculture inputs either on cash basis or realise the value in instalments. The distribution of fertilizers and seeds has been taken over by the cooperatives for quite a long time now. The various agro-industrial corporations in the states seek to supply agriculture machinery on cash, credit and hire-purchase system.

The idea of "in—kind" assistance has been mooted from the simple fact that outright cash grant to the farmer for production is often misused and misdirected in consumption. Even those genuinely interested in buying implements and machinery, have faced numerous problems in purchasing them at reasonable prices. The farmer who is detached from urban life takes time in locating the supplier and picking up the operating technique. Because of "scarcity" of modern machinery, is said that a "black market" has also grown in agricultural inputs.

The purpose of establishing the agro-industrial corporations, therefore, is not only to equip the farmer with modern implements but also to train him in the operation of machines—so essential at the early stages of mechanisation , ensure proper use of funds and protect the farmer from the difficulties involved in purchasing right type of machinery and implements suitable for cultivation in his region. In India, the soil and climate conditions so sharply differ from one region to another that only regional corporations could take a better view and mould the tools according to regional requirements.

Although there has been an impressive development of large-scale industries during the two decades of planned development, India still remains predominantly a country of villages and small industries. About two crore persons are engaged in these industries, of whom nearly 90 lakhs work in the handloom industries, i.e., more than the total number of persons employed in the organised industries and mining put together.

The small-scale and village industries sector covers a wide range of traditional and modern small-scale industries including handloom, khadi, powerloom, sericulture, coir, handicrafts, village industries and mechanised small-scale industries.

This sector consists broadly of (i) traditional cottage and household industries (viz., handloom, khadi & village industries, handicrafts, sericulture and coir industry), and (ii) modern small scale industries (defined as those having investment of up to Rs. 10 lakhs in plant and machinery and Rs. 15 lakhs in the case of ancillary industries). As distinguished from modern small scale industries, the traditional cottage and household industries are located mostly in rural and semi-urban areas. A large number of these traditional industries do not use power-operated appliances and equipment. These also involve relatively lower levels of investment and technology and provide largely part-time employment. A very large number of the persons dependent on traditional industries belong to the poorer sections of the society and live below the poverty line. However, a number of these industries produce certain essential articles required by the masses and also some other items which are exported. The number of persons employed in principal traditional industries is estimated at 140 lakhs, including about 57 lakhs in the handloom industry and about 36 lakhs in sericulture. Much of this employment is neither full-time nor well remunerative. Modern small scale industries are estimated to provide full-time employment to about 28 lakh persons.

The Industrial Policy Resolution of the Government of India, 1948 recognised cottage and small scale industries as an important sector of our economy. The Cottage Industries Board and the Cottage Industries Directorate were accordingly set up. Since each of these industries have their own complexities and problems, separate Boards were also created to look after individual industries such as coir, silk and handicrafts. The Small Scale Industries Organisation was also created to take care of those small enterprises which were outside the orbit of all such Boards. For purposes of definition, it was decided that a unit which has an investment of less than Rs. 5 lakhs and employs less than 50 persons could be classed as small scale. The limit on employment has been removed since then.

In spite of the awareness of the importance of cottage and small scale industries and initiative of the organisational measures as mentioned above nothing much could be achieved during the First Plan period. Some protection was given to handloom and three or four other village industries. But a large number of the cottage industries faced strong competition from mill— and factory-made goods.

In order to review the problems and programmes of such industries, a Village and Small Industries Committee was set up in 1955 under the chairmanship of Prof. D.G. Karve. The recommendations of the Committee deal with the following three objectives:

— Further technological unemployment such as occurs in traditional village industries should be avoided as far as possible.

— Employment opportunities for as large a number as possible should be created through different village and small industries.

— The basis should be prepared for an essentially decentralised society and also for progressive economic development at a fairly rapid rate.

With these objectives in view, the Committee considered that the progressive expansion and modernisation of rural industry could be best brought about by the establishment of small industries units, along with the necessary services in large villages and small towns located all over the country. Industrial expansion on the periphery of large towns could scarcely be said to reduce the concentration of industry. What was needed, therefore, was a pattern of industrial activity in which a group of villages converging on their natural industrial and urban centre, form a unit, what the Committee called "a pyramid of industry broad-based on a progressive rural economy."

The Committee also visualised the introduction of technical improvement even in the traditional village industries. It was recommended that for the future there should be a regular programme of gradual transition to better techniques.

Necessitated by the acceptance of a socialist pattern of society as the national objective and to meet the requirement of the planned economic development, a fresh statement of industrial policy was made on April 30, 1956. "The Resolution accepted the policy of supporting cottage as well as village and small scale industries by restricting the volume of production in the large scale sector by differential taxation or direct subsidies. The aim of state policy was declared as that of ensuring a decentralised sector acquiring sufficient vitality to be self-supporting and integrating its development with that of the large scale industry. The state was thus to concentrate on measures designed to improve the competitive strength of the small scale producer."

The second Five Year Plan could then take bolder steps for the development of small scale and cottage industries, as a means of achieving dispersed industrial growth on the one hand and provide better employment opportunities on the other. The Development Commissioner's Organisation for Small Scale Industries was set up at the Centre as the apex administrative machinery which has since then rendered technical assistance through a network of 15 State Institutions, Branch Institues and 36 Extension Centres already established for this purpose all over the country.

Intensive area and marketing schemes for khadi and village industries were introduced. The scheme aimed at the integrated economic development of selected contiguous areas with a population ranging between 20,000 to 30,000 with a view to developing village industries as an integral part of the rural economy. The number of such intensive areas was increased from 35 in 1955-56 to 200 at the end of the Second Plan.

A provision of Rs. 10 crores was also made for setting up industrial estates. The object was to provide conditions favourable to working efficiency, maintenance of uniform standards in production and economic utilisation of materials and equipment. This was intended to enable the small scale units to have the advantage of common services and other facilities such as good site, electricity, water, gas, steam, compressed air, railway sidings, watch and ward, etc.

It was felt in 1959 that the impact of the small industries programme was more confined to the cities and towns or to areas within close proximity of the headquarters of the Institutes and Extension Centres and had not permeated the countryside. Little advance had been made by this programme into rural areas. The objective of regional and dispersed development of industries as conceived by the Second Plan had not been achieved.

In order to carry the programme to the underdeveloped areas and make the people interested in the development of small industry, an intensive development campaign programme was chalked out.

The programme was primarily to be launched in such areas (districts), which though underdeveloped, offered maximum potentialities for the development of small industries. Closest cooperation was also intended to be provided among the Central Small Industries Organisation including the Small Industries Service Insitute, the State Directorates of Industries, National Small Industries Corporation (P) Ltd. and other official and non-official institutions and agencies. The underlying idea of the campaign was to carry the development programme to the very doors of the potential entrepreneurs and apprise them of the benefits that were likely to accrue to them from taking up small scale industries.

At the end of September 1960 the scheme was in operation in 65 intensive and 18 preintensive areas. The basic unit for working out the scheme was a selected areas comprising 30-40 villages with a population of about 20,000. Warrangal district in Andhra Pradesh and Pali as well as Bhilwara districts in Rajasthan were the first to receive the benefit of this programme.

Forestry research

The work of forestry research is supervised by the Indian Council of Forestry Research and Education (ICFRE). The

Council has six research institutes under it. The major activities carried out currently are:

— Development of suitable technological methods for storage of seeds.

— Clonal variation study on the basis of length, leaf area index and lead number.

— Vegetative propagation studies of Eucalyptus, Casurina, etc.

— Studies to control pests of Bambusa and Dalbergia spp.

— Study mechanical and physical properties of several important commercial species etc.

— Tissue culture technology.

— Bio-diversity conservation etc.

The major problem area in the research activities carried out by ICFRE is not the research content but linkages with the state forest departments. Today, what is happening in ICFRE is not being translated into action at the field level. Unfortunatley, the State forest departments have neither inherited a strong research base nor tried to institutionalise Research and development (R&D).

Forestry policy

The main emphasis of 1894 Forest Policy was management of forest to promote the general well—being of the country. It is further observed that maintenance of adequate forest is dictated primarily for the preservation of climatic and physical condition of the country and secondly to fulfill the demands of the people. However, the above mentioned two objectives were subject to:

— Permanent cultivation should come before forestry.

— Satisfaction of the needs of local population should override all consideration of revenue.

— After fulfilment of the above conditions, the realisation of maximum revenue would be the guiding factor in the management of forest.

The forest policy of 1952 emphasised the need of forests in balanced and complementary land use system. It also realised the need of forests for checking soil erosion and denudation in the mountainous regions, invasion of sea sands on coastal terrain, and shifting sand dunes. The Policy also emphasised on planting and establishing trees for amelioration of physical and climatic conditions and increasing supply of large quantities of small wood and firewood for local population. The value of forests was recognised not only in the physical fields, such conservation of moisture and prevention of erosion, but also in economic fields like development of agriculture, industry and communication by supply of timber to railways, defence, industries etc.

The forest policy of 1952 proposed classfication of forests on functional basis into protected forests, National forests, village forests and tree lands. The policy also laid down that it would be the duty of foresters to awaken interest of people for development, extension and establishment of tree lands or woodlands wherever possible. The policy laid stress on:

— weaning the tribal people away from shiftng cultivation particularly in the North-Eastern states, Andhra Pradesh, Orissa, etc.

— increasing the efficiency of forest administration to maintain adequate forest lands and giving requisite training to staff.

— providing adequae facilities for conducting research in the field of forestry.

— controlling grazing, etc.

Over the years, forests in the country have suffered serious depletion. To overcome these problems the National Forest Policy was revised in 1988.

The principal aim of National Forest Policy is to ensure environmental stability and maintenance of ecological balance. The main features of this Policy are as under:

— The existing forests and forest lands should be fully protected and their productivity should be improved.

— Forest cover should be increased rapidly on hilly slopes, in the catchment areas of rivers, lakes reservoirs and on the semi-arid and desert tracts.

— There is a need for the establishment of National parks, sanctuaries and biosphere reserves and protected areas for the conservation of total biological diversity.

— The country should have a minimum of 33 per cent of total area under forest cover. Hilly and mountainous regions should have 2/3 of the area under forest cover to prevent erosion and land degradation.

— A massive need based and time bound programme of afforestation should be undertaken with particular emphasis on fuelwood and fooder development.

— The rights and concessions including grazing should remain related to carrying capacity of the forests.

— The forestry activities should be designed in such a way that they could work as levers for improvement of the socio-economic conditions of the rural poor and tribal communities.

— Division of forest land for any non-forest purpose should be subject to most careful examination and with stringent conditions.

— The damage to forests from encroachment, fire, grazing, shifting cultivation, etc. needs to be checked.

— Good agriculture land should not be diverted for raising plantations/afforestation.

— The need for more attention for forestry research, personnel management, adequate data base and infrastructure in the field of forestry is realised and recommended.

5

Government Plans Programmes

The Central Ganga Authority (CGA) was set up in 1985 to oversee the implementation of the Ganga Action Plan drawn up for cleaning polluted stretches of the river Ganga. A Steering Committee has identified different schemes to be taken up in Uttar Pradesh, Bihar and West Bengal through which the rive runs and a Monitoring Committee monitors the progress of the schemes and their impact on the river quality.

The Ganga Action Plan proposes to divert the sewage flowing into the river to other locations for treatment and conversion into valuable energy sources. Schemes identified for this purpose include: renovation of existing trunk rivers and outfalls to prevent overflow of sewage into the Ganga, construction of interceptions to divert the flow of sewage and other liquid wastes into the river and renovation and construction of pumping stations and sewage treatment plants to recover maximum possible resources. Smaller schemes such as construction of community toilets, conversion of dry toilets to flush toilets, construction of electric crematoria, development of river Ghats and modernisation of solid waste management system, have also been taken up to reduce domestic waste load on the Ganga. As against the target of creating infrastructure capable of intercepting, diverting and treating 873 million litres per day (mld) of domestic waste, infrastructure capable of intercepting and diverting 628 mld and treating 431 mild of municipal sewage has been created. Out of 261 schemes sanctioned, 237 have been completed and almost all low-cost sanitation schemes and construction of electric crematoria have been completed leading to significant reduction in the polluction load of the river Ganga.

The second phase of the Ganga Action Plan is proposed to be taken up as a Centrally-sponsored scheme with equal contribution from the Centre and the concerned state governments and Yamuna and Gomati Action Plan have been approved under the phase at an estimated cost of Rs. 421 crore.

An approach Paper on the National River Action Plan (NRAP) has been approved at an estimated outlay of Rs. 1,000 crore spread oover a period of 10 years. The NRAP includes grossly polluted stretches of those rivers of the country not covered under both the phases of the Ganga action Plan. The NRAP is to be renamed as the National River Conservation Plan (NRCP).

India's most sacred river, the Ganga, which orginates from the snow-caps of the Himalaya, is one of the most polluted rivers of the country. To address these pollution problems, the Central Ganga Authority (CGA) was constituted to oversee and guide the implementation of a programme for restoring the quality of the river. In addition to carrying out treatment measures, the CGA also conducts awareness programmes for the general masses. Commissioning of the Howrah Sewage Treatment Plant and of electric crematoria in West Bengal are positive steps taken by the Government to help in the cleaning of the Ganga. The Damodar Valley Corporation (DVC) has initiated efforts to clean the river Damodar.

A recent scheme of the Government of India provides for the award of a label known as ECOMARK to environment friendly household and other consumer products. These products will have to meet specified environmental criteria along with the quality requirements laid down by the Bureau of Indian Standards. Criteria have so far been notified in the case of soaps and detergents. Criteria for paints, paper, plastic, aerosols, packing materials and wood substitutes are under consideration. It is hoped that the ECOMARK scheme will motivate the manufacture, use and disposal of commonly used consumer products in a way that would cause less harm to the environment than at present.

The National Environmental Engineering Research Institute, Nagpur, is concerned with issues of quality control in respect of air and water, and disposal of waste water and solids. Its activites include development of analytical capabilities to improve monitoring of pollutants, waste recycling, urban and industrial solid waste management, environmental impact analysis, development of appropriate processes for water treatment and environmental support programmes for integrated rural development to minimize health hazards.

The Housing and Urban Development Corporation (HUDCO) was set up in 1970 as a government owned company to finance or undertake housing or urban development programmes, develop new or satellite towns, set up building materials industries, and extend consultancy assistance for projects in India and abroad. In addition, the State Housing Ministries and Boards along with the Municipal Corporations and Metropolitan Development Authorities also work for the upgradation of urban areas.

To generate public involvement in environmental protection, the Government has decided that the amount paid by a taxpayer to any association or institution for programmes of conservation of natural resources will be exempt from income tax. A depreciation allowance at 50 per cent on devices and systems installed for minimizing pollution or for conservation of natural resources was introduced in 1982. An investment allowance at the rate of 35 per cent, as against the general rate of 25 per cent of the actual cost of new machineery or plant which assists in the control of pollution or protection of environment is also allowed. To encourage industries to shift from urban areas, capital gains arising from transfer of buildings or lands used for the purpose of business are exempt from tax on capital gains if these are used for capital investments for the purpose of business at the new place.

The Water Cess Act 1977, provides for the levy of a cess on water consumed by certain industries and by local authorities. If any of these bodies install plants for the treatment of sewage or effluent, they are entitled to a rebate on the cess.

The Central Pollution Control Board was constituted under the Water (Prevention and Control of Pollution) Act, 1974. All states have their own Pollution Control Boards. The main function of the Boards is to promote cleanliness of different water bodies, to improve the quality of air and to control air pollution in the country. The Environment Protection Act of 1986 has further widened the scope of these Boards. They have also been entrusted with teh additional responsibility of air pollution control under the Air (Prevention and Control of Pollution) Act, 1981.

The Industrial Toxicological Research Centre, Lucknow, is a pioneering institute dealing with effects of industrial and environmental pollutants on environment and human health. Studies on the role of various factors like age, sex, physiological status, nutritional status and genetic make-up in morbidity, hitherto largely unexplored in the Indian context, are being taken up. It also takes up occupational health related studies and environmental monitoring of pollutants.

Ground water depletion and watershed development

The situation has become more serious in states like Haryana and Punjab. The annual ground-water depletion rate in some districts of these states is over 30 cms. As the water-table goes down, the farmers have to take their pumping sets to a higher depth for increasing the delivery of water and this involves much cost. Generally, the pumping set depth is increased once in five years.

The problem of water shortage because of sinking tube-wells has become so acute in some areas like Kurukshetra district of Haryana that the resource-rich farmers have started getting more and more submersible pumps installed which is a very costly affair. The cost involved in installation of one submersible pump is more than Rs. 1.25 lakh. These pumps fetch water from different depths. But there is limit to the depth from which even a submersible pump can tap water. If the water-table goes beyond this limit, the pump can no longer exploit ground water. It was with the introduction of high-yielding genotypes of wheat and rice in mid-sixties that India ushered in the era of what is commonly referred to as 'Green Revolution'. Our country has since made spectacular achievements in the field of agriculture. It is evidence by the fact that we are today not only self-sufficient in matter of food but also in a position to export food grains and other agricultural products, in addition to having comfortable food reserve to meet unforeseen exigencies. We have emerged as the largest producer of fruits and the second largest producer of vegetables in the world. But unfortunately, the efforts made during the last thirty years have not been confined to constructive measures and useful results. Frightful damage has been wrought to the basic natural assets, particularly soil, water and genetic (plant and animal) resources on which agriculture is dependent. Although some of the damage is irreparable, the wide spread growing realization of the disastrous consequences that thoughtless exploitation of nature leads to justify hope for the future. It is a happy situation that the whole world today has become very much concerned about healing the wounds inflicted by the errors committed in the wake of modernization.

Our country is today faced with serous problems of falling ground-water-table in tube-well/pump-set irrigated areas and rising water-table in canal irrigated areas. Although our policy makers, planners, administrators and agricultural scientists are very much aware of these problems, the situation is getting alarming year after year. The remedial measures taken so far do not seem to have touched even the fringe of the problems. The situation demands time-bound aggressive measures to overcome the problems which have cropped up over the years.

"The water-table in much of the country is steadily sinking. The fall in a little over a decade has been two to four metres in many states. Delhi and the surrounding states are worse, the decline being four to eight metres in the decade after 1971, with a further fall in a decade after."

India is one of the countries affected by serious and vast land desertification in the world. Such areas are characterised by severe ecological degradation with denuded forests and poor protective vegetative cover causing soil erosion and decline in the productivity of the land. The water table is receding thus causing shortage of water for irrigation as well as drinking purposes. The increase in human and cattle populaltion has only added to the immense pressue on the already fragile ecosystems.

Signs of reclamation of degraded areas of late have become visible in some parts of the country such as Ralegon Sidhi and Adgaon in Maharashtra, Kabbernala and Mittemari in Karnataka, Jhansi in Uttar Pradesh and Jhabua in Madhya Pradesh. The development of these areas which until recently epitomised poverty, resourceslessness, is characterised by the adoption of watershed based development of the area and active involvement of voluntary organisations in facilitating the participation of local community.

Watershed is a geo-hydrological unit and drains at a common point. It has been accepted the world over as a scientific unit for area development. The long-term objective of watershed development is the rational utilisation of natural resources of soil, water and vegetation for increasing and stabilising the productivity of land on a sustainable basis. The benefits that would flow from the development of watersheds would include increase in sub-soil water regime, recharge of wells along the down stream of watershed and augmentation of drinking water availability. The agricultural production would be enhanced and there will be greater availability of fooder, fuelwood, small timber and raw materials for rural industries. In the process, some intangible benefits like institution building, as people get together to manage the watersheds, and increased bio-diversity of the watershed can also be expected.

Constitution of two High-Powered Committees by Government of India recently, first headed b;y Prof. C.H. Hanumantha Rao and second chaired by Shri Mohan Dharia on drought prone, desert and wastelands development can aptly be termed as turning points in the whole perception of and approach towards area development planning in the country. Both these committees have diagnosed the problem of degradation of land, water and vegetation resources and have recommended in unequivocal terms that waershed as the over—arching principle of area development will have to be adopted by all the concerned departments if 175 million hectares of drought peone, desert and wastelands are to be brought to reasonable level of productivity and ecological balance is to be restored in these areas.

It has been clearly pointed out that without taking into account the local communities' outlook and development builds upon traditional soil and water conservation measures and farming systems, any area development programme is bound to fail.

Watershed approach is currently being followed with different thrusts by different Ministries. Ministry of Agriculture through its National Watershed Development Programme for Rainfed Areas (NWDPRA) seeks to enhance agricultural production in the rainfed areas. Ministry of Environment & Forests has used it for regeneration of vast degraded forests especially in hilly and sloppy regions. Ministry of Rural Areas & Employment h;as gone further in recognising the watershed based developmental planning in its broader sense and has used it as a tool for overall economic development of rural areas by launching the Watershed Development Programme from 1st April, 1995 for implementing Drought Prone Areas Programme (DPAP). Desert Development Programme (DDP), Integrated Wastelands Development Assurance Scheme (EAS). As a result, the flow of funds for development of land, water and vegetative resources is no more a constraint. According to an estimate, approximately Rs. 5000 crore is annually available from various government sponsored development programmes for this purpose. But, co-ordinated efforts to establish longterm strategies that are coherent at all levels would need to be made to achieve the desired objectives.

The submersible pumps extract water from such high depths that they may render shallow tube-wells of other farmers around useless. "The situation is so alarming in some of surveyed villages in Kurukshetra district (Haryana) that small and marginal farmers whose shallow tubewells have dried due to ground water depletion and can not afford submersible tube-wells are getting converted as farm labour by subletting their land to those farmers who have submersible tube-wells." Even those fetching water from wells and hand pumps for drinking and other purposes fall victims to the few haves having submersible pumps around them. Thus, reckless installation of particularly submersible pumps is highly detrimental and unjustified even from the view point of equity and social justice. This is why there is so much cry about the urgency and immediacy of effective measures not only to arrest the depletion of ground water but also to replenish it. Even the Supreme Court has taken cognizance of the problem of continuously dropping water-table. "The continuous ground water exploitation led to another serious problem which is brackish/alkaline water in Haryana. The exploitation of such water spoils not only good quality of water/canal water but it also destroys the soil fertility."

Ground water must be viewed as a national, rather than regional or local, resource and an optimum-use model should be designed for irrigation, drinking and other purposes with due consideration of the interests of all the users. "Even if water is scarce in a region, through more efficient planned use, it is possible to increase the overall benefits to everyone there... To use water properly, you must look at all the trade-offs to all significant users, not must a few and not just one time."

The steady fall of ground water-table is seriously impairing the original productive power of nature. It is highlv disastrous for stable and sustainable agriculture.

The results of over exploitation of ground water is hazardous to even public health. In Calcutta and the rest of the state, "the exploitation has upset the geological balance, with arsenic from the bed rock flowing into the water. In a third of West Bengal's districts, the government admitted in Parliament earlier this year (1996), drinking water has more arsenic than the maximum limit prescribed by the world Health Organisation."

"The affected area is growing by 20 per cent every year. As for the metropolis of Calcutta, heavily dependent on tube-well water, a city university study says, it is on the brink of an arsenic bomb."

The problems caused by excessive use of ground water are visible every where. "In Delhi, for instance, though most residents are blissfully unaware, the level of fluorides in the water, which can have a crippling effect over time, is well above the safe limit in a number of localities. Some places have increasing salinity problems, some have other contamination and many have a mix of all these."

The water supply department of the metropolis of Delhi pumps out 65 million gallons of ground water every day for municipal supply as a result of which water table is continuously dropping.

The pressure on ground water has tremendously increased over the last thirty years because of high-yielding varieties, intensive cultivation involving water-loving crops and dominance of such crops in the cropping patterns which require much water, on one hand and wane of traditional sources and methods of irrigation, on the other. The yield potential of high-yielding varieties in general can not be exploited without adequate and timely irrigation water obviously increases with increase in cropping intensity. Some crops require much water. Paddy is number one among such crops. It requires a very high amount of water. Dominance of crops like paddy and wheat in the cropping patterns necessitates increased use of ground water. Sustainability of agriculture underlines the need for diversion of area from the crops demanding more water, particularly paddy, to the crops requiring less water. Emphasis has to be laid on selecting such crop verities which give equivalent yields with less moisture and are of short duration. Even in respect of crop varieties, cropping patterns and cropping intensity, we must go back to the past and seek in traditional agriculture some solution to the present-day problems.

National Watershed Development Project for Rainfed Areas (NWDPRA) was launched in 1990-91 and to cover 25 states and two union territories. The objective of the project is restoration of ecological balance in rainfed areas and sustainable bio-mass production. It focuses on: (i) Conservation, upgradation and utilisation of natural endowments in integrated manner with low cost replicable technology and (ii) generating employment opportunities for the poverty striken rural masses in the rainfed areas through directly involving the farmers and watershed beneficiaries in planning, execution of all project works in the watershed by developing Self Help Groups of Mitra Krishak Mandals. The farming systems approach on watershed management principles has been adopted in order to conserve rainwater and top soils with people's participation. Animal husbandry, agroforestry, horticulture, fisheries development, sericulture, agro-processing etc., are some of the diverse activities which are also being taken up.

Under this project the target is of treating an area of 28 lakh hectare at a cost of Rs. 1,100 crore. Taking into consideration the project criterion of covering all the blocks where arable areas under assured means of irrigation is less than 30 per cent, 2,621 blocks have been identified in which a micro watershed of 500 to 5,000 hectare has been taken up for treatment. In all 2,497 micro-watershed with an area of 38.41 lakh have been sanctioned by the state governments at an estimated cost of Rs. 1,128.50 crore. So far 1,407 composite, 1,343 Kisan/ Mihila Mandal and 199 government-owned nurseries have been established. The project currently in operation in 25 states and two UTs covering 115 agro-climatic zones, is expected to saturate by the end of the Eighth Plan period.

Salient achievements in the field of integrated watershed development are: (i) unified command approach of multi-disciplinary team has proved to be an effective organisational set up for implementing the watershed managemet development programme; (ii) contour farming in both black and red soil regions has shown encouraging results in increasing the yields of different crops; (iii) different farming systems based on contour vegetative barriers in watershed development programme has shown substantial in situ moisture conservation and yield increase; (iv) cropping intensity has increased significatly following the integrated approach of farming and (v) people's participation has shown encouraging results.

The Integrated Watershed Development Project (Hills) has been in operation from 1991-92 within the states of Haryana, Himachal Pradesh, Jammu and Kashmir and Punjab. The main objectives of the project are to slow down and reverse degradation of natural environment through use of appropriate soil and moisture conservation technology and improve production potential of the area. The duration of the project is seven years. Under this project, an area of 2.30 lakh hectare will be treated with an estimated cost of US dollar 125.6 million. Integrated Watershed Development Project (Plains) has been taken up in the states of Gujarat, Orissa and Rajasthan with a total cost of US dollar 91.8 million to cover an area of 2.65 lakh hectare in a period of seven years from February 1991. The main objectives of this project are to slow down and reverse ecological degradation in a variety of agri-ecological zones by promoting sustainable and replicable production system.

Among the various factors responsible for steady ground water depletion is growing dependence on tube-wells/pumping sets. In fact, it is not be because of tube-wells/pumping sets as such but because of excessive exploitation of ground water through these artificial methods of irrigation that water-table is continuously dropping. There is no recharge of ground water. In order that ground water depletion is checked and effective measures taken for its replenishment, it is imperative to restrict reckless and indiscriminate installation of tube-wells/pumping sets. The number of tube-wells/pumping sets to be installed in an area should be determined considering how many of them can be sustained by ground water reservoirs. It calls for strict legislation with respect to the spacing, the depth and the quantity of the quality of pumped water to prevent its contamination. If fact, mere legislation won't do. More important is forceful implementation of the legislation. Perhaps only three states and one union territory have presently some legislation to regulate ground water exploitation.

In view of fast declining ground water resource, unavailability of adequate energy to tap it by pumping is, in a way, blessing in disguise. Had adequate energy been available, the ground water situation would have become most alarming.

While inadequacy of energy restricts the use of ground water, "the major and medium irrigation system's inefficiency is a big contributor to the ground water recharge. It would indeed be a very costly way of recharging the ground water. Further, the water recharged this way is turning a great extent of the area saline."

"The ultimate source of all water is precipitation, that is snow and rainfall. The precipitation that falls on the ground is dispersed in several ways and ultimately appears in the form of surface and ground water resources."

It is unfortunate that in our zeal and enthusiasm for modernisation, we have become oblivious of the centuries old time-tested system of irrigation where in our farmers depended mostly on surface rain water. As the situation stands today, the dependence on rainfall has drastically reduced because of increasing use of tube-wells/pumping sets and canal. In the traditional systems of irrigation, in-situ conservation of rainfall by way of such practices as bunding, terracing were very common. The excess run-off was stored at appropriate sets in tanks, ponds and natural reservoirs for future use. We had a network of such reservoirs scattered throughout the length and breadth of the country. The impounded water was used for irrigation directly or indirectly through recharge where also used ground water for irrigation and other pursposes, digging wells without adversely affecting the ground water reserve. Numerous references to wells, tanks, ponds and natural reservoirs are found in the Vedas.

When the run-off is stored in widely scattered tanks, ponds and other reservoirs, a sizable portion of the water that infiltrates into the soil percolates deeply and adds to the ground water. So far as rain water is concerned, it has been estimated that approximately 54 per cent of the total amount infiltrates into the soil of which about 23 per cent is added to the ground water. By adopting some simple low-cost measures, it is possible to conserve upto about 65 to 70 per cent of the total rainfall.

The fast declining ground water must be recharged and the best way it can be done is In-situ conservaton of the rain water and storage of excess run-off at appropriate sites by following the age-old traditional practices which have stood the test of time. We wish and hope that decisive steps will soon be taken to revive these practices which is a must for stable and sustainable agriculture.

A key to successful implementation of watershed management is appropriate planning and selection of activities followed by an efficient monitoring and objective evaluation.

The efficient planning for watershed management would require efforts at both policy and implementation levels supported byan effective information analysis system.

Some requisite changes have to be brought in at the policy level so as to remove or, at least, lessen the constraints in the effective watershed management. These are as follows:

Through regularisation of genuine encroachments following a politically suitable and socially accpetable criteria so that people can undertake ecologically sound activities like agro-forestry without fear of being evicted.

Although the needs of local people as well as their management efforts is gradually being recognised as desirable and even essential, their involvement in the process of conceptualising these efforts in a cohesive manner is still only marginal. The local population's aspirations are as important—as a potential benefit or as a potential constraint—as those of the government and, therefore, should find accommodation in the development process through appropriate policy measures.

At the district level various develkopment activities are carried out by different Departments of Central and State Governments in a watershed areas with very little cohesion. Optimum benefits can be obtained by creating a Watershed Mission at the district level which would pool resources and technical expertise and take up the watershed treatment in a comprehensive manner.

It should be appropriately amended to rehabilitate oustees from illegally occupied forest uplands. They should also be given priority in employment under various employment programmes.

The development activities under watershed development being primarily land based, the area development programmes tend to benefit the land owners more than the landless. Though the landless people may benefit to a small extent in terms of wage labour and greater availaability of drinking water, fuelwood, grasses or forest based usufructs from the village common lands, the landed class would be benefitted substantially by way of greater availability of water for irrigation, development of their lands and the improved cropping patterns. This inequity is bound to cause social tensions between the already polarised rual community into the rich and the poor. Any developmental endeavour with such overtones of social inequities would be socially unacceptable and thus would not be able to sustain for long.

An apropriate mechanism with adequate legal and institutional support will have to be devised to provide adequate income generating opportunities to the landless and assetless in the watershed area. This may involve among others. allotment of land to the landless and granting of rights over trees and other usufructs.

Policies in Non-farm sector: these have to be redesigned to diversify the rural economy and provide full benefit of the value addition to the local inhabitants. For example, establishment of wool processing units, tanneries, food processing and other agro-based industries in such areas will raise employment and income for local people. This would also supplement the income generating avenues for the landless.

Following measures may be taken at the implementation level:

It should get greater attention as the degradation of uplands has far reaching ecological consequences especially for low land people. People inhabitating uplands should be given some incentive for not taking up intensive agriculture.

Under the Integrated watershed management, close cooperation and assistance form various government agencies is reqauired, like the Ministries of Rural Areas & Employment, Agriculture and Cooperation, FOrests and Environment, Education and Commerce (for export of agricultural and forest priduce).

Greater productivity from developed watersheds would demand a better and extended marketing facility for the forest and agriculture produce which must be created by appropriate institutional and economic measures.

Target groups for training would be policy planners, administrators, technical experts, extension agents, village leaders and workers. Sufficient books and extension materials should be printed in the local language and made available for trainees.

Awareness raising including dissemination of relevant information to the field functionaries and the community is of prime importance and should be taken up on a regular and continuous basis by a district level task Force drawing persons from amongst technical experts, fold artists and social motivators.

Since watershed management planning would require the collection, storage and analysis of a wide range of physiographic as well as socio-economic data both spatially and temporally, an efficient and state-of-the-art information system is required to be incorporated in the very concept of watershed management. An essential component of planning is to make projections of future situaations under different sets of conditions. A Geographical Information System (GIS) being capable of such simulations can be a valuable tool for planning for watershed management. Recently, Integrated Mission for Sustainable Development (IMSD) launched by the National Remote Sensing Agency (NRSA) of the Department of Space, Government of India, using remote sensing and GIS techniques, has developed treatment plans for comprehensive development of watersheds in a few selected blocks of the country. The scope of the project should be widened to cover more areas so that scientific and technically sound development plans are readily available with the field level agencies. But, the scientific and technical inputs from space imageries and aerial photographs in the planning and implementation of the wateshed development programmes need to be supported by Rapid Rural Appraisal (RRA) and Participatory Rural Appraisal (PRA) involving local people for collection and appraisal of field level data.

Soil and water conservation

Soil and water conservation measures are one of the essential inputs for increasing agricultural ouput in the country. These programmes were first launched during the First Plan. From the very beginning, emphasis has been on development of technology for problem identification, enactment of appropriate legislation and constitution of policy coordination bodies. While conceptual framework of soil and water conservation activities has not changed, concept of programmes has undergone considerable revision during successive Five Year Plans.

Till the end of 1993-94, an area of 2.91 million hectare out of the total treatable area of 17.59 million hectare in the catchments of River Valley Project has been treated, which comes to 16.50 per cent of the treatable area. Similarly in the case of Flood Prone River scheme till the end of the 1993-94, an area of 0.61 million hectare out of the treatable are of 4.37 million hectare has been treated, which comes to about 13.96 per cent of the treatable area.

A Centrally-sponsored scheme for reclamation of alkali (usar) soils initiated during the Seventh Five Year Plan is continuing in Haryana, Punjab and Uttar Pradesh. The major components of the scheme include assured irrigation water on farm development works like land levelling, deep ploughing, community drainage system, application of soils amendment, organic manure, etc. It is a 50:50 funding between the Centre and the concerned state on identified components. Since the inception of the scheme, an area of 3.36 lakh hectare of land has been reclaimed with Central investment of Rs. 41.78 crore upto 1993-94. During 1994-95, it is expected to reclaim 60,000 hectare of land with Central investment of Rs. 7.88 crore.

The scheme for control of shifting cultivation (CSC) was implemented with cent per cent special Central assistance in all the north-eastern states, Andhra Pradesh and Orissa till 1990-91 wherein 26,532 families were selected (out of which 18,842 families in the north-eastern states) for rehabilitation. However, in pursuance of the decision taken in the NDC meeting held in October 1990 the scheme was transferred to the state sector * ture of Rs. 61.72 crore has been reported till 1991-92 against a release of Rs. 55.67 crore.

The Planning Commission has approved for the revival of the scheme only for the north-eastern states from 1994-95. An outlay of Rs. 15 crore has been provided for this purpose. The Scheme for Watershed Development Project in Shifting Cultivation Areas (WDPSCA) of North-Eastern States is to be implemented in accordance with the guidelines of the ongoing Centrally-sponsored scheme for National Watershed Development Project in the Rainfed Areas (NWDPRA). An outlay of Rs. 16 crore has been provided for 1995-96 for this purpose.

In order to make the watershed development programme effective and sustainable efficient monitoring and evaluation oare as crucial as its implementation. Monitoring provides a mechanism to supervose, direct and control the sequence of actions so that the implementation of the programme could be guided to achieve the desired objectives. An effective monitoring helps to detect the shortcomings, if any, in planning and implementation of the Programme and thus makes possible mid-course corrections simultaneously. Similarly, evaluation of the programme helps in assessing the achievements and impact and also identifying the possibilities and constraints which work as incentives or obstructions to successful and speedy implementation of the programme.

In case of watershed management with complex networking of different activities and its implementation as a people's programme, an elaborate monitoring and evaluation system will have to be evolved right through its grounding stage to the implementation phase and post-project period. Important criteria for monitoring the successful grounding of the programme could be the following:

— Institutional framework with adequate people's participation for effective delivery system.

— The existence of the legal and regulatory framework to ensure the protection of rights of different sections of society with special emphasis on the assetless and women.

— Regular and continuous technical support to the programme.

—• The presence of inter-sectoral linkages kfor effective integration and dovetailing of resources.

—• An efficient mechanism for release of funds to the field implementing agencies.

The tools for monitoring the implementation phase of the programme would include:

— Physical and financial achievements through periodical progress reports from the field level implementing agencies.

— Field visits to get a first hand information about the quality of the implementation through interaction with the field functoinaries and the beneficiaries.

— Seminars and workshops to get feedback on the field level difficulties and suggestions for improvement.

— Revies meeting to examine broad policy issues.

Similarly, important indicators for an objective impact evaluation of programme could be:

— Economic indicators such as income level,

purchasing capacity of the inhabitants of the project area and the trend of migration.

— Changes in land use cropping pattern as a result of land development and various water conservation measures taken up in the watershed area.

— Improvement in the geohydrological regime by way of recharge of ground water and surface water bodies and enhancement of sub-soil moisture.

— Capacity building of non-governmental organisations and local community as a result of participatory working.

As the Watershed Development Programmes primarily concentrate on dry regions such as drought prone, desert, wasteland infested and sloppy areas their success would not only bring about improvement in the productivity of land and water resources and restoration of ecological balances but would also help in correcting the regional imbalances caused by the Green Revolution of 60s and 70s between the irrigated and rainfed areas. Moreover, as the Watershed Management is based on the sound principles of sustainability, the enhancement in agricultural production as a result of watershed development is not likely to be acckompanied by such harmful practices as overuse of fertilisers and pesticides, over exploitation of ground water resources and intensive farming resulting in depletion of soil nutrients. We have sufficient funds, technical expertise, instutional infrastructure and policy-framework in the form of well formulated guidelines to treat and develop our vast degraded lands. But what is required is a proper orientation of implementing agencies towards adoption of watershed based planned and integrated aproach and willingness to involve the local people in the right earnestin the whole process. This concerted endeavour by all only would help in realising the dual goals of conserving the legendry splendour and munificence of our natural resources and making of a drought free country with food for all.

Fragile ecosystems

The Government of India started the Crocodile Breeding and Management project in 1976 with FAO/UNDP assistance to save all the three endangered crocodilian species, namely, the freshwater crocodile (crocodylus palustris), saltwater crocodile (C. porosus) and the rare gharial (Gavivalis gangeticus). The project surveyed the remaining crocodile habitats and facilitated their protection through declaration of sanctuaries and national parks. Captive breeding and reintroduction or restocking programmes cover regimented collection of eggs from the wild. Research and training necessary for all these activities are also undertaken. Till 1980, 11 sanctuaries had been declared especially for crocodile protection, including the tri state National Chambal Sanctuary in Madhya Pradesh, one of the largest in India. By then thousands of crocodiles of all three species had been reared at 16 centres. several thousands of these had been released in the wild. This project has thus secured conservation of crocodilians on a long-term basis.

Special initiatives are being taken for the conservation of fragile ecosystems such as wetlands, mangroves and coral reefs. A National Wetland Management Committee has been constituted which has identified 16 wetlands for conservation and management on a priority basis. Steering committees have been set up by the concerned state governmetns in which representatives of the State Government, universities and research institutions are included. A number of research projects on various aspects of wetlands are also being taken up. Notable research on wetlands and waterfowl has been conducted by the Bombay Natural History Society. This effort is strengthened by the new Salim Ali Centre for Ornithology and Natural History, recently set up in Coimbatore (Tamil Nadu). A National Mangrove Committee has been set up which has identified 15 mangrove areas for immediate attention. similarly, four coral areas have been identified for conservation programmes and concerned state governments are preparing management action plans for these. The National Institute of Oceanography, Goa, has undertaken a project to prepare a status report on corals of the Andaman and Nicobar Islands and the Gulf of Kachchh.

An all-India tiger census conducted in 1972 revealed that there were only 1,872 tigers (Panthera tigris) in the country as compared to an estimated 40,000 at the turn of the century. Taking this as an indication of the deteriorating health of India's wilderness, the Government of India launched Project Tiger in 1973 with the support of WWF International. Launching the Project, Prime Minister Indira Gandhi said, "The tiger cannot be preserved in isolation. It is at the apex of a large and complex biotope. Its habitat, threatened by human intrusion, commercial forestry and cattle grazing, must first be made inviolate."

Today there are 18 tiger reserves, comprising an area of 28,017 sq. km, of which the core segment is 12,634 sq. km. Fire protection and habitat development activities have increased the vegetation and improved the water regimes of the reserves.

By 1989 the tiger population had more than doubled to an estimated 4,200. The tiger has not been the only beneficiary. A number of other endangered species such as the swap deer, elephant, rhino and wild buffalo have received protection. The floral diversity of the tiger reserves has also shown a significant improvement. This programme has thus had a direct impact on conservation of biodiversity.

The enhanced programmes introduced in the second phase or Project Tiger include establishment of guidelines for tourism in the tiger reserves, management of buffer areas, integration of local population through ecodevelopment programmes, and establishment of nature interpretation centres.

Biodiversity

Research is the foundation of an effective conservation strategy for the preservation of biodiversity. NGOs in India have played a key role in enhancing knowledge and understanding of the ecology of the country.

The Bombay Natural History Society (BNHS) founded in 1883, is recognized as one of the foremost conservation research organizations in the world. It has undertaken a wide range of projects in conjunction with both local and overseas counterpart organizations on birds, reptiles, mammals, natural history, and of late, on the impact of development programmes on wildlife. BNHS is represented on the Indian Board of Wildlife, and on many State Wildlife Advisory Boards.

The World Wide Fund for Nature—India, was established in 1969 as a charitable trust and with a network of 18 state and divisional offices is the country's largest conservation NGO. WWF—India started as a wildlife conservation organization and has, over the years, broadened the scope of its policy work and field programmes to encompass conservation of ecosystems and support to the management of the country's protected areas network.

The centre for Ecological Sciences at the Indian Institute of Science is supported by the Ministry of Environment and Forests under the Centres of Excellence

Scheme. Its mandate is to focus on the ecological problems of the Western Ghats. It has played an important role in the setting up of the Nilgiri Biosphere Reserve.

The Bombay Natural History Society (BNHS) was formed in 1883 as a forum for exchanging information on natural history. Over the years its members and scientists have helped document India's diversity of wildlife.

The Botanical Survey of India (BSI) was established in 1890 with the objective of surveying and identifying the plant resources of the country and to undertake studies on selected critical and fragile ecosystems. The Survey has nine circles located in different phytogeographical regions of the country. It is headquartered in Calcutta and has several regional offices. It studies coastal vegetation, flora of protected areas, and ecology of endangered species. It s industrial section displays about 15,000 specimens to create appreciation and public awareness of the importance of plants in our daily life and the value of conservation. BSI is also trying to conserve threatened plant species in national parks. Surveys of areas affected by irrigation dams, hydroelectric projects, canals etc., with reference to their impact on the flora, are also undertaken by BSI.

The Zoological Survey of India (ZSI) established in 1916 was assigned the task and responsibility of exploring and determining the faunal wealth of the country. ZSI has been studying the rich and diverse faunal wealth of the country in almost all areas, with respect to taxonomy status, bio-ecological features, bio-geographical pattern of distribution etc.

The inclusion of ZSI under the Minsitry of Environment and Forests in 1981 has enlarged the sphere of its activities, especially in the areas of conservation and protection of rare and endangered animals, the assessment of environmental degradation from the biological viewpoint, and the management of natural resources.

ZSI has conducted studies on wildlife of different regions, sanctuaries and national parks, and population and status surveys of a number of species. It has initiated ecological and environment research to collect baseline data on the characteristic fauna of a biosphere reserve and to gain insight into overall protection and management.

The Forest Survey of India (FSI) came into existence in 1981 as a successor to the Preinvestment Survey of Forest Resources which was established in 1965 with the limited objective of assessing wood and bamboo availability in certain selected industrial catchments. FSI has made several independent assessments of the forest cover in the country by visual interpretation of Landsat imagery. The ground inventories give an indication of the potential productivity of the forests of the country. A digital cartography system installed at the National Forest Data Management Centre, Dehra Dun, facilitates digital processing of remote sensing data.

The barasingha (Cervus duvauceli) was once plentiful in central, northern and eastern India. In 1970 only 66 were left in and around Kanha, in central India. These 66 were the last of their kind, wild or capative. The major reason for this was the progressive reduction in their grassland habitat due to heavy cattle grazing, cultivation and poaching. Fortunately at this point the precarious situation of the Barasingha was realized. In 1969 the Government of Madhya Pradesh, supported by the Government of India, launched the 'Save the Barasingh' campaign. The broad strategy was to regenerate the grasslands and to limit the other factors. Reclaiming areas which were once Barasingha habitat was the first priority. The villages inside were relocated outside the park and cattle grazing was stopped in the park. Later, water bodies wer constructed, which helped to reduce the grazing pressure of other wild herbivores on the Kanha meadows. The tiger baiting sites of Kanha where most of the Barasingha habitat existed were shifted in 1969, and in 1979 tiger baiting was given up altogether.

Anti-poaching measures were also taken up. A 28—hectare enclosure was constructed around a typical Barasingha habitat to ensure the survival of at least a small population of Barasingha in their natural habitat, though in captivity. All these measures proved to be highly satisfactory and the number of Barasingha rose from 66 in 1970 to 547 in 1988.

The Wildlife Institute of India (WII) is an autonomous institute devoted to the development of wildlife science and to suggesting wildlife management in the field. It trains wildlife biologists through a Master's—programme and also in service foresters at the post graduate diploma level. Its short courses provide conservation orientation to others concerned with land use and management.

Wildlife Institue of India has major research programmes which cover biological management and human aspects of wildlife and biodiversity conservation. The topics and sites conform to national priorities so that findings are helpful in improving management. A notable contribution is by way of a detailed biogeographic classification, an examination of the existing network of protected areas, with suggestions for additional sites in order to fill in the gaps in representative biogeographic coverage. It has a rapidly growing wildlife database which includes information on protected areas, status of major habitat types and main species.

New initiatives include development of landscape level integrated management strategies in areas harbouring protected area clusters, and training in planning of ecodevelopment measures around protected areas. Its training programmes show an upward trend in utilization by countries of the region.

Although the first protected areas in this century were set up in the mid thirties their numbers went up susbtantially in the fifties. The onslaught on natural areas in the fifties and sixties led to gazetting of a large number of new areas in the seventies and eighties. The number reached 75 national parks and 419 sanctuaries, covering 138,000 sq km in 1992.

The need for systematic coverage of the full spectrum of the country's biological diversity in the protected area network was, however, strongly felt. In 1988 the Wildlife Institute of India came up with a biogeographic classification system recognizing 10 zones divided into 25 provinces in which over three hundred landforms were identified. The existing network was then tested for its representativeness vis-a-vis the classification system. Sites were identified to fill the gaps and the suggested network now recommends 148 national parks and 503 sanctuaries covering an area of 151,000 sq km or about 4.6 per cent of the country's geographic area. These suggestions have found extensive support and already the present network covers 75 national parks and 419 sanctuaries, equivalent to about 4 per cent of India's land area.

Tourism is now recognised as an industry generating a number of social and economic benefits. It promotes national integration and international understanding, creates employment opportunities and augments foreign exchange earnings. Tourism also gives support to local handicrats and cultural activities.

International tourism in India has grown substantially over the last three decades. Foreign tourist arrivals including the nationals of Pakistan and Bangladesh during 1994 were 18,86,433 as compared to 17,64,830 during 1993, registering an increase of 6.9 per cent. India's share in the world tourist market at the beginning of the Seventh Plan was 0.39 per cent, and it remained almost the same by the end of the Plan. Foreign exchange earnings from tourism during 1993-94 were provisionally estimated at Rs. 6,509 crore and for 1994-95 at Rs. 7,449 crore. Thus, tourism has become one of the largest foreign exchange earner of the country. With the increase in income levels and emergence of powerful middle class, the potential for domestic tourism has grown substantially during the last few years.

In order to further accelerate the development of tourism in the country, the thrust during the Eighth Five Year Plan on various activities are enumerated as under: (a) development of selected tourist places/areas; (b) diversification from culture-oriented tourism to holiday and leisure tourism; (c) development of trekking, winter sports, wildlife and beach resort tourism; (d) exploring new source markets in regions and countries having cultural affinity; (e) restoration of national heritage projects; (f) launching of national image building and marketing plans in key markets; (g) providing inexpensive accommodation in different tourist centres; (h) improving service efficiency in public sector corporations; and (i) streamlining of facilitation procedures at airports.

The organisations involved in the development of tourism at the Centre are Department of Tourism, Indian Institute of Tourism and Travel Management, National Council for Hotel Management and Catering Technology and Indian Tourism Development Corporation Limited.

The Department of Tourism under the Ministry of Civil Aviation and Tourism is responsible for the formulation and implementation of policies and programmes for the development of tourism within the country and for attracting foreign tourists to India by way of developing tourist infrastructure, publicity and promotion overseas, dissemination of information on tourist places, coordination and supervision of activities of various segments of industry and travel trade such as hotels, trave agencies, tour operators, etc.

There are 20 tourist offices in India, which include four regional offices located at New Delhi, Bombay, Calcutta and Madras. These offices supervise the functioning of other offices at Aurangabad, Goa, Khajuraho, Jaipur, Varanasi, Agra, Patna, Bhubeneswar, Bangalore, Hyderabad, Cochin and Port Blair. there is also a sub-regional tourist office in the north eastern region at Guawahati which supervises the work of tourist offices at Shillong, Imphal and Itanagar. Tourist offices in India and abroad handle tourist equiries, diseeminate tourist information, undertake promotion by means of advertising and publicity, maintain liasion with trade and press. Tourist offices abroad also counter the adverse publicity by the foreign media in respect of various events taking place in India. The feed-back which is received from tourist offices abroad helps in determining the overseas marketing policy of the Government. With the objective of achieving optimum impact, the Department of Tourism and Air India under the operational scheme are engaged in joint promotional efforts in Europe, UK, America, East Asia, West Asia and Australia through 18 tourist offices located in various parts of the world.

The India Tourism Development Corporation (ITDC), a public sector undertaking, was established in October 1966. The activities of the Corporation include:

(a) construction, management and marketing of hotels, restaurants, travellers lodges for tourist at various places in the country; (b) provision of tourist transport facilities; (c) production, distribution and sale of tourist publicity materials; (d) provision of entertainment facilities such as light and sound shows, music concerts, etc; (e) provision of shopping facilities including duty free shops; and (f) provision of consultancy-cum-managerial service in India and aborad.

The Indian Institute of Tourism and Travel Management is an autonomous body set up to impart post-graduate level education in Tourism and Travel Management to meet the demands of professionally trained personnel in the tourism industry. It also organises executive development programmes, seminars and workships relating to tourism and travel management. The Institute has also assisted several universities for running courses at the post-graduate level. The Department of Tourism has accorded high priority to the development of manpower to meet the growing needs of hotels, restaurants and other tourism industries. For this purpose, the Department has set up 31 intitutes of hotel management and catering technology and food crafts in the country. These institutes conduct diploma courses in the fields of hotel management, catering technology and applied nutrition and craft courses in food and beverage services. Food craft institutes conduct craft courses for a duration ranging from six months to one year for operational staff.

In order to encourage adventure tourism, the Department of Tourism has set up a National Institute of Water Spots at Goa and the IISM at Gulmarg. The Indain Institutes of Skiing and Mountaineering conducted five courses at Auli, Patnitop, Gulmarg and Kulu and trained 330 persons during 1994-95. The National Institute of Water Sports conducted 15 courses for 166 participants in various activities, sailing, scuba diving, water skiing, etc. The institutes act as a nodal institute for adventure and sports oriented tourism activities in the country. These assist the state governments in building up tourism infrastructure in water sports and winter sports activities.

Development of tourism is primarily the responsibility of the state governments. However, the Central Department of Tourism extends financial assistance for the augmentation of tourism infrastructural facilities like yatri niwas, tourist lodges, wayside facilities, restaurants, cafeterias, tourist bungalows, etc. In addition, financial assistance is extended for adventure sports activities, tourist transport, tented accommodation, etc. To consolidate the development of tourism infrastructure, 17 circuits/areas have been identified for intensive development. It has been decided to take up five focus centres as 'special tourism areas' for integrated development.

The hotel sector from one of the most important segments of the tourism industry with high potential for employment generation and foreign exchange earnings. To give impetus to this sector, the Government provides tax benefits and other incentives to encourage the hotel industry. The Industrial Policy has now placed the hotels and tourism related activities as a priority industry. Foreign investmet and collaborations are now facilitated under the new economic policy. Upto 51 per cent foreign equity is now granted automatically. Non-resident Indians are allowed cent per cent investment.

Tourism promotion

In recent years, the Indian Railways have shown an interest in assisting and promoting the country's rich tourism industry. A beginning in this direction was made with the introduction of the Palace on Wheels trains on the Rajasthan sector. Now special trains are run to centres of both tourism and pilgrimage. Lately, the private sector has also been invited to aid the tourism efforts of the Indian Railways.

With the Government deciding to open up the economy in a big way, the private sector has been invited to assist the Indian Railways. Two major schemes are "own your wagon" and "build, operate lease and transfer (BOLT)" schemes.

Not every effort of the Indian Railways in improving its performance has been successful. For instance, there continues to be concern over the failure to lure back sufficient goods traffic from the road transport sector. Despite all the measures, the safety record of Indian Railways is not examplary. The woes of ordinary passengers hve not declined to any considerable extent. Despite its excellent work, the research and development activity also need to do better to meet newer callanges. On its own part, the Ministry of Railways continues to pine for higher budgetary support which has dropped to 15 per cent from a high of 75 per cent in the Third Plan, while some of its actions are seen as reckless by economists.

The Indian Railways, however, feel confident of meeting the needs of the 21st century. Its Corporate Plan, for the year 1985-2000 A.D., has outlined seven broad strategies: Optimise investment and improve productivity of assets; upgrade technology; bring down costs by reducing fuel consumption, material costs etc.; adopt cost-based tarrif policy; rehabilitate and maintain assets, particularly track and rolling stock; develop human resource and divest auxiliary activities. Perhaps a pursuit of this strategy might ensure a better ride for the Indian Railways in the next century.

India also started taking part in international tourism events like annual meetings of Pacific Asia

Travel Association, the American Society of Travel Agents, the International Tourism Exchange in Berlin and trade marts. Besides, Indian delegations participating in international conferences on a wide range of disciplines invited these bodies to hold their future meetings in India thereby giving an exposure to the manifold facets of the Indian tourism product.

Until the 70s the accent had been on cultural tourism. It still remains a major draw. At the same time, the need was felt to respond to global trends in tourism preferences by diversifing the roduct. The preferences varied according to age groups, origin of the market and the economic opportunites available at different places. Thus new attractions like beach holidays, wild life viewing, adventure travel and special interest tours were developed. Northern Europe shivering in winter sees a great exodus of holiday makers in search of sun and sand. Most of them used to go to the Mediterranean coast or islands off northern Africa or the Caribbean. For the first time, the Indian beaches at Kovalam, Goa, Mammalapuram, and Puri were marketed. These places used to receive only an occasional visitor from abroad until new facilitations were introduced and publicised. A measure of the progress of beach tourism is that charter flights by the dozen are operating every week to Goa and Kovalam (Kerala). New beaches have also been developed at Bekal, also in Kerala, Diu and Ahmed Mandvi on the Gujarat coast and quite a few resorts in Orissa in the Konark-Puri area.

For the more adventurous, trekking in the mountains as well as river rafting, kayaking and canoeing, skiing and hang gliding are being popularised and these find ever increasing stream of annual visitors. So much so, a section of the travel trade today finds it a profitable business to concentrate on this segment only. In promoting mountains and beaches a new accent is being laid on preservation of environment. And tourists are encouraged only to the limits of carrying capacity of these places. Still, happily the country is so extensively endowed with natural assets that it could welcome many more thousands of nature lovers is another thrust area fast being promoted in hills, islands and other remote areas.

In the wake of economic reforms yet another market segment has been enlarged. This is corporate travel. Investment and other business opportunities presented by the opening up of the Indian economy have set thousands of travellers in industrialised countries on their journey to India. A visible evidence of the spurt in business travel is the high occupancy rate in the classy hotels of metro cities—Delhi, Mumbai, Calcutta, Chennai and Bangalore. There has been an acute shortage of rooms in these places where in the last fifty years since Independence the accommodation sector has grown five hundred times. The position today is that the country is short of 65,000 rooms to reach a goal of 125,000 rooms just four years away when the number of international arrivals is targeted to reach a still modest figure of five million—a far cry from the officially listed 17,000 at the time of Independence.

Arrivals are going up gradually while there is phenomenal expansion in domestic travel. With increase in numbers of people having disposable income, change in life style, holiday outing is becoming a part of life. Destinations for the domestic visitor are no longer limited to pilgrim centres and hill stations. They go to other vacation spots with their families as far away as the Andamans and the Lakshadweep. The introduction of leave travel allowance for millions of employees of the Central and State governments as well as public sector undertakings and also holiday schemes in the private sector have added incentives for leisure time journeys.

To meet the demands of this vast movement of people a series of steps have been taken by the Union Ministry of Tourism as well as State governments. Incidentally, tourism remains a State subject. To encourage investment by entrepreneurs at least 22 States have declared tourism an industry entitling promoters to various tax concessions and other incentives. These are Andra Pradesh, Assam, Bihar, Haryana, Himachal Pradesh, Jammu & Kashmir, Kerala, Madhya Pradesh, Tamil Nadu, Tripura, Karnataka, Uttar Pradesh, Pondicherry, Maharashtra, Mizoram, Arunachal Pradesh, Andaman & Nicobar Islands, Rajasthan, Lakshadweep, Orissa, Chandigarh and West Bengal. The other states too are offering a range of incentives. New destinations are being developed as in Himachal to take the pressure off from places like Shimla and Manali. New products are also being developed like house boats in Kerala backwaters which have become an instant hit with both domestic and foreign tourists.

A National Action Plan for tourism was unfolded in 1992 to cover the development of infra-structure projects as well as promotion. In a follow up, a strategy paper has also been formulated calling for investment in different segments of infrastructure from approach roads to airport development. The private sector will be the major player in this exercise involving an estimated outlay of Rs. 31,000 crore. To promote international tourism new marketing strategies are being studied and enforced as also more international airlines are allowed to operate through India. Most of these carriers see a great future in the Indian market and for that reason want more frequencies and landing rights.

Thus, tourism has come into its own in India. International agencies forecast the Asia-Pacific region as the centerpiece of tomorrow's tourism and India is part of it. It opens up new challenges and opportunities. As part of the ongoing economic liberalisation, foreign investment from 51 to 100 per cent has been allowed in tourism related projects. Nonetheless, for such expanding multidimensional activity new directions and fresh initiatives are constantly called for particularly for up gradation of the product. A central tourism authority with powers to coordinate policy decisions by a multiplicity of agencies at the centre and in the States is called for. Strong political will and commitment is also an imperative for the tourism sector to fulfil the expectations from it.

Sectoral programmes

Both at the central and state level, the Government has initiated and supports many efforts towards capacity-building. The major thrust of development is on the implementation of sectoral programmes, particularly those related to agriculture and allied sectors. Programmes such as the National Rural Employment Programmes (NREP), Rural Landless Employment Guarantee Programme* (IRDP) aim to alleviate rural poverty. Programmes such as Hill Area Development are designed to tackle hostile environmental factors which affect development of certain areas. In the Drought-Prone Areas Programme (DPAP) and Desert Development Programme (DDP), the emphasis is on water and moisture conservation.

India has sovereign rights and jurisdiction in the economic zone extending 200 nautical miles from the coastline. The Government has established a wide-ranging network of legislative and institutional frameworks for protecting and preserving the marine environment.

The programme of the Department of Ocean Development and associated organizations include Development of Coastal Zones and Islands, Monitoring and modelling of the Marine Environment, Control of Marine Pollution, Wave Power Generation, Ocean Modelling, Sea Level Monitoring and Modelling, and Coastal Mapping.

Marine Satellite Information Secvice centres and a multi-institutional Marine Pollution Coastal Ocean Monitoring and Predictive System have been established.

The National Environmental Awareness Campaign (NEAC), which began in 1986, is a major programme of the Ministry of Environment and forests. The programme seeks to increase environmental awareness through the involvement of governmental and non-governmental organizations. Activities under the NEAC include seminars, workshops, rallies, teacher training, eco-clubs, environmental campus etc.

The Ministry of Environment and Forests set up the Environmental Information System (ENVIS) in 1982 as a decentralized system using a network of databases to ensure integration of national efforts in collecting information related to environment. ENVIS has ten centres working in diverse areas such as pollution control, coastal ecology, environmentally sound and appropriate technology etc. It has a documentation service and processes queries from national and international useres. A quarterly abstracting journal Paryavaran Abstracts is published after scanning nearly five hundred scientific journals. ENVIS maintians a close liaison with other national information systems like National Information System on Science and Technology (NISSAT) and Biotechnology Information System (BTIS).

The Central Arid Zone Research Institute (CAZRI) was set up at Jodhpur in Rajasthan by the Government of India to undertake studies on land, soil water and vegetation resources of arid and semi-arid areas. The Institute carries out studies on precipitation, the regional dynamics of the landscape and the impact of climatic conditions and man-animal activities on it in order to determind the optimal natural plant community of major environments, and to optimize the use of water and land. CAZRI is also involved in transfer of technology, publicity and extension work to create awareness about the desertification process, and to achieve public participation in the development programmes of arid and semi-arid regions.

In the area of formal education, the National Policy on Education (1986) stresses the paramount need to create consciousness about the environment. This must permeate all ages and sections of the society, beginning with the child. The Policy gives unqualified priority to universalization of elementary eduction and substantial improvement in the quality of education. Detailed school mapping exercises have been planned under a master plan for universal provision of facilities for environment education. The National Council of Educational Research and Training (NCERT) has been assigned the responsibility of developing model syllabi and instructional packages in ten core cureicular ares, of which protection of environment is one.

The Ministry of Human Resource Development (MHRD) has taken a major initiative in the field of environment education through the launching of the Environment Orientation to School Education scheme. Under this scheme special cells have been created in the state departments of education. Support is also extended to NGOs to facilitate the development of locale-specific programmes and materials.

The Ministry of Environment and Forests supports two centres of excellence in the area of environmental educationl. These are the Centre for Environment Education, Ahmedabad, and the CPR Environmental

Education Centre, Madras. The Centre for Environment Education, Ahmedabad, is involved in developing innovative programmes and materials to increase awareness about the environment.

The National Museum of Natural History (NMNH), New Delhi, is a unique facility which provides people an opportunity to acquire a direct understanding of the world of nature, the inter relationships among plants, animals, and the environment, and the need to develop a new approach and ethic towards the natural environment. NMNH also has centres at Mysore, Bhubaneshwar and Bhopal.

The Government of India supports research projects for the study of ecosystems and the causes of their degradation. In this regard, two committees—the Environmental Research Committee (ERC) and Man and the Biosphere (MAB) Research Committee function as advisory bodies under the Ministry of Environment and Forests. The research is followed up by formulation of action plans for optimal utilistion of resources leading to sustainable development.

Man and the Biosphere programme is an inter-disciplinary programme of research and training which emphasized and ecological approach to the study of inter-relationships between humans and their environment. The programme aims to provide scientific basis to solve practical problems of resource management through understanding the environmental problems in the ecosystem context.

The Environmental Research Committee addresses problems of chemical, engineering and technological aspects of environmental management, and promotes research in all subjexts concerned with the human environment that are not covered by the MAB programme. ERCs thrust areas include environmental aspects of rural and urban settlemens, resource management, environmental degradation, planning, training and education. It promotes integrated action-oriented programmes which deal not only with research but also its demonstration and extension. Such action-oriented research has been taken up in the Himalayan region, and in the Western and Eastern Ghats, besides multinational project of integrated studies on the Kaveri river.

The Ministry of Environment and Forests has so far supported about 500 environmental research projects in different parts of the country. Of these, about 300 had been completed by March 1990.

The findings of the research projects are published in a departmental publication and also in scientific journals and the popular press. Some of the findings have direct applicability while others contribute to the data base for environmental planning and management.

Various other research organizations set up by the Government and other agencies are concerned with different aspects of evnironment. The physical Research Laboratory (PRL) Ahmedabad, is a premier national centre for research in space and allied sciences; the Indian Institute of Remote Sensing (IIRS), Hyderabad, imparts training in remote sensing techniques and promotes research in areas like thematic mapping of land.

The functions of the Council of Scientific and Industrial Research (CSIR) include institutional financing, awarding fellowships, collecting and disseminating information on research and industrial matters. It has a chain of 39 laboratories and about 80 field centres. From aeronautical products to oceanography, and from drugs to salt and marine chemicals research, CSIR is involved in helping the country enter frontier areas of research. Its centres include the Central Drug Research Institute, Lucknow; National Environmental Engineering Research Institute, Nagpur; Indian National Scientific Documentation Centre, New Delhi; National Chemical laboratory, Pune; Central Institute of Medicinal and Aromatic Plants, Lucknow; Industrial Toxicology Research Centre, Lucknow; Indian Institute of Chemical Technology, Hyderabad; and Central Food Technology Research Institute, Mysore.

Council for Advencement of People's Action and Rural Technology (CAPART), set up in 1986 is the central agency for funding rural development projects of voluntary agencies. It assists voluntary efforts which aim to implement locale-specific rural development projects. Funding for projects coming under several government programmes like the Drought Prone Area programme, Integrated Rural Development Programme etc., are disbursed through CAPART.

CAPART gives financial assistance to registered voluntary organization. Up to 80 per cent of the project expenditure is made available and the remaining has to be raised by the organization for other sources.

The Department of Science and Technology, Government of India, is involved in research and development related to several environmental issues throuhg its institutions.

The Indian Institute of Tropical Meteorology, Pune, is involved in studies of atmospheric ozone, effect of aerosols on climate change, effect of stratospheric changes and anthropogenic activities on climate change, carbon dioxide studies etc.

The Birbal Sahni Institute of Paleobotany, Lucknow, is engaged in paleobotanical research which aims to build up an evlutionary sequence charting the history of modern vegetation. It is also involved in investigating past climates.

The Wadia Institute of Himalayan Geology, Dehra Dun, has been studying various aspects of the chemistry of Himalayan glaciers. It has also conducted studies on the impact of growing human population on the Himalayan ecology.

The Indian institute of Astrophysics, Bangalore, studies solar activity while the Indian Institute of Geomagnetism, Bombay, has a programme for the study of atmospheric and solar terrestrial weather relationships.

The Survey of India, Dehra Dun, is responsible, among other things, for tide gauge observations along the Indian coastline and for the study of anticipated problems of sea-level rise and impact on coastal environment.

The Centre for Atmospheric Studies at the Indian Institute of Technology, New Delhi, studies the effect of aerosols on climate change, air pollution over India, and other related issues.

The Department of Science and Technology is also actively involved in the national efforts of the International Geosphere-Biosphere programme.

The practice of scientific forestry in India dates back to over 120 years. Systamatic research and trainign in foresting commenced nearly 70 years ago. Research and forestry education now come under the purview of the Indian Council of Forestry Research and Education, which conducts its programmes through six regional institutions and a number of universitites and other organizations. Its six regional institutions, including the Forest Research Institute at Dehra Dun which is a premier institution in forestry, carry out extensive field and laboratory research. The Indian Institute of Forest

Management (IIFM) Bhopal, was established in 1982 to meet the growing need for managerial expertise in forestry and allied sectors. The institute also runs management development programmes for in—service managers of forest departments, forest development corporations, forest based industries, financial institutions and voluntary organizations. In addition, the Institute is involved in applied research and provides consultancy service.

Forest management in the field is planned and implemented by the Indian Forest Service (IFS). Two year postgraduate training in forestry is imparted to IFS officers at the Indira Gandhi National Forest Academy, Dehra Dun. There are also three regional State Forest Service colleges and numerous rangers' colleges for training middle level and field professionals.

NGOs in India have played a vital role in raising awareness about the issues related to environment and development, and in mobilizing people to take action. They have employed a variety of techniques and media. The Kerala Sastra Sahitya Parishat, which was the catelytic agency involved in mobilizing public opinion agaisnt the Silent Valley hydroelectric project, uses traditional and folk media to communicate its messages. The Centre for Science and Environment (CSE), New Delhi, has brought out three widely circulated volumes on the state of India's environment, in addition to several other publication. CSE has also played a key role in bringing in the South perspective in International discussions of environment and development issues. Eklavya, Bhopal, develops innovative and relevant school programmes and material. The Assam Science Society which has a membership of professional and students, attempts to enhance science education.

The Narmada Bachao Andolan has brought together scattered voices of protest against the damming of the river Narmada and has raised awarness not only in the affected area and in the rest of India, but alos among the international community. The Vivekanand Kendra, Tamil Nadu, trains hundreds of workers in the fields of health, education and development. A major focus of its activities is in Arunachal Pradesh where it runs 14 residential schools for tribal children. The People's Commission on Environment and Development, New Delhi, is a forum creatd to bring together and articulate citizen's concerns to put before the UNCED. Kalpavriksh, New Delhi, organizes awareness programmes and carries out campaigns on specific issues by lobbying, holding demonstrations and fighting legal cases.

The Ministry of Environment and Forests has instituted a number of awards to recognize outstanding contributions of individuals and organizations in various environment related endeavours.

National Awards for Prevention and Control of Pollution have been instituted to recognize the achievements of industries for their contribution in the prevention and control of pollution.

Indira Priyadarshini Vrikshmitra Awards are given to individuals and organizations for outstanding work in the field of afforestation and wastelands development.

Indira Gandhi Paryavaran Puraskar is awarded to either an individual or organization for contribution in the field of environment.

Pitamber Pant National Fellowship recognizes excellence in research in any branch of environmental science.

The Centre for Mining Environment at Dhanbad (Bihar) was establised in 1987 by the Ministry of environment and Forests to generate scientific data for sustainable mining in the country. The Centre conducts postgraduate and doctoral level courses, as well as training programmes for in service professionals. Research areas include land use management, noise and vibration problems in mining areas, air pollution in fire areas and its effects on health.

Remote sensing for survey of resources is carried out by India's earth observation satellite system, the IRS series of satellites. Projections of crop yields, land-use mapping, monitorin of forest cover and biomass, identification of agro-climatic zones are today possible, and provide a basis for micro-level planning. Drought monitoring on a real time basis is also becoming possible, as is the use of remote sensing for mitigating damage due to floods. Detailed remote sensing surveys have also helped to considerably narrow down areas for groundwater exploration. Satellite based glacier inventory of the Himalayan states has been found promising for planning and operating mini and micro hydroelectric stations.

Fishers prospect charts, derived from satellite monitoring of sea surface temperature anamolies, are in regular use. Remote sensing has also been used extensively for forest mapping, in India. It is through this that a correct picture of the extent of forest cover and the relative changes in it have been obtained.

The National Natural Resource Management System of the Ministry of Environment and Forests involves utilization of remote sensing technology for accurate inventory of resources such as land, water, forests, minerals, ocean, etc., and to utilize this information for monitoring changes in ecological systems.

The objective of all development is to add to the economic well-being of the people so that their standard of living can be improved. Development projects are, therefore, taken up to convert the natural resources into right at the inception stage to prevent the erosion of the resouces base itself. Impact assessment is a handy tool to assess the environmental compatibility of the projects in terms of their location, suitability of technology, efficiency in resource utilisation and recycling etc. Impact assessment was introduced in 1978 and now covers almost all major projects.

At present environmental impact assessment is being done for the following types of project: (a) (i) river valley; (ii) thermal power; (iii) mining; (iv) industries; (v) atomic power; (vi) rail, road, highways, bridges; (vii) ports and harbours; (viii) airport; (iv) new towns and (x) communication projects, (b) projects which require approval of the Public Investment Board/Planning Commission/Central Electricity Authority; (c) projects referred to the Ministry of Environment and Forests by other ministries; (d) projects which are sensitive and located in environmentally degraded areas; (e) public sector undertakings of the Centre where the project cost is more than Rs. 50 crore. A notification has been issued in January 1994 which makes Environmental Impact Assessement statutory for 29 categories of developmental projects under various sectors such as industrial, mining, irrigation, power, transport, tourism, communication, etc. The notification contains details aimed at rationalising and standarding the procedure for environmental clearance. Extensive delegations to the stae governments are also provided in this notification. An amendment to this notification stipulates inter alia that all applications complete in every material aspect have to be examined and decision conveyed to the applicants within 30 days in the case of site clearances and 120 days in the case of environmental clearnce of projects. Once an application has been submitted by project authority the preliminary scrutiny of the project is done by the respective technical divisions and the overall appraisal of the projects is undertaken by specially constituted environmental appraisal committees of experts. In addition, special groups/committees and task forces are constituted as and when needed for expert inputs on major projects. After a detailed scrutiny and assessment, the appraisal committee makes its recommendation for approval or rejection of the projects. Depending on the nature of the project, certain safeguards are recommended. For monitoring and timely implementation of safeguards suggested, six regional centres have been set up by the Ministry at Shillong, Bhubaneswar, Chandigarh, Bangalore, Lucknow and Bhopal.

Under the Forests (Conservation) Act, 1980 diversion of forest land for non-forest purpose requires prior approval from the Central Government. While proposals involving forest land less than 20 hectare can be decided by the state forest departments, proposals involving more than that are appriased by the Advisory Committee of the Ministry, constituted under the Forests (Conservation) Act, 1980 as amended in 1988.

When a project requires both environemental and forest clearance, the proposals are simultaneously processed under the Single Window Celearance Scheme. All cases with complete environmental data and action plans are decided within three months. In the case of diversion of forest land, the decision is taken within six months.

Major environmental impacts of river vally projects which need consideration are: (i) degradation of catchment areas; (ii) command area development; (iii) rehabilitation of those affected; (iv) incresed incidence of water-borne diseases; (v) reservoir induced seismicity; and (vi) deforestation and loss of flora and fauna including gene-pool reserves.

Major environmental impacts of mining operations are: (i) degradation of land; (ii) pollution of surface and ground water resources; (iii) pollution of air; (iv) deforestation including loss of flora and fauna; (v) rehabilitation of affected populationincluding tribals; and (vi) impact on historical monuments and religious places. A major component of the mining operations in India is the opencast mining which severely affects land use pattern. Mining operations have serious adverse impact on the growth of vegetation and general landscape. Minerals extracted interact with surface and ground water thus polluting the water resources. Loss of top-soil due to deforestation also depletes ground water resources and results in drying up of perennial sources like springs and streams especially in hill areas.

Major environmental impacts of thermal power projects include; (a) air pollution; (b) water pollution; (c) deforestation; (d) rehabilitation; and (e) land degradation. Flue gases emerging from stacks containing sulphur dioxide, oxides of nitrogen, carbon monoxide, etc., are detrimental to human beings and vegetation. Water pollution from thermal stations can due to release of slurry which is a mixture of flyash and water. Thermal pollution is due to release of cooling water which can affect acquatic life. Solution to disposal of ash problem is in its recycling by converting it into building blocks and its use in other construction works. Another step which helps in abating pollution cuased by ash is stabilisation of ash dumps through suitable vegetation.

Major environmenal impacts of industrial projects include (i) are pollution; (ii) water pollution; and (iii) disposal and utilisation of solid waste. Impacts of projects in specific areas are examined in great detail and suitable control measures suggested. Linkages of project requirements to utilisation of resources in an optimal way is an essential pre-requisite. Concept of recycling, reuse and adoption of clean technologies is increasingly becoming predominant.

Projects considered under the transport sector include laying of railway lines, roads and bridge construction, airport construction and establishing of ports and harbours. The environmental parameters affected by the transport projects have been classified into (i) natural physical resources; (ii) natural ecological resources; (iii) human/economic development resources; and (iv) quality of life values including aesthetic and cultural values. Adverse impacts on above environmental parameters are to be identified and mitigation measures provided for to offset such impacts.

Under the Environment (Protection) Act, 1986, a notification on Coastal Zone Regulation has been issued declaring coastal stretches of seas, bays, estuaries, creaks, rivers and backwater within 500 meter of High Tide line as Coastal Regulation Zones. Setting up of new industries or expansion of existing industies except those directly related to waterfront, manufacturing, handling, storage or disposal of hazardous substances and setting up and expansion of units/mechanisms for disposal of wastes and effluents etc., are prohibited in these Costal Regulation Zone. All the seven coastal states are required to prepare coastal management plans which would provide protection to ecologically fragile coastal areas rich in biological diversity and provide for land use zoning. The Coastal Regulation Zone notification, 1991, has been amended.

In nuclear power plants, safety from radiation during the operation of the plants and after, and disposal of nuclear wastes are of prime concern. Major environmental impacts of nuclear power projects which need consideration are; (i) radio-active contamination of air, water and soil; (ii) thermal pollution due to discharge of cooling water; (iii) deforestation and loss of flora and fauna; (iv) rehabilitation; and (v) radio-active waste disposal. Exposure to radio-active radiations in excess of the prescribed limits are detrimental to human beings, aquatic life, flora and fauna. The long half life periods for radio-active decay necessitate sealing of the reactor vessel and components for a dormant period of about 30 years after decommissioning of the plant.

Indira Gandhi Nahar Project in Rajasthan, though completed partially has rejuvenated the economy of the Thar desert region by improving the living conditions and brining prosperity. The completed stage I of the project provided irrigation and drinking water and raising the annual agricultural production to the level of Rs. 800 crore. Consumption of fertilizers and modern cultivation methods result in the per hectare yield of 1820 kg. of cotton and 1810 kg. of ground nut, which are the highest in the country.

The conversion of desert land into fertile land has led to phenomenal appreciation in land value and the widespread green fields is the growing indication of visible prosperity. A number of mandies have sprung up facilitating disposal of farm produce. A large number of agro based industaries have come up and allied activities like opening of banks, insurance companies, warehouses, chilling plants etc. are indications of development and growing employment opportunities.

At present the stage II of the canal is under construction. The main canal comprising 649 km was completed in 1986, including 256 km in stage II. On completion of 5780 km of distribution system and five lift canals by the year 2005, a further area of 13.16 lakh ha will be brought under irrigation.

The Indira Gandhi Nahar Project (formerly) known as Rajasthan Canal Project) was conceived by Rajasthan to utilise its share of surplus Ravi-Beas waters, with the objective of improving the living conditions in the Western Desert region of Rajasthan. After the inter-state agreement of 1955 regarding allocation of Ravi-Beas waters, the project report was first formulated and submitted in 1957 for an estimated cost of Rs.66.43 crore. The first revision of the project was done in 1963, evisaging construction of the entire project in two stages, stage I and stage II.

A sum of Rs.1425 crore has already been spent in canal construction since 1958, out of which three hundred crore area on stage I. According to official sources the total estimate expenditure of 1993 constant prices is going to be Rs. 2600 crore, whereas it will be Rs. 3522 crore incuding escalation when the project is completed in the year 2005.

Any project of such a big dimension having multipurpose objectives cannot be free from problems and Indira Gandhi Canal is not an exception.

The allotment and sale of land in the command area is being governed by Rajasthan Colonisation (allotment and sale of government land in Rajasthan canal colony area) Rules, 1975. The policy has laid down certain priorities for allotment of land. In stage, an area of 6.66 lakh has and in stage II, 2.58 lakh has been alloted so far. More than one lakh families have been benefited.

Twelve hundered cusecs of drinking water is earmarked for use in stage I (300 cusecs) and stage II (900 cusecs). The State government has so far implemented schemes to supply water to 40 villages in Jodhpur district, 30 villages in Jaisalmer district and 140 villages in Churu district. The Kanwar Sain Lift irrigation Scheme is already providing drinking water to about 180 villages. The Jodhpur water supply scheme which has been completed is to provide 10.6 cusecs of water to 158 villages and 80 cusecs to Jodhpur town.

There has been a constant demand of funds for this project. Being a project of inter state nature, this has acquired national importance. One of the reasons for delayed completion of the project is lack of funds. The Government of India has been liberally assisting the project since the Seventh Plan under various programmes. Under the Border Area Development Programme an amount of Rs. 254 crore has been provided since the beginning of Seventh Plan. The Government of India has assured continued assistance for an early completion of the project. The Rajasthan government too is making substantial plan provision so that the project does not have financial constraints. The Indira Gandhi Nahar Project all these years has not received any financial assistance from World Bank or any other international financing agency.

The project once completed in the year 2005, will improve household income and expenditure structure by bringing substantial changes in attitude and life style of people.

Afforestation, horticulture, pasture,l agro forestry are the areas which will attract huge investment. Innovative scientific and technology inputs for irrigation, production technology growing of commercial and pharmaceutical crops, coming of agro based processing units are going to be the predominant field of growth.

The State government is making sufficient provisions for Command Area Development Works in stage II, which were commenced in VII Plan.

Once stage II of the project is completed, it is going to yield immense benefits to the economy of the region. An additional irrigation in 9.64 lakh has yielding an annual agricultural production of the value of Rs. 2200 crore, making available drinking water for 14.0 million of human population and big stock of cattle besides bringing an area 3.62 lakh ha under afforestation are going to be the laudable achievements of this project.

Alongwith meeting the requirements of human beings, making available fooder for 5.2 million herd of cattle and generating employment are the other benefits which will accure. It is estimated that direct employment to five lakh people will be provided. The rejuvenation resources, establishment of large number of industries, and thus being an allround socio-economic development of the region.

Though there was no uniform pattern of outlay and investment, it is evident that the performance of social forestry programme in terms of investment (as a proportion to targeted amount) was fairly high, largely due to the devaluation of the Indian rupee but, there was a sharp decline in terms of investment (both in absolute terms and as a proportion of targeted amount) between 1992-94 reflecting the resource crunch on the part of the government and a lack of interest in the scheme.

The basic feature of the scheme being to plant seldings where CPRs were available, afforestation was carried out in the State on different categories of land.

Since the commencement of the programme, the Karnataka Forest Department has brought a larger area under this scheme. Up to the end of 1993-94, 50,234 ha of land were planted under different models. A major proportion of this was achieved under the World bank sponsored programme in the first two phases. After the end of the World Bank sponsorship, the State continued the scheme. It is too early to judge whether the State government would be able to carry on the programme effectively considering the fact that there was a drastic cut in the investment during 1992-94. Whatever amount was spent during this period has mostly gone to maintenance of the existing plantation rather planting new area. Of the total plantations raised under various categories of land (for which the data is available category wise up to 1991-92), the C&D lands account for the largest area with 16,291 ha, closely followed by Gomal land (11,383 ha) and tank foreshore (7,669 ha). Though a large area was under the component of C&D lands, it still fell short of the targeted area. The same is the case with other categories of land. According to an estimate, up to 1989-90, the total area available for development of forest was 499, 498 ha (Wasteland Development in Karnataka). Out of this, only 50,234 ha wre covered by trees which account for only six per cent of the available potential.

It is also significant to note that in the first phase of the scheme (1983-84 to 1987-88) aided by World Bank and ODA, annually about 5,703.33 ha of land were brought under plantation. However, a fairly sharp decline in the area brought under plantations during the II (in spite of devaluation effect) and III phases (during which the State government took on itself the responsibility of financing the SFP) reflects on the government dependence on the agency funds (though the government claims that a huge portion of the funds has to be spent towards maintaining the existing plantations and hence the decline in the fresh area brought under plantations).

In Katnataka, 13 villages spread over a few districts were selected for the study. In each village, a structured questionnaire was employed at different levels. Information was also collected through informal discussions with village elders, village-level officers and through our own observation.

It was observed that most people in Karnataka were not aware of the SFP. All that they knew vaguely was that the Forest Department had planted some trees on the village commons and the villagers were not allowed to graze their livestock in the enclosed lands; and the efforts of the forest officials in enducating the people on the importance of social forest through displaying billboards in some strategic points have had little impact on them.

Before taking up common lands for regeneration, the government felt the need for setting up Village Social Forestry Committee (VSFC) consisting of members drawn from different sections of society. The VSFC was conceived as a link between the Forest Department and the local community. The committee was to be responsible for all decisions—from identification of plantation sites to laying down of norms for the distribution of usufructs.

It was also envisaged to make the social forestry scheme a community-based one, as the success of revival of CPRs depended to a large extent on the co-operation of the people.

But it was noticed that there were problems in the formation and composition of VSFCs. In most of the sample villages, the VSFC was not formed before undertaking the plantation work. In Karnataka, of the 13 sample villages, only a couple of them—Siddapura in Chitradurga district and Bathsandra in Tumkur district—had VSFC formed before start of the work. In Siddapura, a non-government organization—Taralabalu Rural Development Foundation (TRDF)—managed to form a VSFC thanks to the head of the community and involved the village community in the development of the plantation right from the beginning. But in Bathsandra, the VSFC existed only on paper with hardly any meeting convened during the year. In one village, Chilkur in Hassan district, Efforts made by the Deputy Conservator of Forests to form a VSFC failed due to sheer indifference on the part of the Zilla Parishad and the village leaders concerned.

We are faced with a sort of paradoxical situation in that though recent trends indevelopment administration are ine favour of strengthening democratic institutions at the grass roots level for ensuring sustainable development, it was observed that in the sample villages in Karnataka, people were against inclusion of Mandal Panchayat members or other politicians as members of the VSFC because this wuld, as they perceived, politicize the institution. Further, some of the committee members were generally not interested in implementing the programme. Inclusion of politicians in VSFCs, belated formation of VSFCs and the indifferent attitude of the members have, to some extent, affected the effective management of the SFP in the State.

It is also observed that the Forest Department has initiated efforts to hand over the forests raised under the SFP to decentralized governments for maintenance, so that they can get a substantial portion of income when the forest produce is harvested. But many Panchayats have not come forward to take up the responsibility as maintenance requires some expenditure which they claim is difficult to bear, as they always face a 'resource crunch.'

In Karnataka, in the absence of VSFCs barring a coupie of villages, forest officials did not consult local people in choosing plantation sites and seedlings to be raised on the proposed plantations. The reasons advanced by the forest officials were that there was the possibility of the people objecting to such an idea on the ground that they might lose access to common lands for graxing livestock and for collecting fodder, firewood, etc. The forst officials also felt that private encroachers might go to court for redressal thereby delaying the project. Such fears on the part of the forest officials led the villagers to think that their common lands were being taken away the Forest Department. In this ironical situation, community participation in CPR development suffered a set-back.

Normally the VSFC at its meeting passes resolution requesting Social Forestry authorities to undertake plantation on common lands. But, it was observed that indoing so, the VSFCs allocated sites far away from habitation and devoid of access to water source. Since achievement of the target was the main driving force, big plots were selected rather than appropriate ones. Here again care was seldom taken to look into the soil suitable or environmental problems.

Enroachment of common lands was found to be quite high in the sample villages of the State. Of the 4.654 acres of of CPRs available across the sample villages, the poor people had encroached on about 525 acres (accounting for about 11.3 per cent of the total available CPRs), while the rich had enroached on about 1,220 acres (about 26.2 per cent). As the common lands belong to the village community, the big farmers who usually wield considerable influence over village affairs by virtue of their position in society, encroached on these lands as if it was their natural right. The small and marginal farmers also encroached on these lands as they provided foood to them. The efforts of forest officials to evacuate the encroachers met with little success. Thus privatization of CPRs reflected a total lack of societal responsibility to protect what was common property.

The massive plantation scheme has posed a big problem to the village community in general and the IRDP beneficiaries in specific as they are not allowed to graze their large and small runinants on the plantation areas at least in the first three to four years. Faced with a scarcity of grazing lands, the villagers are forced to graze their livestock on these plantation areas (in the initial years of plantation) resulting in the destruction of saplings and frequent quarrels between the rural community and the forest authorities.

Forest officials allow people to collect loppings and dry twigs from plantations after a certain stage of growth. However, it was brought to the notice of the research team that most of the housedolds were not allowed by the forest officials to collect dried tops from the plantation areas. When the issue was discussed with the officials, they came out with the observation that the people felled trees illegally while collecting dried leves, lops and tops from the plantations. In some sample villages in Karnataka, people belonging to SCs/STs brought toour notice that just because they belonged to lower castes, they were not allowed to collect even fodder from the plantation areas. (This needs further probing).

One of the objectives of the Social Forestry Programme was to provide employment to rural people during off-season. But observations in coastal and Maland Karnataka reveal that though there was substantial labour force available in rural areas, it was not enough to meet the needs of plantation work during critical periods as most labourers would be busy in agricultural operations, demand for which being very high during rainy season. To carry out plantation work during he rainy season, therefore, it was necessary to bring in workers from neighbouring areas and this invited objection from the local community. Thus overlapping of social forestry activities and agricultural operations defeated the very purpose of providing employment to the local people. On the contrary, the farmers in southern Karnataka expressed that their agricultural operations would get affected due to SFP. They say that under the scheme, several local rural agricultural labourers were employed for the purpose of digging poits, boundary trenches, planting of seedings, weeding and maintenance of forestry. This type of work isusually carried out during the rainy season. The higher wage rate offered by the Forest Department for plantation operations attracts local labourers. This has considerably affected the agricultural operations during the sowing and weeding season. The scarcity of labour during the sowing season not only forced some of the farmers to go in for other crops which require less labour input but also force them to switch over from labour-intensive crops to labour saving crops. This may be one of the reasons for the declining trend in investment in agriculture. (See Business Standard, December 30, 1994). In this kind of controversial situation, it is difficult to say whether the villagers are benefited by the programme or not. Therefore, an in-depth study is required to explore further.

Removal of silt and sand from tank-bed plantations by villagers is causing soil erosion and withering of trees. Sand and limestone are carried away by people, mostly for house construction and pot-making. Even government agencies take sand to fill up seepages and breaches in other places. In hillock plantations, government as well as private parties remove blocks of granite.

The village social forestry workers and plantation watchers ae the bridge between officials and local people. They interact closely with village people and as such there is greater scope for spreading the message of social forestry to all the villages thrugh them. But unfortunately, the drop-outs among them are more as the nature of the job is temporary and very tiresome.

It was observed that massive planting operation was carried out wherever wasteland was available. The roadsides have been extensively used for raising various species such as eucalyptus, subabul and most of tank foreshores have been planted with Acacia Nilotica as it has the capacity to survive prolonged drought conditions and prolonged submersion. Although these species may have solved, to some extent, the problem of firewood and small timber to the local people, such amicro help is inadequate in a growing society; perhaps people could have benefited to a large extent if the Forest Department had planted fruit-bearing species such as mango and tamarind on a large scale along with other species.

6

Environmental Concerns

In a wide spectrum of industry and agriculture and the entire gamut of services, there has been great progress in the country during the post-Independence era. The growth in several sectors have indeed been spectacular and in several others it has been modest while in a few others outright dismal. On Monday, 10 November 1996, the foundation stone for the automobile plant of the Hyundai Motor Company of South Korea, was laid at Irungattukottai, some 40 km from Chennai. The plant involves an outlay of $ 700 million (around Rs. 2500 crore) in the first phase; and another $ 400 million (around Rs. 1440 crore) in the second phase. A production capacity of around 100,000 passenger cars in the 1300 cc-1500 cc range is envisaged. The first car is expected to roll out of the assembly line by October 1998. Most importantly, HMC promises a 70 per cent indigenous content from the first car. Which means prospects for dozens of additonal collaboration arrangements and investments for the production of components. At full production, the turnover of HMC will be in the region of Rs. 6000 crore.

This is the third mega investment in the automobile sector involving outlays exceeding Rs. 1500 crore each. The other two relate to the Mahinndra-Ford India Ltd. project to produce passenger cars of similar capacity and in same medium segment; and by Ashok Leyland Ltd., planning to invest on facilities to expand capacity to 100,000 commercial vehicles.

In recent months total investments promised in Tamil Nadu exceed Rs. 5000 crore–an outlay that perhaps exceed all investments made on new projects in the first instance all through the past 50 years.

In all these areas, and in a wide spectrum of industry and agriculture and the entire gamut of services, there has been great progress through the years of Independent India. The growth in several sectors have indeed been spectacular and in several others, it had been modest; and in a few others outright dismal. The bench-making has been done both in regard to the potential offered by India and by developments in several other countries which started on industrialisation much later than we did. South Korea offers a ready example.

In looking at growth, over the last five decades, we can segment these into five distinct phase that roughly correspond with decennial slots.

India has made rapid strides in industrialization, and today is one of the ten most industrialized nations of the world. But industrialization, as in the rest of the world, has brought with it unwanted and unanticipated consequences. These include unplanned urbanization, pollution and risk of accidents. Industrialization moreover not only affects the immediate environment, but has consequences for a larger region whose resources get intimately tied to new industrial development.

Yet as the country continues to industrialize and new plants come up, some of the underlying issues remain. Dirty industries continue moving South. Hazardous chemicals are dumped or brought for reprocessing to developing countries. Often, in developed countries, different values are attached to human life in the North and in the South. Different standards are applied, and processes and factories being discarded in developed countries get relocated in the developing ones.

The Bhopal disaster, when methyl isocyanate crept into the houses of sleeping residents on the morning of 3 December, 1984, killing over 3,000 people and maiming countless others for life, brought many of these issues into sharp focus. It was a tragic testimony of just how much could go wrong. The hazardous side of industry became painfully apparent to countless people in India and abroad. It questioned location policies, safety requirements of industries, the responsibilities of North-based multinational corporations, the preparedness for dealing with disasters, citizens' right to know about the industrial process and the risks involved.

Near the industries, water and air pollution problems are very serious. Water pollution not only affects surface water but also groundwater. It is estimated that 70 per cent of India's surface water is seriously polluted and 80 per cent of the population does not have access to safe drinking water. For instance in Patancheru in Andhra Pradesh, over 60 factories—most of them chemical units—discharge their toxic wastes into freshwater streams. In Bichhri in Rajasthan, chemical effluents from textile and chemical industries pollute the waters of rivers and wells. The health impact of such cases is serious and the incidence of cancer, lung and skin diseases, and deformities is high in these areas. While they are restricted in extent, air pollution levels are high in industrial areas. For instance the average levels of particulate matter in the four metropolitan cities exceeds 360 mg/m while the WHO standard is 150 mg/m.

Another concern relates to occupational health incertain industries. Asbestosis, byssinosis and pneumo-noconiosis are some of the occupational diseases reported. Silicosis has been reported in mines and other industries.

Several central and state statues, such as the Industrial Development Act, the Labour Acts, the Factories Act and the Municipal Acts have environmental provisions in them. However it was the enactment of the Water (Prevention and Control of Pollution) Act, 1974, and the Air (Prevention and Control of Pollution) Act, 1981, which made these environmental factors the principal object of legislation. The Bhopal tragedy caused a surge in environmental legislation and an umbrella Environment (Protection) Act was passed in 1986. This covers hazardous activities in addition to pollution.

Under the Environment (Protection) Act, 1986, the Central Government is responsible for laying down procedures and safeguards for handling hazardous substances. Rules have been made for the manufactures, storage and import of hazardous chemicals, their management and handling, as well as for the manufacture, use, import and storage of micro-organisms and genetically engineered organisms. Radioactive waste disposal is controlled through a regulatory board managed by the Bhabha Atomic Research Centre. The Government has also established a Central Crises Group Alert System with a control room at New Delhi to deal with major chemical accidents in the country.

Many industries and large projects need environmental clearance. The State Pollution Control Boards monitor industrial areas. The Government of India has made it mandatory to assess the environmental impact of new large undertaking in the country. The impact assessment covers not only air, water and soil polluiton, but also damage to historical monuments, wildlife, forests, and to natural resources in general. Unique to India is the recently enacted Mandatory Public Liability Insurance which makes it imperative for units dealing with hazardous substances to take insurance cover against damage to health or property of the community in the vicinity of the industry.

Industrial location policy is a crucial element in determining the impact of industry on the environment. Unplanned industrial growth has in some cases led to industrail conglomerates and urban sprawl. This has often led to prime agricultural and forest land being diverted for urban and industrial use. Near forests, urban areas have led to deforestation. For certain industries, a two-stage clearance procedure has been adopted by the Ministry of Environment and Forests, considering the site specific nature.

While legislation today has enabled authorities to step in, this alone cannot lead to improved environment in and around industries. For this to happen public awareness, as well as awareness and concern among the decision-makers is required. Where people have been consicous they have protested and not let polluting industries spoil their environment. Where industries have been conscious they have got together and taken initiatives for effluent treatment. A typical example of joint efforts by industry in the safe disposal of effluents is the Baroda Effluent Channel in Gujarat, managed by the Gujarat Industrial Development Corporation.

There is urgent need to create widespread awareness. Towards this end the Ministry of Environment and Forests has made a beginning by introducing a scheme for an Ecomark to lable environm-ent-friendly products. NGOs too have several programmes to create environmental consciouness. School programmes to involve students in environmental quality monitoring have begun.

But finally environmental factors will only be taken into account where alternatives are availabel. Today with Indai opening up its economy to greater internationl participation in the industrialization of the country, it si important to ensure that the best and cleansest technologies are available for htis growth, so that industrialization occurs with the minimum of negative consequences.

In accordance with the prevailing thinking, the First Five year Plan stated that the objective of industrial planning was to make good the deficiencies in production of key industrial items and to initiated development, which would enable cumulative expansion of such basic production. There was better appreciation in the First Plan of the need for coordination of industrial planning with the formulation of other economic policies, such as customs and excise tariff structure, import and export policy, investment and technology policy and monetary and financial policy. The Second Plan and later plans have been encreasingly concerned with the allocation of public resources and much less with indications and policies to direct the whole economy indesired directions.

The Industrial Policy Statement of 1973, inter alia, identified high-priority industries where investment from large industrial houses and foreign companies would be permitted. The Industrial Policy Statement of 1980 focussed attention on the need for promoting competition in domestice market, technological upgradation and modernisation. The policy laid the foundation for an increasingly competitive export base and for encouraging foreign investment in high priority technology areas. This found expression in the Sixth Five Year Plan, which emphasised the need for productivity to be the central concern in all economic and production activities.

Nevertheless the sector continued to provide the thrust for the development of heavy industries. In critical areas such as power, railways, coal, petroleum, steel and fertilisers, the public sector has been intensely involved in setting the pace of development. Apart from public investments in basic industry and infrastructure, the expansion of the private sector in line with Plan objectives and priorities were greatly facilitated by financial institutions. An elaborate network of specialised development banking institutions with the Industrial Development Bank of India at the apex was established to help finance industrial investment in the private sector. These institutions, numbering over 50, have become the major source of long-term finance for the corporate sector.

As the statement on Industrial Policy, 1991 says, "These policies created a climate for rapid industrial growth in the country. Thus on the eve of the Seventh Five year Plan, a broad-based infractructure had been built up. Basic industries had been established. A high degree of self-reliance in a large number of items–raw materials, intermediates, finished goods—had been achieved. New growth centres of industrial activity had emerged, as had a new generation of entrepreneurs. A large number of engineers, technicians and skilled workers has been trained."

The Sixth Plan had achieved augmentation of new capacity more or less in consonance with the targets in alarge number of insdustries including, among others, aluminium, zinc, lead thermoplastics, yarn, petrochemical intermediates, electrical equipment, cement and consumer durables. However shortfall in production had taken place in some basic industries, such as steel, cement, non-ferrous metals, fertilisers and certain other industries, including textiles, jute manufactures, sugar, drugs and pharmaceuticals, commercial vehicles and railway wagons. Production targets were exceed in a few industries like machine toos, passenger cars, motor cycles and scooters, consumer electronics and communication equipment. Domestic imbalances resulting from shortfalls in production hasd to be corrected through imports of essential commodities, like steel, cement, fertilisers and sugar.

A technological thrust was given during the Plan period in certain industries in the engineering sector. The first 500 MW thermal generating unit was commissioned and the manufacture of 500 MW turbo generators and boilers had commenced. There has been a systematic upgradation of production technology for other equipment, needed by the power sector. The manufacture of equipment for 1350 tonnes per day fertiliser units and blast furnaces of 3200 cubic metres capacity for steel plants was being undertaken in the country. A strong base had been laid for the rapid development of the electronics sector.

The Seventh Plan recognised the need to consolidate on these strengths and to take initiatives to prepare Indian industry to respond effectively to the emerging challenges. A number of policy and procedural changes which were introduced in 1985-86 aimed at increasing productivity, reducing costs and improving quality. Production capacity restrictions on the industries were gradually reduced and broad banding, which enabled a manufacturer to choose and produce any product mix which suited him in the context of the prevailing market conditions was introduced. In 1986, as against a policy of re-endorsement of existing capacity, the scheme of minimum economic scale of production was introduced with Letters of Intent prescribing a minimum economic size for a single unit. The accent was on opening the domestic market to increased competition and readying the industry to stand on its own in the face of international competition. The public sector was freed from a number of constraints and given a large measure of autonomy. The technological and managerial modernisation of industry was pursued as the key instrument for increasing productivity and improving competitiveness in the world.

As a result of the policies pursued since Independence, the long term trend of industrial growth for over forty years since 1950 is a trend annual growth of just over 6 per cent. This, says rakesh MOhan in an essay in Bimal Jalan's book on Indian Economy, "is quite an achievement, given the magnitude of distortions built into the system." He divides the growth record into three distinct periods: 7.7 per cent annual growth over the first three plan periods (1950-1965), four per cent annual growth over the holiday (1966-69) and the Fourth and Fifth Plan periods (1969-79), and finally the recovery to about 7.7 per cent growth over the Sixth and Seventh periods.

The period 1966-1980, says Mohan is effectively the dark period for Indian economy. This period encompassed a number of exogenous shocks: the devastating three-year drought of 1965-68, the aftermath of increased defence espenditures resulting from 1962 was with China and two wars with Pakistan, the oil price shocks of 1973 and 1979, and the downturn in the availability of foreign resources. During this period, the Indian economy was constantly struggling to adjust.

As a result of policy changes, the composition of Indian industry had undergone great transformation. At Independence, the consumer goods industry accounted for almost half of all industrial production. In 1991 such industries accounted for only about 20 per cent. In contrast, capital goods production was less than 4 per cent of total industrial production. In 1991, it had gone up to 24 per cent. Similarly basic goods share had increased from 20 per cent to 40 per cent.

Metals and minerals

India is richly endowed with minerals. Under the Constitution, minerals rights and the administration of mining laws are vested in the state governments. The Centre, however, regulates the development of minerals under the Mines and Minerals (Regulation and Development) Act, 1957 and the rules and regulations framed under it. This Statute empowers the Centre to formulate rules for: (i) the grant of prospecting licences and mining leases for schedule minerals, (ii) the conservation and development of minerals., and (iii) the modification of old leases. The Act, came into force on 1 June 1958. Amendments to this Act were made in 1972, 1986, and 1994.

Principal mineral found in the country along with their estimated reserves are given below.

Coal is India's largest mineral resource and presently India is the fifth largest producer of coal in the world. Vast deposits of coal of Gondwana formations occur in West Bengal, Orissa, Bihar, Madhya Pradesh, Andhra Pradesh, Uttar Pradesh and Maharashtra. It also occurs in tertiary formation in Assam, Arunachal Pradesh, Meghalaya and Nagaland. Total known reserves of all types of coals in Gondwana and tertiary coalfields estimated stands at 192 billion tonnes. Out of these, reserves of prime-coking coal have been estimated at 5.3 billion tonnes. Total reserves of lignite stands at 6.5 billion tonnes, located in Tamil Nadu, Gujarat, Rajasthan, Kerala, Pondichery and Jammu and Kashmir.

The total recoverable reserves of bauxite in the country are placed at 2,525 million tonnes while the total in situ reserves are 3,037 million tonnes. The conditional resources of bauxite are about five lakh tonnes. In addition, prospective resources are placed at 90 million tonnes. Orissa, Andhra Pradesh, Madhya Pradesh,

Gujarat, Maharashtra and Bihar are the principal states where bauxite deposits are located. Major reserves are concentrated in the East Coast Bauxite deposits of Orissa and Andhra Pradesh.

Total recoverable reserves of chromite are estimated at 8.8 million tonnes. Deposits of economic significance occur in Andhra Pradesh, Bihar, Karnataka, Maharashtra, Manipur, Orissa and Tamil Nadu. However, refractory grade reserves of chromite are very meagre.

The total recoverable reserves of copper ore in the country are 415.86 million tonnes equivalent to 4.14 million tonnes of metal content. The all-India conditional resources of copper are 695.29 million tonnes (1.99 million tonnes of copper metal) and prospective resources are 769.9 million tonnes of copper ore. Major and important copper ore deposits are located in Singhbhum district (Bihar), Balaghat (Madhya Pradesh) and Jhunjhunu and Alwar (Rajasthan). In addition, small copper ore deposits are in Andhra Pradesh, Gujarat, Karnataka, Sikkim, Orissa, Uttar Pradesh and West Bengal.

There are three important gold fields in the country, namely, Kolar Gold Field, Kolar disrict, Hutti Gold Fields in Raichur district (both in Karnataka) and Ramgiri Gold field in Anantpur district (Andhra Pradesh). Total gold metal ore reserves are estimated at 176.9 lakh tonnes.

The total recoverable reserves of iron ore in the country are about 9,606 million tonnes of haematite and 3,143 million tonnes of magnetite. Haematite resources are located in Andhra Prades, Bihar, Goa, Karnataka, Madhya Pradesh, Maharashtra, Orissa and Rajasthan. Magnetite resources are located in Andhra Pradesh, Bihar, Goa, Karnataka and Kerala.

Lead-zinc resources are located in Rajasthan, Gujarat, West Bengal, Andhra Pradesh, Meghalaya,

Orissa, Sikkim, Tamil Nadu and Uttar Pradesh. Total recoverable reserves (all grades) of lead and zinc ores are 198.5 million tonnes comprising of metal content of 2,390 thousand tonnes of lead and 9,866 thousand tonnes of zinc metal. The conditonal resources of lead-zinc are 200.29 million tonnes in the country.

The total recoverable reserves of manganese ore are 233.33 million tonnes out of which 41.05 million tonnes are proved , 142.03 million tonnes probable and 50.25 million tonnes of possible category. Main reserves are in Karnataka followed by Orissa, Madhya Pradesh, Maharashtra and Goa. Minor occurences of manganese are in Andhra Pradesh, Bihar, Gujarat, Rajasthan and West Bengal.

The total estimated conditional resource of nickel ore is 294 million tonnes located in Orissa (285 million tonnes) and Bihar (9 million tonnes). Minor occurrence of nickel in Tamil Nadu, Maharashtra and Goa are indicated.

The recoverable reserves of tungsten ore have been estimated at 25.89 million tonnes or 77.32 thousand tonnes of WO_3 content. The main reserves are at Degana, Rajasthan. It also occurs in Maharashtra, Karnataka, West Bengal and Uttar Pradesh.

The recoverable reserves of barytes are 70.15 million tonnes. The Mangampet deposit occuring in Cuddapah djistrict (Andhra Pradesh) is the single largest deposit in the world containing 67 million tonnes of recoverable reserves. Minor occurences of barytes are located in Rajasthan, Madhya Pradesh, Maharashtra, Himachal Pradesh, Tamil Nadu, Uttar Pradesh and Bihar.

Diamond deposits occur in three types of geological settings such as kimberlite pipes, conglomerate beds and alluvial gravels. The main diamond bearing areas in

India are Panna belt in Madhya Pradesh, Munimadugu-Banganapalle conglomerate in Kurnool district, Wajrakarur kimberlite pipe in Anantpur district and the gravels of Krishna river basin in Andhra Pradesh. Reserves of about a million carats, there are conditional submarginal of 265 thousand carats.

Dolomite occurrences are widespread in almost all part of the country. The total recoverable reserves of all grades of dolomite are 4,967 million tonnes. Of the total all India recoverable reserves, major share of about 92 per cent reserves is distributed in seven states– Madhya Pradesh, Orissa, Gujarat, Karnataka, West Bengal, Uttar Pradesh and Maharashtra.

Fireclay occurs as a bedded deposit, mostly associated with measures of Gondwana and Tertiary periods. Important deposits are associated with Jharia and Raniganj coalfields in Bihar and West Bengal, Korba coalfields in Madhya Pradesh and Neyveli Lignite field in Tamil Nadu. Notable occurrences of fireclay not associated with coal measures are known in Gujarat, Jabalpur region of Madhya Pradesh and Belpahar-Sundergarh areas of Orissa. The recoverable reserves of fireclay are about 697 million tonnes.

Total recoverable reserves of fluorspar in India are 2.15 million tonnes. Rajasthan and Gujarat are the only producing states in India. Fluorspar occurs in Gujarat, Madhya Pradesh, Maharashtra and Rajasthan.

The recoverable reserves of gypsum are estimated at 239 million tonnes. Out of the above, 70,000 tonnes surgical plaster grade, 39 million tonnes of fertilizer/pottery grade, 38.6 million tonnes of cement/paint grade, four million tonnes of soil reclamation grade and the rest is unclassified. The production of gypsum is confined to Rajasthan, Tamil Nadu, Jammu and Kashmir, Uttar Pradesh, Himachal Pradesh and Gujarat. Rajasthan is the main producer of gypsum followed by Tamil Nadu.

The recoverable reserves of graphite are 3.11 million tonnes. Orissa is the major producers of graphite. Almost the entire reserves under proved category are in Ramanathapuram district, Tamil Nadu. Resources of graphite are in Andhra Pradesh, Orissa, Tamil Nadu, Kerala, Bihar, Gujarat, Rajasthan, Madhya Pradesh and Maharashtra.

The recoverable reserves of ilmenite are 86.75 million tonnes. Ilmenite occurs mainly in beach sand deposits right from Ratnagiri coast in the west to Orissa coast in the east. These minerals are found in Kerala, Tamil Nadu and Orissa.

The all India recoverable reserves of kaolin, including white clay of all categories are about 986 million tonnes. Principal producing states are Bihar, Gujarat, Rajasthan and West Bengal. Kerala, Haryana, Orissa and Madhya Pradesh also produce significant quantities and ball clay is mainly produced in Rajasthan, Andhra Pradesh and Gujarat.

The total recoverable reserves of limestone of all categories and grades are placed at 76,446 million tonnes. The conditional reserves have been estimated at 360 million tonnes. Major producing states are Madhya Pradesh, tamil Nadu, Andhra Pradesh, Gujarat, Bihar, Orissa, Rajasthan and Karnataka.

India is the world's leading producer of sheet mica and accounts for about 60 per cent of global mica trade. Economic deposits of mica occur in three important belts in Bihar, Andhra Pradesh and Rajasthan.

The total recoverable reserves of magnesite are about 233 million tonnes of which 41 million tonnes are in theproved category. Magnesite is found in Uttar Pradesh, Tamil Nadu and Rajasthan while minor occurrences are in Karnataka, Jammu and Kashmir and Himachal Pradesh.

The total recoverable reserves of kyanite and sillimanite in the country are 2.7 million tonnes respectively. Besides, conditional resources of 175.84 million tonnes of kyanite are also estimated. For sillimanite conditional resources of 5.9 million tonnes and prospective resources of 0.8 million tonnes have been estimated. Kyanite deposits are located in Andhra Pradesh, Bihar, Karnataka and Maharashtra. Sillimanite resources are in Kerala, Orissa, Madhya Pradesh, tamil Nadu and minor occurrences in Andhra Pradesh, Assam, Bihar, Karnataka, Maharashtra, Meghalaya, Rajasthan and West Bengal.

Deposits of phosphorites are located in Madhya Pradesh, Rajasthan and Uttar Pradesh. Besides, apatite deposits of commercial importance are reported from Bihar, Andhra Pradesh, Rajasthan, West Bengal and Tamil Nadu. Recoverable reserves of rock-phosphate are estimated at 146.95 million tonnes of all grades and of apatite at 13 million tonnes.

Other minerals occuring in significant quantities in India are bentonite (Gujarat, Rajasthan, Bihar, Jammu and Kashmir and Tamil Nadu), corundum (Maharashtra, Madhya Pradesh, Andhra Pradesh * and Gujarat), fullers earth (Rajasthan, Karnataka and Andhra Pradesh), garnet (Tamil Nadu, Rajasthan and Andhra Pradesh Pradesh), pyrites (Bihar and Rajasthan), steatite (Rajasthan, Uttar Pradesh, Andhra Pradesh, Tamil Nadu and Bihar), wollastonite (Rajasthan and Gujarat), zircon (beach sand of Tamil Nadu, Kerala and Orissa) and quartz and silica minerals are wide spread and occur in about all states. Besides, the country has vast resources of building dimension and ornamental stones such as granite, marble and slate. Granite is mainly mined in Tamil Nadu, Karnataka, Andhra Pradesh and Rajasthan, marble in Rajasthan, Uttar Pradesh and Gujarat and slate in Madhya Pradesh, Andhra Pradesh and Haryana.

Oil and natural gas

As India is one of the lowest cost refiners in the world, experts believe that it might become a net exporter of petroleum products in the coming century and a "swing producer" to stabilise global product markets. Though the first oil well in India was completed late in the last century—drilling for the oil well at Digboi in Assam was begun in September 1889 and completed in November 1890—the search for oil in a big way started only after the country gained Independence. The first well at Digboi was drilled by the Assam Railway and Trading Company. Later the Assam Oil Company (AOC) came into existence, which sold its rights to the Burmah Oil Company.

These were the beginnings of Oil India Limited, which became a fully-owned Government company in the early eighties. Thus at the time of Independence, indigenous production of crude oil was confined to Assam.

Since this was hardly enough to meet the country's needs for petroleum products, the Government of India took a conscious decision to develop the country's oil resources, both onshore and offshore.

Creating a Petroleum Division within the Geological Survey of India in October 1955, exclusively for country-wide oil exploration, was the first step. It did not take much time for GSI's Petroleum Division to grow into the Directorate of Oil and Natural Gas, and subsequently into an autonomous Oil & Natural Gas Commisssion through an act of Parliament in October 1959. Now, of course, the Commission is known as Oil & Natural Gas Corporation Limited.

The real fillip to the development of the indigenous petroleum industry was given by the late Keshav Deo Malaviya, who gave ONGC the necessary push and was also responsible for the creation of Indian Oil Corporation, India's first national refining and marketing corporation.

Later, of course, the refineries and marketing companies owned by Burmah-Shell, Esso and Caltex (not to talk of the small Digboirefinery owned by Burmah Oil Company) were nationalised giving birth to two more national oil companies, i.e. Bharat Petroleum and Hindustan Petroleum. Today there are 14 refineries (including the two mentioned above)—13 in the public sector and one in the joint sector. The Gas Authority of India Limited (GALL) was set up in 1984 for planned utilisation of gas reserves and was given the responsibility to set up the HBJ pipeline.

These are briefly the main operators in the oil and natural gas sector, which is basically a public sector monopoly now. While Oil India's operations, in the initial stages, were confined to the north-eastern region, ONGC's initial successes came in the western region. The first discovery of oil and gas made by ONGC was in 1958 in the Cambay onshore basin in Gujarat. Also in Gujarat, the first giant oilfield was discovered at Ankleshwar in 1960.

In what was termed as "Samudra Manthan" in the early sixties, ONGC decided to step up its offshore exploration activity in earnest. Seismic surveys helped in the discovery of the Aliabet structure at the mouth of the Narmada and later in "Bombay High". A big debate raged in the late sixties whether we should develop "Bombay High" on our own or entrust the job to foreign compaines. The first option was chosen and ONGC acquired its first jack-up type rig "Sagar Samrat" (built for the Commission in Japan) in 1973. "Sagar Samrat" started drilling in "Bombay High" in January 1974 and about a month later oil was discovered at the very first well it drilled in this oilfield, which has met part of the country's crude needs for the past 15 years or so.

This writer was fortunate enough to be among the group of reporters who were on board the "Sagar Samrat" in early 1974 to witness the drilling for the first well. By the time we returned to shore and about to report this first experiment in offshore drilling, news arrived that oil has been found. February 1974 will thus be a landmark in the development of offshore oil production in India.

ONGC has travelled quite far in the 22 years since oil was established in "Bombay High". Crude oil production from offshore areas (which is solely from ONGC) has risen from five million tonnes in 1980-81 to a high of 21.2 million tonnes in 1990-91. It was around 20.2 million tonnes 1994-95. Total crude production both from onshore and offshore areas (i.e. the total output of OIL and ONGC) was around 35.2 million tonnes in 1995-96.

But the country's requirements of petroleum products have grown at a rapid rate, from 30 million tonnes in 1980-81 to almost 75 million tonnes in 1995-96. Current estimates indicate that it would reach a level of about 113 million tonnes by 2001-02.

Looked at from a different perspective. India's domestic oil production vis-a-vis petroleum product consumption indicate that the percentage of slef-sufficiency has declined from 55.6 per cent in 1990-91 to 43.7 per cent in 1995-96 and is estimated to decline further to 23.5 per cent by 2006-7. In other words, the percentage of self-sufficiency in another 10 years (which is not far away) will be half of what it was in 1990-91.

This emphasises the immense task ahead for all the institutions involved in meeting the country's petroleum product requirements. According to the report of the

Strategic Planning Group on Restructuring of Oil Industries (referred to as the R group), mobilisation of Rs. 180,000 crore is required as venture capital for investment in the exploration and production sector alone in the next few years.

Several policy initiatives are required to tackle the gigantic task ahead. Delivering the Third Lovraj Kumar Memorial lecture on India's oil policy in the coming century, Dr. Vijay Kelkar, Secretary, Ministry of Petroleum and Natural Gas, visualises that in the coming century, India will be one of the great industrial powers and obviously oil policy will have to subserve this goal.

Talking about India's oil policy not only from a long-term perspective but also in the international context, Dr. Kelkar is of the view that if the 20th century was the century of oil, the 21 st century would be the century of natural gas.

Not only natural gas is more abundant in terms of reserves but also it is more evenly spread in terms of geographical distribution of these reserves and thus offering greater security of supplies. At the present rate of depletion, Dr. Kelkar points out, the global reserves of crude oil will last 43 years and natural gas 66 years.

Pointing out that India's current consumption of petroleum products is around 78 million tonnes and will be growing at the rate of about 10 per cent or so per annum over the next decades and exceed 270 million tonnes by 2020, Dr. Kelkar says that even by early part of the next century itself India would have already become one of the top five consumers of petroleum products, ahead of a number of major OECD countries such as France, U.K. and just behind China and Russia. In other words, India's import requirements would be growing faster with total demand exceeding total supply resulting in increased import dependence for oil and also for natural gas.

Comparing India's situation with other countries which have very little domestic hydrocarbon resources, Dr. Kelkar has pointed out the first element of policy thrust has to be accelerated exploration programme within the country. In this India is fortunately placed because over the last several decades, the country has created a great institutional base in exploration, production and refining. But Indian institutions have to become more efficient, internationally competitive and try to maximise India's share in global equity oil (like some of the other countries have done who have very little hydrocarbon resources).

Another policy element is to review the present administered pricing mechanism (APM) under which a number of petroleum products are heavily subsidised. This aspect has been gone into at length by the R Group, which has suggested a phased withdrawal of the present administrative pricing mechanism, under which the main operators in the petroleum sector have little inducement to become more efficient as the return is based on a cost-plus formula.

Even from the point of view of generating more resources for re-investment in the industry to meet future demands of the country, a review of APM should form an integral part of future oil policy.

Addressing the economic editors conference in Delhi in November, Mr. T. Baalu, Minister of State for Petroleum and Natural Gas, highlighted that the cumulative outstanding claims of oil companies from the oil pool account are likely to touch Rs. 15,500 crore by March 31, 1997.

On of the reasons he cited for this mounting outstanding claims is the non-adjustment of selling prices of petroleum products in the context of increased imports and rise in international prices of crude oil.

Gross imports of crude oil and petroleum products at 47.68 million tonnes in 1995-96 were 15.4 per cent higher than in the previous year. If the value of these imports was Rs. 17,838 crore in 1994-95, the bill rose to Rs. 24,095 crore in 1995-96.

According to the R Group report, the contribution to the exchequer both Centre and States) from the oil and gas industry by way of royalty on crude oil and gas, oil development cess, excise and customs duties, corporate taxes and dividends worked out to Rs. 24,493 crore in 1994-95. If one excludes the share of the States out of these levies, the Centre is already spending more on imports of oil and petroleum products than the contribution being made by oil and gas industry to the exchequer.

Here, it must also be noted that the Central Government mopped up 47 per cent of oil revenue in 1993-94 by way of taxes, royalties, etc. Oil and gas industry is thus a large source of revenue for the Centre.

Organisational structure

A number of organisations are engaged in exploration and development of mineral resources in India. These include Geolgical survey of India (GSI), Indian Bureau of Mines (IBM) and a number of public sector undertakings under the administrative control of the Ministry of Mines.

Geological Survey of India functions as the premier national organisation for earth science, entrusted with the task of scientific survey and research for locating mineral resources (except oil, natural gas and atomic minerals), systematic generation and continous updating of geoscience information through ground, airborne and marine survey, the entire gamut of activities being related to multifarious developmental needs of the country. The survey operates within the ambit of its charter 1873 and priorities laid down by the Government. The other important functions of the organisation cover management of natural hazards like earthquake, floods, landslides, volcanism etc., providing geotechnical advice to all the major civil engineering, communication and urban development projects, geoenvironmental resource appraisal, upgradation of geoscientific expertise through training. The results of GSI investigations are documented in the form of scientific and technical reports, professional papers, maps, inventories and various types of publications.

The survey with its central headquarters at Calcutta, functions through six geographically based regions, three activity based Wings (Marine, Coal and Airborne Survey) and one training Institute. In each of the region/wings towards greater collaboration and setting up of consultancy and commercial endeavours in the third world countries.

The Indian Bureau of Mines (IBM) is the national organisation under Ministry of Mines and engaged in promotion, conservation and scientific development of mineral resources of the country other than coal, petroleum and natural gas, atomic minerals and minor minerals. It performs regulatory functions, namely enforcement of Mines and Minerals (Regulation & Development Rules and the provision of Environmental Protection Act. It also undertakes scientific techno-economic, research-orientid studies in various aspects such as geological, mining ore beneficiation and environment. IBM provides technical consultancy services to the mining industry for geological appraisal of mineral resources and preparation of feasibility reports of mining projects including beneficiation plants. It prepares mineral maps and countrywide inventory of minerals resources of leasehold and freehold areas. IBM also functions as data bank for mines and minerals and publishes statistical periodicals and brings out technical publications/monogrphs on individual mineral commodities and bulletins on different connected subjects. it advises the Central and state governments on all aspects of mineral industry, trade and legislation. It imparts training to technical and non-technical officials of IBM and also persons from mineral industry and other agencies in India and abroad. IBM is organised into six functional agencies in India and abroad. IBM is organised into six functional divisions. It has its headquarters at Nagpur and 11 regional offices and well equipped ore-dressing laboratories and Pilot Plant at Nagpur, besides, two regional ore-dressing laboratories at Ajmer and Bangalore. IBM also has a big Central Library with about 61,000 books.

Minral Exploration Corporation Limited (MECL) was created in 1972 with the main objective of bridging the gap between the discovery of mineral prospect and its eventual exploitation. Its identified major functions are to plan, promote, organise and implement programme for the exploration of mineral resources and to perform such functions as Central Government may from time to time, assign to the company in connection with exploration of the mineral resources in and outside the country. The Corporation has its headquarters at Nagpur. MECL has fulfilled its main objective by establishing over 55,000 million tonnes of reserves of higher confidence for veriety of minerals. The drilling capacity of 72,000 m per annum at the time of inception in 1972 has increased to 4.25 lakh metre of drilling and mining capacity has increased from 1200 mtr in 1972 to 9000 m in the last year of Seventh Five Year Plan. During 1993-94, the turnover of the company was Rs. 40.73 crore.

Bharat Aluminium Company Limited (BALCO) was incorporated on 27 November 1965 as the first primary aluminium producing undertaking in the public sector.

The Company is operating Korba Aluminium Complex in Bilaspur district of Madhya Pradesh and Bidhanbag Unit in Asanosl in west Bengal. It has a capacity to produce one lakh tonnes of aluminium metal/products. During the past few years, the Company's production of saleable metal/products has been about 92,000 tonnes per annum. Its net profit has been going up steadily and during 1994-95, it earned a net profit of Rs. 90.51 crore (provisional). The new projects of the Company include installation of a new Cold Rolling Mill having an installed capacity to produce 40,000 TPA of thin quality sheets/coils. The Comapny is also in the process of modernisation of their smelter plant at Korba for increased productivity and reduction of power consumption, which is a major factor in input costs.

National Aluminium Company Limited (NALCO) was incorporated on 7 January 1981 with the objective to produce alumina and aluminium. Its registerd office is at Bhubaneswar. It operates a bauxite mine to raise 24 lakh tonnes per annum of bauxite from the Parnchpatnali (Koraput) deposits, an eight lakh tonnes per annum alumina refinery at Damanjodi (Koraput), a 2,18,000 tonnes per annum aluminium smelter at Angul (Dhenkanal) and six 120 MW captive power plants at Angul to feed the smelter. Aluminium Pechiney of France was the technical consultants for the project and had supplied the technical know-how and basic engineering package.

NALCO received ISO 9002 Certification from IROS for Alumina Refinery on 21 November 1994 and ISO 9002 Certification for quality system for Smelter Plan in March 1995 from RWTUV. Highest production of calcined alumina of 81,000 MT during January 1995 exceeding the rated capacity. NALCO produced 1,78,072 tonnes of aluminium and earned net profit of Rs. 294.62 (provisional) during the same period.

Hindustan Zinc Limited (HZL) was incorporated on 10 January 1966 to take over operations of the earstwhile Metal Corporation of India Limited and to develop mining and smelting capacities to substantially meet the domestic demand of zinc and lead metals. With headquarters at Udaipur, HZL's operations are spread over in the states of Rajasthan, Andhra Pradesh, Orissa and Bihar consisting of five mines with a total lead-zinc ore production capacity of 3.04 million tpa and four smelters with combined installed capacity of 1,49,000 tpa zinc and 65,000 tpa lead besides a rock phosphate and tungsten mine. The company offers a wide range of zinc and lead metal grades to its customers, besides a range of by-products. The production of zinc metal by the company during the last four years has ranged between 84,600 tpa and 1,19,810 tpa. The lead production during the same period has ranged between 30,300 tpa and 34,500 tpa. The sales turnover of the company during 1994-95 was Rs. 97,274 lakh and its net profit (after tax) during the same period was Rs. 7,643 lakh.

HZL signed a Memorandum of Understanding with M/s. Niugini Mining Limited.Australia, to identify gold resources in India and later on if resources are found viable, to set up a joint venture. It has also signed an MoU with M/s. BHP Minerals, Austrails, for exploration and development of base and procious metals in Rajasthan. Besides, HZL and BRGM, France, have reached an agreement with Vietnam Rare and Precious Metal Corporation (VMC) for setting up of joint venture for exploration and development of Pac Lang Gold Prospect in Vietnam.

Hindustan Copper Limited (HCL) is the sole producer of primary copper metal in the country. It was incorporated on 7 November 1967, to take over from the National Mineral Development Corporation, projects, schemes and studies pertaining to exploration, exploitation, mining and smelting of copper. In 1972, the erstwhile Indian Copper Corporation Limit, a company incorporated in England was nationalised and merged with HCl. The main projects of the company are: (i) Khetri Copper Complex (KCC) in Rajasthan comprising Khetri, Kolihan, Chandmari and Dariba mines (since closed), concentrators at Dariba (since closed) and Khetri, Metallurgical and fertilizer plants at Khetri; (ii) Indian Copper Complex (ICC) at Ghatsila in Bihar comprising Mosaboni, Fathargora, Kendadih and Rakha Mines, three concentrators at Mosaboni, Moubhandar (since closed) and Rakha and metallurgical plants for copper and by-product recovery at Moubhandari (iii) Malanjkhand Copper Project (MCP) at Malanjkhand in Madhya Pradesh comprising an open pit mine, concentrator and leach copper plant; and (iv) Taloja Copper Project (TCP) at Taloja in Maharashtra for conversion of cathodes both imported and part of our own into continuous cast copper wirerods as value added product. The company produces primary copper products in the form of cathodes, wirebars, wirerods and is also engaged in manufacturing of single super phosphate, sulphuric acid, gold, silver, selenium, tellurium, palladium, copper sulphate and nickel sulphate as by-products.

The current operation plants of the company are to produce and market about 70,000 Mt copper in different forms out of which 45,000 MT of refined copper is produced from indigenous ore resources. With the changed economic scenario in the country, HCL has initiated process of restructuring of companies to remain competitive. During 1994-95, the turnover of the company was Rs. 932.95 and its production of refined copper was 46,134 MT.

Bharat Gold Mines Limited operates the world famous century old Kolar Gold Mines in Karnataka State. The company was nationalised in 1956 and was incorporated as a public sector company under the Department of Mines, Government of India in March 1972. Though the gold mining is the principal activity of the company, as a corporate stategy, it has diversified into the field of mine construction and contract works, manufacture of mining machinery and components of equipment.

The company has three major activities namely: (i) Gold mining: Two mines in Kolar Gold Fields, Karntaka-Mysore Champion Amalgamated mine and Nundydroog mine, and three mines in Andhra Pradesh, Yeppamana mine, (Anantapur); Chigargunta mine; and Old Bisanatham mine, (Chittoor); (ii) Mine Project and Construction Division-Taking up mine construction and development works for other mining (coal and metal mines) industries all over India, and (iii) Workshop Diversification-The workshops manufacture mining machineries and components of certain equipment and undertake jobbing works, like machining and fabrication for major industries in the country.

The company's registered office is at Koar Gold Fields and its liaison office is at New Delhi. In 1994-95, the company produced 650.28 kg of gold. The continued financial losses over the decade has resulted in the company being declared as a sick industry and consequently referred to Board for Industrial and Financial Reconstruction (BIFR) who have appointed ICICI as Operating Agency to formulate a rehabilitation package envisaging increase in gold production from the existing shallow mines to ensure economic viability, exploration and exploitation of gold from the BGML lease-hold areas in collaboration with a suitable joint venture partner and to recover gold from old mill tailings accumulated over the years by constructing a suitable gold recovery plant by BGML.

Sikkim Mining Corporation was established as joint venture of Sikkim State and Government of India in 1960 by proclamation of erstwhile "Sikkim Darbar". the objective of the Corporation is to mine multimental ore for production of copper, lead and zinc concentrates. The Corporation has only one mine (Bhotang Mine) Situated at Rangpo (East Sikkim). During 1994-95, the Corporation produced 270 mt tonnes of copper concentrate, 85 mt of lead concentrate and 568 mt of zinc concentrate. Zinc concentrate is being sold to M/s. Hindustan Zinc Ltd. since April 1994. Hindustan Copper Limited has stopped taking copper concentrate, M/s. HAMCO Mining and Smelting Limited, Calcutta, has lifted 3,500 tonnes of lead, 200 tonnes of copper and 200 tonnes of zono concentrates on trial basis in the year 1994-95.

Policy issues

The National Mineral Policy, 1993, announced on 5 March 1993, in brief, had dispensed with the reservation of all the minerals reserved for exclusive exploitation by public sector and also for the first time, sought to invite foreign investment in the mining sector. The amendments to the Mines and Minerals (Regulation & Development) Act, 1957 seek to further elaborate the principles enunciated in the National Mineral Policy by, among others, devolving more powers to the state governments, providing greater stability of tenure in mining leases and by accelerating inflow of private capital, both domestic and foreign, as also the state-of-the-art technology into the mineral sector.

The amended Act has deleted 15 minerals hitherto listed in the First Schedule of the MM (R&D) Act, 1957 requiring prior approval of the Central Government before the state government could grant a prospecting licence of a mining lease. The minerals so deleted are apatite and phosphatic ores, barytes, dolomite, gypsum, kyanite, magnesite, molybdenum, nickel, platimum and other precious metals, sillimanite, silver, sulphur and its ores, tin, tungsten and vanadium ore. With this deletion (excepting the atomic minerals and fuel minerals), there would only be 11 minerals left for which the state government would require prior approval of the Central Government. These are asbestos, bauxite, chrome ore, copper ore, gold, iron ore, lead, limestone (except where it is used in kilns for the manufacute of lime as building materials) manganese ore, precious stones and zinc. the amended Act has removed any restriction on equity holding by foreign nationals in a mining company. As of now, any company registered or incorporated in India can apply for a prospecting licence of a mining lease from the concerned state government. For the first time, a minimum period of lease of 20 years, has been made mandatory. The maximum period for grant of lease has been increased to 30 years. Further renewals are possible with approval of the Central Government. The period for which prospecting licence can be granted has been increased to three years and these licences can be renewed at the discretion of the state governments so that the total period does not exceed five years. The amended Act also provides that no appeal or revision will lie to the Central Government against orders passed by the state governments with regard to minor minerals. State governments have also been empowered to terminate leases of minor minerals without prior approval of the Central Government. The amended Act also introduces a new section, whch gives powers to carry out searches to check unauthorised mining. The Act, was amended to increase the period before which a lease can lapse from one year to two years. In addition, the amendment also provides that notifications issued by state governments under their minor minerals concession rules must be placed before the State Legislature and also empowers the Central Government to modify leases not in conformity with the Act to bring them in line with the provisions of the MMR&D Act, 1957.

While of course it is true that it is the Centre's responsibility to find adequate funds to develop the oil and gas industry, the above figures only highlight the need to let the oil and gas industry generate more internal resources to finance its future development. It is an open secret that the Government of India's finances are none too rosy and there are too many competing claims on the limited kitty available with the Centre.

All the more reason for immediate reforms in the hydrocarbons sector. Though it is difficult to quantify in monetary terms the benefits of reforms, the R Group has estimated that the net present value of the reforms it has suggested would amount to around Rs. 100,000 crore. And that is a lot of money.

The controversy that is raging at the moment over raising the prices of some of the heavily subsidised petroleum products only serve to highlight the problems that arise in opening up the oil and gas sector in line with the changes that are taking place in other sectors of the economy.

For instance, it is widely admitted (even in official publicity material) that a level playing field should be given to national oil companies "particularly by paying them international market price of oil". This will help them to raise more revenue, but this good intention still remains on paper only.

"If discovered fields are offered in future for improving economic viabiloity, the national oil companies, who have discovered the fields, should be reimbursed the past costs incurred by them", says an official note explaining the short-term measures to be taken for development of the oil sector. This is another contentious issue on which there is more noise than action.

The Government has allowed entry of private sector in a major way into the oil refining sector (proposals, including export-oriented refineries, adding up to 70 million tonnes per annum have been cleared so far). Similarly, parallel marketing in gas has been allowed (though this has yet to pick up) and with the approval in principle for the Southern Gas Grid, several policy decisions with regard to the natural gas sector have also to be taken. For instance, natural gas is underpriced and there is a recommendation that it should be raised.

Development of the natural gas sector (which will, as per present indications, will be largely based on imported gas) means heavy investment in pipelines, port and storage facililties, etc. It takes years to set up these. Here again, to facilitate and encourage investment, a rational pricing policy must be in place, the sooner the better.

Since the country has mastered the art and science of setting up refineries as well as running them, experts believe that india might become a net exporter of petroleum products in the coming century and a "swing producer" to stabilise global product markets. This expectation is based on the fact that India is one of the lowest cost refiners in the world.

But, to quote Dr. Kelkar again, "our present administered prices regime is non-transparent and certainly not efficency compatible. Further, our current tariffs provide negative rate of protection for the refining sector and as such it discourages provate investors to bring in new investments". Hence, what is required is comprehensive reforms of pricing and tariff policy as that alone can promote adequate infusion of capital and efficient use of these resources, he argues.

Now, that prescription applies not only to the refining sector, but to the entire oil and natural gas sector. This is not the place to go into specific details, but a visionary approach is needed similar tot he one shown by many of those who have helped paying the foundation for the oil and gas industry.

The great institutional base built up within the country over the past several decades in exploration, production and refining should be strengthened further, along with the entry of a range of new actors. Major investments are taking place in sectors like automobiles, but these can become infructuous if the main engine of growth (here one means both industrial and agricultural growth) i.e. the oil and gas sector, is not properly taken care of. It is time we put this sector on a faster track.

Alternative fuels

Ministry of Non-Conventional Energy Sources is endeavouring to develop alternatives to diesel and motor sprit in order to reduce their consumption and outflow of precious foreign exchange. The main alternatives are battery-operated vehicles (BOV); use of alcohol, methanol/ethanol as a fuel in diesel and petrol vehicles; and use of compressed natural gas (CNG) as a fuel. In different areas of the country, 235 battery-operated and 105 alcohol-operated vehicles have been taken up for demonstration. Apart from this, a new project to develop 100 alcohol based vehicles has been taken up in Gujarat.

FIPB had cleared in February 1994 a joint venture proposal for manufacture of solar battery car developed by M/s Frazer-Nash, UK, in India in collaboration with M/s Peerless Limited, Calcutta. It has been reported that the performance of the four wheel drive solar battery car is quite compatible to Indian autorickshaws and it can find the market potential in India among educated unemployed for rural and city mass transport, postal department, industrial sectors and various shuttle service applications.

Use of hydrogen as an energy source involves five basic issues i.e. production, storage and transportation, utilisation, safety management and economy. A 100 cc four stroke hydrogen/hydride fuelled motorcycle has been developed and development efforts to increase the range of the motor cycle is under way. The plan for hydrogen fuelled three-wheelers and motor-cars is at planning stage. The other important use of hydrogen energy is in heat pumps and refrigeration. The projects on heat pumps have been progressing well at Indian Institute of Technology, Madras. The production and storage of hydrogen has been pursued at Banaras Hindu University, Varanasi, Osmania University, Hyderabad and Rajasthan University, Jaipur.

The conversion of solar energy into chemical energy is an imortant route for tapping solar energy as it allows storage of solar energy also. As many as 50 research and development projects in the area of photovoltaic chemical cells, photovoltaics and photosynthesis have been funded and good results have been achieved in these areas. The other two areas pursued under chemical sources of energy are duel cell and electro-chemical storage batteries. A 2.5 kw phosphoric acid fuel cell (PAFC) has been developed and is under test. Plan for 200 kw PAFC has been prepared. The programme on storage batteries is for development of storage systems needed for intermittent energy sources like solar, wind, etc., and for vehicular use. Amongst commercial batteries currently available, lead acid battery seems to hold attractive position. However, lead resources in India are rather limited. The other battery systems are such as nickel-cadmium, dilver-zinc, nickel-hydrogen, etc. Materials and construction methods are too expensive fo find application.

A project on 'Development of Sodium Sulphur Batteries' suitable for electric vehicles, satellite communications, photovoltaic energy storage and submarine power etc., has been undertaken at Central Electrochemical Research Institute, (CERI) Karaikudi and NPL, New Delhi

The Ministry is actively pursuing the proposal for setting up a tidal power plant for 900 mw in the Gulf of Kachchh at an estimated cost of Rs. 4,000 crore. The tidal power potential in the country is estimated to be of the order of 8,000 mw to 9,00 mw (approximatley 7,000 mw in Gulf of Cambay, 1,000 mw in Gulf of Kachchh and 100 mw in Sundarbans). A techno economic feasibility report has been prepared by the CEA/NHPC for a 900 mw tidal power plant at Gulf of Kachchh. This project is proposed to be included as a command area development project in the state sector.

India is having large potential of Ocean Thermal Energy Conversion (OTEC) which could be of the order about 50,000 mw. M/s Sea Solar Power Inc., USA, is promoting the use of ocean thermal energy conversion technlogy and the first plant is proposed off the coast of Tamil Nadu with a capacity of 100 mw at a cost of about Rs. 750 crore, the finance being entirely brought in by the overseas entrepreneurs. The company has signed the MOU for this project with TEDA and TNEB of Government of Tamil Nadu in January 1994.

Wave Energy Potential in India is estimated about 40,000 mw. One wave energy power plant of 150 kw (maximum) capacity based on OWC has been installed in Vzhinjam near Thiruvananthapuram by IIT, Madras under a sponsored project by Department of Ocean Development. The power plant has been commissioned and is under trial. One Swedish organisation Sea Power (HWPC) concept. Harnessing a wave energy on this principle in India is being explored and a one mw wave energy plant is being set up in the Andaman and Nicobar Islands.

Geothermal manifestations are widespread in India, in the form of 340 identified hot springs localities, many of these having temperature near boiling point at their places of occurrence. There is considerable scope for the development and exploitation of geothermal energy resources. The ongoing activities include the survey and assessment of geothermal potential, utilization of geothermal energy for direct heat and power generation. A five kw geothermal pilot power plant has been commissioned at Manikaran in Kullu district of Himachal Pradesh. The assessment of geothermal power potential in Puga Valley Ladakh in Jammu and Kashmir has been done through Manageto-Telluric surveys and geo-scientific studies. A potential of 4-5 mw geothermal power has been estimated in the Valley. Proposal to explore this potential for power generation and utilization for nearly localities is being finaslised. The use of geothermal energy for space heating and green house effect has been demonstrated. A project on mushroom cultivation and poultry framing using geothermal fluid is under implementation at Regional Research Laboratory, Jammu.

The main objective of Indian Renewable Energy Development Agency (IREDA) is to act as a catalyst agent for accelerating commercialization of new and renewable rources of energy. IREDA has been assigned the main task of administering a revolving fund to promote, develop and finance on soft terms the NRSE technologies. The resources base of IREDA mainly consists of equity support from the Government of India, grants from foreign and international organisations, borrowings and internal accruals. The authorised share capital has been raised from Rs. 25 crore to Rs. 100 crore during 1994-95. In addition, the Government of Netherlands have already given to IREDA grant-in-aid of 17 million Guilders for assisting NRSE projects. It has further committed an amount of 23 million Guilders.

The World Bank has also agreed to provide US dollar 195 million which includes a grant-in-aid component of US dollar 30 million to be contributed by Global Environment Trust Fund and Swiss Development Cooperation for financing projects to generate power through wind energy, small hydro and solar photovoltaic schemes. IREDA has also signed an agreement with the Asian Development Bank to receive technical assistance of US dollar 3.54 lakh and a credit of US dollar 150 million is under finalisation.

The Ministry of Non-Conventional Energy Sources has established a Solar Energy Centre as an institute dedicated to the development and testing of solar energy products. The Centre has state-of-art facilities for the testing of both solar thermal and solar photovoltaic devices. Asia's largest indoor sun simulator for measurements on solar thermal collectors has been dedicated to the Centre in May 1994. In addition, there are specialised simulators for measurements on solar cells and photovoltaic modules as well as equipment for testing of systems for different applications. The Centre is coordinating cooperative activities in solar energy among G-15 countries. It is being developed as a centre of excellence of international standard.

India a vast potential of renewable energy sources and a number of technologies have been developed to harness them. A sizeable industrial base has been created in the country in the various renewable energy technologies such as solar thermal, solar photovoltaics, wind, small hydro, biomass etc. An aggregate capacity of about 900 MW has been installed, based on these technologies.

The Indian Renewable Energy Development Agency Ltd. (IREDA) was established in March, 1987 as a public sector enterprise for the promotion, development and financing of New and Renewable Sources of Energy (NRSE) technologies. During 1995-96, IREDA sanctioned laon assistance of Rs. 602.22 crore in respect of 265 projects. Thus, the total number of projects financed by IREDA reached 728 with IREDA's loan commitment of Rs. 1107.48 crore and cumulative disbursement of Rs. 472.49 crore as on March, 31, 1996.

National Project Biogas Development (NPBD) was taken up in the Contral Sector during 1981-82 on a country-wide basis. Against the potential of 120 lakh numbers of family tye biogas plants the installation has reached 23.59 lakh by 1995-96. Against the target of 1.60 lakh family type biogas plants during 1995-96, achievement was at 1.71 lakh plants. Besides family size biogas plants, the Ministry of Non-Conventional Energy Sources is also promoting the setting up of community, institutional and nightsoil based biogas plants (CBP/IBP/NBP) in the country. About 1400 institutional CBP/IBP and NBP plants were installled up to 1994-95. Against annual target of 200 plants during 1995-96, completion has been reported at 228 plants at a cost of Rs. 2.48 crore.

National Programme on Improved Chulha (NPIC) was taken up as a national programme since 1985 and also included in the 20-Point Programme of the Government. Against the potential of 1200 lakh chulhas in the country, 227.35 lakh nos. of chulahs have been installed upto the end of March, 1996. Over 26 lakh improved chulhas have been installed during 1995-96 against the target of 24 lakh chulhas with budget estimates of Rs. 15 crore.

Biomass programme offer an environmental advantage over conventional fuels for various applications as they are by and large ecofriendly. A number of technologies have been commercialised such as briquetting, gastification etc. Incentive are being given for gasifier systems developed from 5 HP to 10 HP for mechanical energy, 3 KW to 5 KW for electrical applications and 7,500 k cal/hr. to 12.5 lakh k.cal/hr for thermal application. work is also in progress on 70 fast growing fuelwood tree species for raising yield and acreage in the country.

India has achieved considerable progress in the exploitation of wind energy during the last few years. A total capacity of 732 MW has been installed by the end of the year 1995-96 of which 684 MW has been installed by the private sector. It is expected to reach 1000 MW by the end of the Eighth Plan and that would place India in the second position in Wind Energy, after USA.

A total capacity of 121 MW has been constructed under the Small Hydro Power Projects (SHP) and 234 MW capacity is under construction. A numbur of financial and fiscal incentives are provided for the speedy implementation of Small Hydro Projects based on water falls, canals, small rivers and streams. Portable mini hydel sets of 10-50 KW capacity have also been introduced by the Ministry. Under the World Bank line of credit, soft loans upto 15 MW capacity are available to private developers from IREDA.

The solar Photovoltaic (SPV) programmes has now progressed from projects of a few KW to hundreds of KW installation for power generation. Two grid connected projects of 100 KW each have been installed at Kalyan Pur in Aligarh and Sarai Saadi in Mau Districts of U.P. These plants, besides meeting the requirements of concerned villages are also providing 25 KW power each to the state grid. Three solar photovoltaic projects to generate electricity of higher ratings are under consideration for the State of Rajasthan.

For accelerated development of solar photovoltaic production, Government has introduced socially oriented and market oriented schemes. The socially oriented sheme is implemented through State Nodal Agencies and involves Central subsidy. The market oriented scheme is implemented through IREDA by providing soft loan assistance. In addition. IREDA is implementing the World Bank assisted SPV Market Development Project. Under the socially oriented scheme subsidy to the extent of 50% of the cost of the system is allowed to all categories of beneficiaries. The special category covers States/UTs with desert areas, islands, hilly regions, as well as Scheduled Castes, Scheduled Tribes, Fishermen, Handloom workerts, village artisans and handicapped persons throughout the country. During tyhe year 1995-96, 680 street lighting systems, 7,470 domestic lighting systems, 44,938 solar lanterns and power plants of an aggregate capacity of 89 Kwp were unstalled.

A National programme has been launched since June 1995 for proper treatment of urban and industrial wastes and the resultant recovery of energy from these sources. In order to speed up the various programmes, a National Bioenergy Board (NBB) has been set up for evolving policy guidance and direction. A number of State Government and Nodal Agencies have initiated projects for energy recovery from industrial and municipal wastes in the country. The Integrated Rural Energy Programme (IREP) is utilising locally available energy resources at the village level which has been extended to 108 blocks, taking the total number to 660 in 1995-96.

Plan and policy

The non-conventional sources of energy are capable of solving the twin problems of energy supply in a decentralised manner and helping in sustaining cleaner environment.

A new strategy and action plan for the remaining period of the Eighth Plan has been formulated. Against the original Plan target of 500-600 mw, the new action plan envisages a four-fold increase aiming at a target of 2,000 mv of renewable energy, through mobilization of institutional financing (including bilateral and multilateral funding) and purely private sector investments stimulated through entrepreneur development and a package of incentives. Policy changes have been made in both solar photovoltaics and solar thermal fields to encourage market development and minimize dorect subsidies. This opening up of the market especially for solar photovoltaics, has resulted in greater competition, modernization and cost reduction and in overcoming programme infirmities and encouraging genuine entrepreneurs. Rapid growth of solar photovoltaic and solar hot water industry has started as a result of introduction of incentives and soft loans against the budget-drive subsidy programme. Policies have been pursued to encourage direct foreign investment and collaborations including tapping of NRIs have shown interest and are in the process of setting up of projects such as wind farms, solar plants in the states of Andhra Pradesh, Gujarat, Karnataka, Madhya Pradesh and Kerala.

Inter-agency and inter-ministerial contacts have been pursued to bring about greater involvement of user agencies. Initiatives have been taken to promote renewable energy applications in Defence, Railways, Tele-communications and similar establishments. Initiatives have also been taken to develop joint programmes with the Rural Electrification Corporation for promotion of decentralised renewable systems in villages still remaining unelectrified.

India is today recognised as one of the pioneer country in the field of renewable sources of energy. A three-fold strategy has been pursued by the Ministry of Non-conventional Energy Sources (MNES) for the promotion of new and renewable sources of energy (NRSE). This includes: (a) providing budgetary resources of Government for demonstration projects; (b) extending institutional finance from Renewable Indian Energy Development Agency (IREDA) and other financial institutions, for commercially viable projects, with private sector participation and external assistance from multilateral agencies like World Bank, GEF, ADB etc.; and (c) promoting private investment through fiscal incentives, tax holidays, depreciation allowance, facilities for wheeling and banking power for the grid and remunerative price for the power provided for the grid. The MNES intends to promote a new community of 'energy entrepreneurs' whereas the Government will act as the 'mission leader' giving a special focus and direction to the NRSE sector.

The total potential for wind energy in the country is estimated to be 20,000 mw. The Central Government intends to create a wind energy capacity of 500 mw in the Eighth Five year Plan. With the achievement of this target India would become a major wind power producer in the world. Asia's largest wind farm cluster of 150 mw is located at Muppandal in Tamil Nadu.

A comprehensive wind mapoing programme to identify prospective sites for wind farming has been undertaken, 179 wind mapping and 83 wind monitoring stations are operational in the country. Eighty sites have so far been identified in the states of Tamil Nadu, Andhra Pradesh, Gujarat, Karnataka, Kerala, Madhya Pradesh, Maharashtra and Lakshadweep. The total capacity of wind energy to be generated is expected to be 3,000 mw in these areas. The installed capacity in the wind farm sector is 370 mw and a number of projects are under installation in tamil Nadu, Gujarat, Andhra

Pradesh, Kerala, Karnataka and Madhya Pradesh. Several major developers, particularly from United States such as Cannon, Ford, Seawest, Carter Wind Turbines, Optimum Power, etc., are actively working on large proposals. So far 500 million units of energy has been generated and fed to the grids.

MNES is dealing with the implementation of small hydro power projects upto three mw. The new strategy and action plan aims at achieving a goal of 600 mw of energy power generation during the Eight Plan period through small hydro power projects. This is three times the target originally envisaged for the Eighth Five Year Plan. Around 2,000 potential sites with an estimated capacity of 5,000 mw have been identified in various states including potential states of Uttar Pradesh, Arunachal Pradesh, Orissa, Andhra Pradesh, Kerala, Madhya Pradesh, Himachal Pradesh, Punjab and the target of 600 mw in the Eighth Plan is expected to cover almost 1,000 sites in different states. To encourage exploitation of this potential, Ministry has announced a composite scheme for survey, investigation and DPR preparation under which cent per cent cost of survey and investigations and 50 per cent of the cost of DPR preparation is provided as grant, 44 projects aggregating 29 mw for survey and investigation, 36 projects aggregating 52 mw for DPR preparation and in addition 87 projects aggregating to 94.5 mw have been sanctioned under the Ministry's capital subsidy scheme for actual implementation of SHP projects.

Projects of 114 mw capacity have so far been installed and projects worth 220 mw capacity are under implementation. It is anticipated that the potential of small hydro power projects upto 15 mw per site in the country may exceed 10,000 mw. The state governments of Kerala, Karnataka and Tamil Nadu have already signed MOUs with private developers and agreed to lease out a number of sites for private investments in small hydro power projects.

In view of the remoteness and lack of infrastructure and grid in various areas, particularly in the hilly areas, an innovative scheme for providing 50 portable micro-hydel sets upto 15 kw capacity each for local communities in these areas was also launched. A UNDP/GEF project on optimizing development of small hydel resources in the Himalayan and sub-Himalayan regions become operational with a UNDP contribution of US dollar 7.5 million and counterpart funding of Rs. 22 crore. Thirteen hilly states will participate in the project under which a Master Plan will be evolved and twenty demonstration projects will be installed.

Bagasse based co-generation new programme, launched in January 1994, envisages creation of 300 mw power generation capacity during the Eighth Plan. The programme is targeted at around 420 existing and around 90 new sugar mills, where a potential of 3,500 mw of power generation is estimated. The thrust of the programme is towards upgradation of existing co-generation facilities of sugar mills, which basically cater to captive steam and power requirements, to ensure generation of surplus power. A salient feature of the programme is the demonstration project scheme, under which 10-12 selected state-of-the-art projects in major sugar producing states will be provided with 30 per cent subsidy by the Ministry. USAID/GEF have approved a project for alternative biomass co-generation during off-season with funding support of US dollar 12.5 million for technical assistance and to leverage financing for such projects in selected sugar mills. Programmes are also being developed for direct biomass combustion and grid-connected gasification projects using woody biomass and agricultural residues.

The solar photovoltaic systems are currently being used in the country on a commercial basis for powering a variety of lower power applications in rural, remote and un-electrified areas for lighting and water pumping, power for railway signalling, rural telephones, microwave repeater stations and TV transmissions. Under the new strategy and action plan, one lakh number of solar lanterns initiated for both socially oriented and market oriented schemes. So far, 30,000 solar lanterns have been distributed under the programme. Over 60,000 solar photovoltaic systems with total capacity of four mw have been installed in the country. The socially oriented programme specially meant for designated areas and provide subsidy of 50 per cent of the cost. Solar photovoltaic systems with total capacity of 25 mw are proposed to be installed during the Eighth Plan period.

In August 1993 the Ministry has launched a demonstration project for the deployment of 1,000 solar photovoltaic (SPV) water pumps for agriculture and related uses at a cost of about Rs. 28 crore. So far, 397 pumps have been installed and orders for 625 have been booked. Seven manufacturers have finalilsed business plans and some of them have secured loans from IREDA.

The first two 100 kw partial grid interactive solar photovoltaic power projects at Kalyanpur in Aligarh district and Saraisadi in Mau district of Uttar Pradesh have been commissioned. A concept of strengthening of substations with small additions of 20 to 25 kw PV capacity to enhance grid stability is also under examination. In pursuance of the special emphasis being accorded by Government of India for generation of grid quality power from non-conventional energy sources, the Ministry has received several proposals of about 10 mw capacity from prospective promoters in the private sector for establishing grid interactive solar photovoltaic power plants which are being negotiated on build, own and operate (BOO) basis. Three preliminary proposals from American companies have already been received.

Technologies for solar water heating systems and solar cookers have been developed and are being commercialized. Solar thermal systems for various other applications like, solar air heating, crop drying, timber seasoning and water desalination have also been developed and the new action plan envisages their commercialization. Solar thermal systems are today supplementing thermal energy requirements at various temperatures from 60-380 degree celsius for different domestic and industrial applications including process heating and power generation. One lakh LPD solar water heating system at 8 degrees celsius installed at the Hindustan Spinning and Weaving Mill, Bombay. About three lakh sq.mt collector area has been installed in the country for various domestic and industrial applications. There are about 3.5 lakh solar cookers used in the country. Solar water heating systems have vast potential to save electricity in domestic and commercial sectors and furnace oil in industrial sector which otherwise are being used for hot water supply. A provision in municipal law is beingmade for mandatory installation of solar water heating systems in functional buildings. All state governments have been requested to issue directives to local bodies under their control to extend this decision to buildings in private sector by making suitable provision in building bye-laws.

A proposal for setting up a 35 mw size solar thermal power project at Maithania village, Jodhpur, Rajasthan based on line focussing collectors has been under the consideration of the Ministry. Detailed feasibility and project reports have been prepared which are under discussion with World Bank, GEF and Government of Germany for soft loan financing.

So far 21.85 lakh numbers of family type biogas plants and 196 lakh improved chulhas havebeen installed. Under the new strategy and action plan, it is envisaged to install 10 lakh numbers of bio-gas plants during the Eighth Plan period as against 7.5 lakh numbers envisaged earlier. The strategy for the universalisation of rural cooking energy programmes envisages covering 20-25 per cent of the potential beneficiaries by the end of Eighth Plan.

Integrated Rural Energy Programme (IREP) has been transferred to the Ministry of Non-Conventional Energy Sources from Planning Commission with effect from 1 April 1994. The IREP provides a comprehensive framework for macro level planning of energy requirements of rural areas. The programme is being implemented taking block as a unit, and has been extended in 552 blocks so far. To enhance the effectiveness of the programme at the field levels, inputs from ongoing rural energy programmes are being harmonized and increased involvement and concentration of renewable energy programmes is being planned.

Biomass occupies a predominant place as an energy source in rural India. Fuel-wood requirement has gone upto around 166 million tonnes per year, the availability has declined to about 28 million tonnes, resulting in a deficit of 138 million tonnes per annum. It has been estimated that India is having about 93.69 million hectare of waste lands out of which about 20 million hectare is productive non-forest land which would be able to produce 400 million tonnes fuel-wood per year equivalent to 60,000 mw of power. Ministry of Non-Comventional Energy Sources have initiated biomass programme with a view to increase bio-productivity fast-growing short rotation fuel-wood species, suitable for plantation under the given set of agro-climatic conditions through scientific input and to evolve methodologies/ package of practices forincreasing the productivity to around 40 tonnes per hectare per year compared to the average forest tree production rate of 0.5 tonnes per hectare per year. Biomass yield ranging from 12 tonnes to 36.8 tonnes per hectare per year have been achieved by the established Biomass Research Centres.

Of the total energy generated in the country, the contribution of animal energy is close to 50 per cent. This is mailny for farming operations and transportation. The MNES has launched a national programme in this field in March 1994. The programme is implemented in close coordination with the Ministry of Agriculture and involve comunity awareness campaigns about the role of animal energy, support for improvement in equipment, devices and transport vehicles which are animal driven. Under the programme, 15 models of improved bullock carts have been developed.

Energy from wastes

Large quantities of wastes (solids and liquids) are generated in India in urban, municipal and industrial sectors and mostly find their way into the environment with little or no treatment which results in their natural biodegradation with consequent release of methane into the atmosphere. These resources can offer viable option for energy generation with attendant benefits of reducing emission green house gases and minimising environmental pollution. Considering the far reaching environmental benefits by proper utilisation of various wastes hitherto causing pollution problem, UNDP have agreed to provide technical grant out of GEF fund for development of high rate biomethantion process for energy recovery from all such wastes. In the first phase of the activity concerning utilisation of wastes, a national programme under the GEF assisted project for development of high rate biomethantion processes has been initiated in the Ministry. A National Energy Board has been set up as an apex body to formulate policy and over all management.

While exploring newer forms of renewable sources of energy is no doubt the ultimate remedy to this global malady, improving energy efficiency is the most urgent task to be addressed by our planners and administrators. Especially when it is simultaneously pursued along with substitution of scarce oil by coal by a quick shift from oil-fired power plants to coal-fired and nuclear-powered ones in a phased manner, there is a chance of making a reasonable dent on the issue of global warming.

Improved energy efficiency conserves the precious non-renewable sources of energy like coal and oils on one hand, and reduces the total carbon emissions indirectly on the other. In fact, no other approach offers as cost-effective an opportunity for limiting carbon emissions as energy efficiency does.

Shifting to more fuel-efficient transportation can sharply reduce carbon emissions, which if left untouched may double by AD 2010 capable of causing considerable rise in global temperature. In fact, the efficiency of US buildings industry and transportation had resulted in freezing the carbon emissions at 1.2 billion tonnes per year between 1973 and 1987. Taking cue from such success stories we in the less fortunate part of the globe could as well employ a combination of energy-efficient methods like improved mass transit, greater use of bicycles for short trips along with a continuous accent on fuel-efficient automobiles to keep the carbon emissions in check.

With 64 per cent of the world's electricity being produced from fossil fuels such as coal and oil contributing as much as 27 per cent of global carbon emissions, it is time we became conscious of the efficiency of motors. It is estimated that the electric motors currently in use can be made 40 per cent more effective and refrigerators 75 per cent more energy efficient without a major shift in technology. What all our technicians and technocrats have to do is to be conscious about the growing importance of preventie maintenance schedules that are often given the go-by due to callousness and abject neglect on the part of the operating staff.

Worldwide, lighting accounts for as much as 17 per cent of electricity use that is responsible for 250 million tonnes of carbon emissions in an year. With the vast scope for expansion of lighting into the rural scene in Indian villages as also the rest of the developing world, the potential hazard on this count is very high by the turn of the century. With a little concern on the part of our electrical engineers and policy-makers of public and private business, it should be possible to cut the consumption of electricity to the tune of 75 per cent even with the present level of technology, according to Hofemeister and Rosenfeld (1988).

Doubling the efficiency of lighting through the use of compact fluroscent bulbs consuming 11-18 watts of electricity to provide as much illumination as the incandescent bulbs that are mostly in use in domestic as well as public buildings that consume at least 60 watts of power is a practical solution to power shortage as well as pollution.

Priority is accorded by the Ministry of Environment and Forests to promote evironmental education, create environmental awareness among various age groups and to disseminate information through Environmental Information System (ENVIS) network to all concerned. Special emphasis is given to non-formal environmental education through seminars/symposia/workshops, training programmes, eco-camps, audio-visual shows etc. The

Ministry has been organising a National Environment Awareness Campaign (NEAC) since July 1986. As a part of this Capaign, 19 Novmber to 18 December every year is observed as the National Environment Month. Students/youth, techers, women, tribals, administrators, professionals, legislators, industrial workers, Armed Forces and the general public are covered under this Campaign. During 1994-95 about 2,200 organisations have been granted financial assistance by the Ministry to organise various activities for creating environmental awareness. The Ministry also provides financial support for setting up eco-clubs at schools and for production on films on environment.

A new scheme "Paryavaran Vahini" has been launched during 1992-93 to create environmental awareness and to ensure active public participations by involving the local people in activities relating to environmental protection. Parayavaran Vahinis are proposed to be constituted in 183 selected districts all over the country which have high incidence of pollution and density of tribal and forest population. The Vahinis also play a watch dog role by reporting instances of environmental pollution, deforestation, poaching, etc. They function under the charge of District Collectors with active cooperation of the state/union territory governments. this scheme is entirely financed by the Ministry of Environment and Forests.

The National Museum of Natural History (NMNH) set up in New Delhi in 1978, is concerned with the promotion of non-formal education in the area of environment and conservation. Besides permanent exhibit galleries on various aspects of environment, the museum also conducts temporary exhibitions and a large number of educational programmes and activities for school children, college youth and the general public. A Regional Museum of Natural History has been established at Mysore and two more and planned at Bhopal and Bhubaneswar.

The Indian Council for Forestry Research and Education is the focal point for forestry education and extension developmnet in the country. Indira Gandhi National Forest Academy, Dehra Dun imparts in-service professional training to Indian Forest Service (IFS) professionals. State forest service colleges provide training to the officers of the State Forest Service (SFS). The Indian Plywood Industries Research and Training Institute, Bangalore organises short-term courses in the area of wood science. The Indian Institute of Forest Management, Bhopal, also provides training in forest management and allied subjects to persons from the Indian Forest Service, forest development corporations and forest related industries to develop forestry management skills. The Wildlife Institute of India, Dehra Dun conducts various programmes to provide in-service training in wildlife management for forest officers, wildlife ecologists and other professionals.

Environmental Information System (ENVIS) has been set up by the Ministry in 1982 as a decentralised information system network for collection, storage, retrieval and dissemination of environmental information to decision makers, policy planners, scientists, engineers, environmentalists, research workers and the general public all over the country. Besides the Focal Point in the Ministry, the ENVIS network presently consists of 20 subject oriented centres known as ENVIS centres, set up in various institutions/organisations of the country on priority areas of environment such as environmentally sound and appropriate technology, bio-degradation of wastes, desertification, estuary, mangroves, corals and lagoons, media and environment, environmental education, solid wastes disposal, animal ecology, Himalayan ecology, etc. The Focal Point brings out a quarterly abstracting journal "Paryavaran Abstracts" containing information about environmental research in the Indian context.

ENVIS has been designated as National Focal Point (NFP) and Regional Service Centre (RSC) for South Asia sub-regional countries by INFORTERRA (an international referral system for sources of information on environment) of United Nations Environment Programme (UNEP). As NEP, ENVIS updated more than 250 Indian Potential Sources in the International Directory of UNEP for providing information in the field of environment and its related areas.

The Ministry functions as a nodal agency for United Nations Environment Programme (UNEP), South Asia Cooperation Environment Programme (SACEP) and International Centre for Integrated Mountain and Development (ICIMOD) and various international agencies, regional bodies and multilateral institutions. In coordinates all bilateral cooperation in the field of invironment. India has such cooperation programmes with the Netherlands, Norway, Sweden, Denmark, Great Britain, USA, the Russian Federation, Canada, Japan and FRG in addition to forestry programmes with external assistance.

India is signatory to the following important international treaties/agreements in the field of environment: (i) International Convention for the regulation of Whaling; (ii) International Plant Protection Convention; (iii) The Antarctic Treaty; (iv) Conventon on Wetlands of internatonal importance especially as waterfowl habitat; (v) International Convention on international trade in endangered species of wild flora and fauna; (vi) Protocol of 1978 relating to the international convention for the prevention of pollution from ships, 1973; (vii) Vienna Convention for the protection of the ozone layer; (viii) Convention on Migratory Species; (ix) Basel Convention on trans-boundary movement of hazardous substances; (x) Framework Convention on climatic change; (xi) convention on conservation of bio-diversity; (xii) Montreal Protocol on the substances that deplete the ozone layer and (xiii) International Convention for Combating Desertification.

Instituted in 1987, the Indira Gandhi Prayavaran Puraskar, consisting of a cash component of rupees one lakh, a silver trophy and a citation, is awarded every year to an organisation and to an individual for significant contributions in the field of environment.

The Indira Priyadarshini Vrikshamitra Awards have been constituted by the Ministry of Environment and Forests in 1986 to recognise outstanding contributions of individuals and organisations in the field of afforestation and wastelands development. Ten awards are given every year to individuals, educational institutes, Panchayats, voluntary agencies and government agencies. Each award carries a medallion, a citation and a cash component of Rs. 50,000.

The Maha Vriksha Puraskar, instituted by the NAEB during 1993-94 will be given every year to individuals/ organisations for trees of notified species having the largest girth and height and in good health and vigour. These awards would consist of a cash prize of Rs. 25,000, a plaque and a citation.

Since 1991, national awards are being presented every year to eligible industries in recognition of their contributions to the prevention and control of evnvironmental pollution.

Grouping of women has increased their awareness and eliminated exploitation by the middleman, in the case of 'active' groups. In many trades like weaving, processing food items...giving women access to finance through revolving funds and cheap credit has resulted in women directly procuring raw materials and producing and marketing goods without having to depend on the middleman for raw materials to process on measly daily wages, that too at disadvantageously lower levels for women. Incomes have also increased in the process. Studies by the Self Employed Women's Associaton (SEWA), Ahmedabad on the DWCRA groups helped by them in respect of crafts women and gum collectors clearly show that these groups have strengthened women's economic position, increased their bargaining powers, self sufficiency and thereby social status. Women are held in esteen now and men have become more cooperative on the domestic front and even help women in fuel and fodder collection. Women n turn feel more confident and have a sense of belonging. These self helf groups are a new source of social security with the crumbling of the joint family system. Other field level experiences and studies have clearly shown that despite all its limitations, the group strategy has empowered women to approach functionaries and banks to their advantage.

Given the potential power of groups, it serves us well to increase their cover. The government has sincerely tried to generate formation of informal groups. But this is a time consuming process requiring a high degree of social awareness of the local area. Finally, the regions which have highly successful groups are those with highly committed Gram Sevikas and Project Officers. Such functionaries who are invaluabel assets are however not too large in numbers. The government's efforts therefore need to be supplemented to a far larger extent than at present. In the current context, this could best be handled through involvement of local and Non—

Government Organisations in a big way. Intervention by Non Governmental Organisations with a feel for the people and their problems, in some areas, has brought about very successful and functional groups.

This brings us to the next related issue—Committed Non Governmental and Voluntary Organisations are not in abundance and involvement of greater numbers of committed people is essential.

The process of group formation could thus take the following from: The starting point should be the settingup of local 'Skill Exchanges'. Women possessing various skills like craftwork, tailoring, toy making etc. could register themselves for employment. Their motivation to work would be spontaneous as registration is a voluntary act. Also many of the skilled labourers would belong to the poorer sections though not necessatily below the poverty line. There is a strong justification for this, because as gender experts have pointed out, when we talk of the poverty line we talk in aggregates i.e. of a family as a whole being below or above it. While this is absolutely logical in the aggregate sense, it overlooks the inequities in intra household distribution of income and consumption, since women may not have access to a large part of the spouse's income but they may be responsible i seeing that all the children and family member are well fed. So technically though the family may be slightly above poverty line, most of its members may be living in below poverty line conditions. Merely picking up women without skills or motivation from the list of 'Below Poverty Line' families has resulted in many cases in total waste of effort.

From these skill exchanges, Non Governmental local organisations could group women by homogeneity of skills and location for functional success. Such groups of motivated and simimlarly skilled women may perform better and result in faster may perform better and result in faster spread of groups through 'Demonstration Effect'. Further, in due course some of the more successful of these groups could themselves become local voluntary organisations and help in formation of groups in their neighbourhoods.

The government would have to play the role of overseer and facilitator in this entire process—a role that it is most competent to play. The government should first group its activities for a coordinated delivery system of services at the local level. District level teams could be formed with personnel drawn from various departments like health, education etc.—not the higher planning oriented personnel but middle and lower level implementing functionaries. These teams could cater to various blocks for referral services and problem solving through nodal local organisations or group leaders. The Indira Mahila Yojana is a step forward in this direction.

The above system could be tried out along with the existing system which boils down to government gram sevikas exploring possibilities of setting up groups, then motivating the women, selecting an activity for them, arranging for training in some cases and so on without ultimate guarantee of the sustainibility of the group.

Once economic empowerment is achieved it would have major implications on the overall empowerment of women. Intra family relationships and domestic work culture would dnage resulting in social empowerment and a more equitable participation of women in decisions concerning the family. Leadership and active participation in group culture would improve political acumen and eventually help successful political empowerment. Political empowerment in turn would result in more representiative planning for women and a strengthening and sustaining of the process of overall empowerment of women.

Rural growth

Given enough resources with the government, there is no reason why rural development and through it the eradication of rural poverty cannot be achieved during the five year period of the Plan with hundred per cent success. There is need for continued direct State intervention for poverty alleviation. While the programmes for self-employment and supplementary wage employment would continue in the Ninth Plan, these would be redesingned in order to make them more effective as instruments of poverty alleviation. It is necessary that these programmes are integrated with the various sectoral programmes as well as the area development programmes within the umbrella of the Panchayati Raj institutions.

An important change envisaged in the Ninth Plan is to make self-employment programmes more effective through a shift in strategy under Integrated Rural Developnment Programme (IRDP), from an individual benefiviary approach to a group and/or cluster approach would include development of skills of the rural poor through an inbuilt training component, upgradation of technology, establishment of forward and backward linkages, availability of appropriate infrastructure and markekt tie-ups. It is good that the scheme of Training of Rural Youth for Self-Employment (TRYSEM) is now going to be revamped thoroughly in order to improve the employment opportunities of the poor. It is common knowledge that the artisans in rural areas, despite their rich heritage and skills, belong to the poverty group. Therefore, to improve their skills and production capabilities, they would be provided with modern tool kits as well.

A significant aspect of rural growth would be the improvement in the status of rural women. In this context, already the Development of Women and

Children in Rural Areas (DWCRA) has been quite a siccess story in empowering women and in improving their economic status, though only in selected States so far. A mechanism for replicating the successful DWCRA groups would be evolved during the NInth Plan, while it would be integrated with IRDP and TRYSEM to provide womens' groups with greater access to financial resources and training. A country wide Employment Assurance Scheme is also intended to be launched during the Ninth Plan so that during the lean agricultural season, some manual work of casual naure may be given.

Rural poverty is largely among the landless and marginal farmers. Therefore, access to land remains a key element of the anti-poverty strategy in rural areas. Ninth Plan has laid down th e following programme of action for land reforms during the plan period:

— Detection as well as redistribution of ceiling surputs land;

— Upgradation of land records on a regular basis;

— Tenancy reforms providing for recording the rights of tenants and share-croppers;

— Consolidation of holding;

— Preventing alienation of tribal lands;

— Providing access on a group basis to the poor on wastelands and common property resources;

— Leasing-in and leasing-out of land will be permitted within the ceiling limits; and

— Perfernce to women in the distribution of ceiling surplus land and legal provisions for protecting their rights on land.

Social sector

Seven basic services have been identified for priority attention with an all-out effort for their complete coverage in a time-bound manner. These are safe drinking water, availability of primary health service facilities, universalisation of primary education, provision of public housing assistance to all shelterless poor families, nuturitional spport to children, and such other aspects as already mentiones before. The Panchayati Raj institutions will function as effective institutions for olcal self-government and social justice and implement schemes in social services.

The village and small industries sector (VSI) has rightly been chosen as the focal point for triggering off the growth process. Industries of this sector will be provided sufficient incentives and support to facilitate their growth and employment potential. Quite importantly, foreing investment will not be allowed to displace these industries. Investment limit for such industries has now already been raised by the government in order to enabele them to achieve economies of scale. It is hoped that the items reserved for production in them will continue to remain so. The VSI sector is to meke a dent in the regional disparities in terms of industrial and overall growth all over the country.

With all the sectoral financial and physical targets laid down, any plan cannot be successful unless the strategy to achieve its various targets is quite sound, practical and does not go awry. The approach paper contents that while it is feasible to achieve a seven per cent growth rate on the basis of the existing behavioural paramenters for private savings and investment, regular and significant revision of the pervasive underpricing of irrigation services, electricity, railway passenger fares, postal and telecommunication rates, perroleum and other mineral prices is required so that both the value-added and savings of these sectors improve substantially and are not eroded.

It is important to realize that for the target growth rate of seven per cent, investment would need to be of the order of 28.6 per ment of GDP. And this would have to be achieved despite a drop in the incremental capital-output ratio (ICOR, its decline shows improvement in efficiency) from 4.34 per cent.This, therfore, brings us to the aspect of allocation and optimal use of funds for doing so. It is expected that this cecline in ICOR would be achieved due to economic reforms, elimination of outdated technologies, higher energy and material efficiency in the industrial sector.

It is also imperative to maintain a balance between thg capital-intensive industry and labour-intensive industry to achieve the plan targets.Ancillary industries should take over manufacture of the componets of the industry set-up through the foreign direct investment route. All said and done, there fully aware of the dimension of resource mobilization. Therefore, it is necessary that both the Centre and the States work out programmes in concrete terms to meet the financing requirements of both infrastructure development and poverty alleviation schemes.

Rural development

Rural development planning in India was introdrced in the light of experiments for rural uplift prior to Independence by the Father of the Nation, Mahatma Gandhi in Sevagram, Rabindranath Tagore in villages around Santiniketan, Spencer Hatch in Travancore (erstwhile), V.T. Krishnamachari in Kasamba near Baroda, and F.L. Brayne in Gurgaon in the 1920s and after Independence by Prakasham, Albert Mayer and Horace Holmes, S.K. Dey et al. The first massive rural development endeavour called the Community Development Programme was launched with the beginning of the First Five Year Plan itself. This was a co-operative partnership between the government and the people for the all-round development of the people in a particular area. With the commencement of Panchayati Raj, it had to become the programme for the people, of the people, and by the Third Five Year Plan, the entire country was covered with community development blocks numbering over 5,000. The community development blocks became the units of administration, planning, co-ordination, and development for rural people with the focus on integrated rural development, comprising agriculture and allied activities, rural industries, education, health socail welfare, communications, supplementary employment with special focus on self-help and public partcipation. A schematic budget of Rs. 17 lakh per block—Rs. 12 lakh for stage one (5 years) and Rs. 5 lakh for stage two (another 5 years)—was provided. The staffing patern comprised the Block Development Officer (BDO) 8 Extension Officers (in agriculture, animal husbandry, co-operative, Panchayats, rural industries, engineering, social education, and programmes for women and children), 10 Gram Sevaks, 2 Gram Sevikas, a Programme Assistant, a Storekeeper-cum-Accountant, with some support staff on the ministerial side prescribed for a standard block.

The integrated approach to rural development, however, got gradually diluted with the work relating to village industries being handed over to the Khadi and Village Industries Commission (KVIC) and the growing need for self-reliance in food. The greater emphasis on food production resulted in the launching of the Intensive Agriculture Development Programme (IADP) in selected districts followed by the Intensive Agriculture

Areas Programme (IAAP), and the High Yield in Varieties Programme (HYVP). By the late sixties, and the early seventies, it was perceived that even though the intensive effort in agriculture had led to the Green Revolution, the benefits of this remained largely confined to the big farmers and areas which were better placed to receive the benefits of high yielding varieties techonlogy.

Therefore, the need to take special measures for benefiting the poorer sections of the population and for development of backward and disadvantaged areas was felt. As a result, programmes like Small Farmers and Agricultural Labourers (MFAL), Crash Scheme for Rural Employment, Pilot Intensive Rural Employment Programme, Food for Work Programme, Drought-Prone Areas and Desert Development Programmes, and the Minimum Needs Programme were launched.

With the launching of the Sixth Plan the attempts at tackling the problems of the deprived sections of the population and geographical areas were further consolidated, rationalized, and expanded. The SFDA and MFAL were replaced by the Integrated Rural Development Programme (IRDP) which was extended to cover the entire country and its scope expanded to all activities in the primary, secondary, and tertiary sectors. Under this programme, income-base criteria for identification of the target group was prescribed and household approach was adopted. The programme also aimed to provide skills through Training of Rural Youth for Self-Employment (TRYSEM) and assets (through a mix of subsidy and credit with the ultimate objective of raising people above the poverty line. A special programme for economic betterment of rural women, popularly known as Development of Women and Children in Rural Areas (DWCRA), was also developed and linked to the self-employment programme (IRDP). The Food for Work Programme was restructured in the form of wage employment programme known as National Rural Employment Programme, the Rural Landless Employment Guarantee Programme (RLEGP) was launched in 1983-84 with the specific objective of providing up to 100 dats of employment per annum to at least one member of each rural landless household. The programmes of the Sixth Plan were continued with a sharper focus and higher outlays during the Seventh and the Eighth Plan periods. The aforesaid wage employment programmes (NREP & ROEGP) were merged into Jawahar Rozgar Yojana (JRY) and Indira Awaas Yojana (IAY)—a component of JRY—was strengthened both qualitatively and quantitatively. Subsequently, Employment Assurance Scheme (EAS) was introduced for assured employment up to 100 days in the lean agricultural season.

Rural development mey be construed as total all-round socio-economic development of the rural people and not merely the ongoing programmes such as self-emplyment, wage employment, area development, land reforms, etc. A significant step has already been taken to revitalize the Panchhayati Raj institutions with the enactment of the Constitution (Seventy--third Amendment) Act, 1992 so that 'operation by the people and co-operation by the government' becomes a reality. Accordingly, the State goverment mey, by law, endow the Panchayats with such powers and authority as may be necessary to enastitutions of self-government and such law may contain provisions for devolution of powers and responsibilities upon Panchayats at the appropriate level, subject to such conditions as may be specified therein, with respect to the preparation of plans and implmentation of schemes for economic development and social justice as may be entrusted to them including those in relation to matters listed, as follows, in the XI schedule to the Constitution (Article 243G):

- Agriculture including agricultural extension.
- Land improvement, implementation of land reforms, land consolidation, and soil conservation.
- Minor irrigation, water management, and watershed development.
- Animal husbandry, dairying, and poultry.
- Fisheries.
- Social forest produce.
- Minor forest produce.
- Small-scale industries, including food processing industries.
- Khadi, village, and cottage industries.
- Rural housing.
- Drinking water.
- Fuel and fodder.
- Roads, culverts, bridges, ferries, waterways, and other means of communication.
- Rural electrification, including distribution of electricity.
- Non-conventional energy sources.
- Poverty alleviation programmes.
- Education including primary and secondary school.
- Technical training and vocational education.
- Adult and non-formal education.
- Libraries.
- Cultural activities.
- Markets and fairs.

- Health and sanitation, including hospitals, primary health centres, and dispensaries.
- Family welfare.
- Women and child development.
- Social welfare including welfare of the handicapped and mentally retarded.
- Welfare of the weaker sections, and in particular, of the Scheduled Castes and Scheduled Tribes.
- Public distribution system.
- Maintenance of community assets.

Integrating strategies

A each agro-climatic level, educational, health or connectivity stratigies will have to be integrated with agricultural and rural edvelopment strategies. Take the Eastern Plateau and Hill agro-climatic region extending from destricts like Kalahandi in Orissa to Gadchiroli and Chandrapur in Western Maharashtra and including large tribal districts in Madhya Pradesh, the growth strategy is to conserve the rainfall of around 50 cm through waershed programmes and to follow through with forest conservation and optimal cropping patterns. However, the female literacy rate in this region is less than 15 per gcent and so no techology-oriented strategy is possible without remedying this. A destinguished Vice-Chancellor from an agricultural university told me that "sowing" dates were decided by the local Bhuva (witch doctor) rather than the agricultural scientists of the region.

Community organizations are essential for both aspects as at best co-operation is an educational process and limited sharing of rights on land and water is a way out of landlessness and rack renting. It becomes difficult, if not imposible, to channel structural and limited subsidies and priority credit, to the kind of activities described above, if the land rights of the tiller of land are not clear enforceable. Collateral needed by financial institutions, for example, becomes very difficult to organize, if tenancy arrangements are not recorded. Co-operative arrangements provide a way out. Even when farming and other economic decisions are left to the initiative of the peasant, and the signals of the market,, for well-defined purpose, for example, land shaping, acquifer management, lower land water delivery systems or even specific mardeting, quality, grading or input supply requirenents, the peasant can co-operate. Self-help co-operateves with will well-defined objectives can than become the crucial interface between the country's manpower, its limited natural endowments and regional and global markets.

While developing macro-economic parameters for the Ninth Five Year Plan, emphasis will th3e overal GDP growth rate is visualized at seven per cent per annum, then the growth in the agricultural sector wil have to be around 3.5 per cent to 4 per cent per annum in valueadded terms and the growth rate of output will be higher. The precise contours of growth in agricultural sector will be highlighted in the Agricultural Submodel of the Ninth Plan. However, as a preliminary observation, it could be stated that growth in agricultural sector would emanate from improvements in the per hectare yields of crop sector. It is also visualized that diversification and modernization of the various subsets of the agricultural sector would gain momintum in the Ninth Plan and the dynamics of agricultural growth would emanate from growth in non-food grain secters, eg cotton, oil seeds, sugar-cane, fruits and vegetables, spices, plantation crops, etc. along with the development of fesheries, animal husbandry and dairying.

On the assumption that per capita income during the Ninth Plan period will continue to show an annual growth of around 4 per cent, greater emphasis on diversification of the non-food grain sector involving crops like sugar-cane, oil seeds, cotton, fruits and vegetables seems inescapable. Also the output levels in the non-crop based agriculture would rise faster due to (a) increasing flexibility of resource use; (b) response to changing emand conditions; and (c) the technological changes. In fact, these variables would determine the growth process in the economy during the next decade.

The assumption regarding faster growth of non-crop based agriculture is supported by the annual growth rates of output visualized for the Eighth Plan which have been highlighted in the technical note on the eighth Plan, in which agriculture was visualized to grow at an annual rate of 3.25 per cent in value-added terms, feshing at 5.45 per cent, textiles at 5.87 per cent, wood and paper products at 7.63 per cent and leather and rubber products at 16.03 per cent. This structure of output is in tune with the structure of demand anticipated for the economy during the Eighth Plan period.

The other major development that has taken place is the fast growthof agricultural exports. It has been estimated that while a growth of 15 per cent plus annually ibn agricultural export may be difficult to sustain in the long run, a growth path of around 12 per cent annualy in dollar terms should be aimed at. The output implications of cven fast growth of exports are marginal in an economy of India's size, given the magnitude discussed earlier, but in selected regions, the impacts on income and imployment can be high and the technological implications anyway can be important both on agricultural production and processing and distribution.

Rural electrification schemes are financed by the state governments as well as Rural Electrification

Corporation. Upto the end of the Seventh Five Year Plan, 4,70,836 villages were electrified and 83,58,363 pumpsets were energised. As on 31 March 1995, 4,97,796 villages stand electrified representing 85.8 per cent of the total villages in the country. About 107,21,104 pumpsets have been energised. The target for electrification of villages and energisation of pumpsets for 1994-95 was 2,897 and 2,77,008 respectivley. Against this, upto 31 March 1995, 3,238 villages were electrified and 4,35,909 pumpsets were energised. Electrification of tribal villages and Harijan Bastis are also being given special attention. Out of a total of 1,11,886 tribal villages, 78,813 have been electrified and street light facilities extended to 2,65,217 Harijan bastis by the end of March 1995.

To improve the quality of life of rural families, below the poverty line, including Harijan and Adivasi families, the Government of India in 1988 launched a programme called Kutiriyoti for extending single point light connections to the households of such poor families. During 1994-95, about 1.22 lakh single point light connections were released, while cumulatively about 16 lakh connections have been released upto March 1995.

Rural Electrification Corporation (REC) was set up in July 1969 for promoting rural electrification. The Corporation finances rural electrification schemes and rural electric cooperatives in the states. REC had given loans aggregating to about Rs. 8,200 crore to states and state electricity boards for rural electrification upto the end of March 1995.

National Thermal Power Corporation Limited (NTPC) was set up in 1975 as a Central sector generating company for the development of thermal power. NTPC at present has an installed capacity of over 16,000 mw, representing about 30 per cent of the all India thermal capacity. The Corporation has successfully commmiss-ioned super thermal power projects at Singrauli (UP)

2,000 mw; Korba (MP) 2,100 mw; Ramagundam (AP) 2,100 mw; Farakka (WB) 1,600 mw; Vindhyachal (MP) 1,26 mw; Rihand (UP) 1,000 mw; Dadri (UP) 860 mw; and five combined cycle gas power projects at Anta (Rajasthan) 413 mw; Auraiya (UP) 652 mw; Dadri (UP) 817 mw; Kawas (Gujarat) 645 mw and Gandhar (Gujarat) 648 mw. In addition, the Corporation has taken over 420 mw project at Unchahar (UP) and 460 mw project at Talcher (Orissa).

NTPC has also been entrusted with the management of 720 mw Badarpur Thermal Power Station (BTPS) in Delhi since 1978 and with the implementation and management of 270 mw BALCO's captive power plants near Korba. The generating units of NTPC have been performing efficiently and reliably with most of the efficiency parameters for these units/stations being above the all India average for thermal stations. It has been making profits since the commissioning of its station at Singrauli. During 1994-95, the Corporation earned an estimated profit of Rs. 1,112 crore. The turnover of the Corporation has also risen to Rs. 6,373 crore. The sustained high level of performance ofthe Corporation in all areas has made it the largest beneficiary of World Bank assistance in the world. A large number of other multilateral and bilateral financial institutions and external commercial banks have also reposed their confidence in NTPC. It has drawn up an ambitious corporate plan to create new generating capacity to the extent of 10,0000 mw in the next eight years.

The Corporation has gained expertise for providing consultancy services for executing projects from concept to commissioning, including large capacity combined cycle gas projects and associated transmission system, besides setting up coal-based super thermal power projects. In line with Government of India's policy for encouraging greater role for private sector in the power sector, NTPC has also diversified its expertise. Various power projects presently under consideration, are being considered as joint ventures with equity participation by NTPC.

National Hydroelectric Power Corporation (NHPC) was set up in 1975 to promote the development of hydro-electric power in the Central sector in all its aspects including investigation, construction, generation, operation and maintenance of hydro-electric power stations, transmission, distribution and sale of power and also to undertake, wherever necessary, the construction of inter-state transmission lines for timely and coordinated inter-state exchange of power.

The Corporation has so far completed construction of six hydroelectric projects, namely, Baira Siul (Himachal Pradesh)-198 mw; Loktak (Manipur)-105 mw; Salal Stage-I (Jammu and Kashmir)-345 mw; Tanakpur (Uttar Pradesh)-120 mw; Chamera-I (Himachal Pradesh)-540 mw and Devighat (Nepal)-14 mw installed capacity. Devighat project was done on agency basis, while the remaining five projects are in the ownership of the Corporation. NHPC is presently engaged in the construction of Dulhasti (J&K), Uri (J&K), Rngit (Sikkim), Dhauliganga (UP) and Kurichu (as an executive agency) (Bhutan) hydel projects.

Power Grid Corporation of India Limited (POWERGRID), earlier known as National Power Transmission Corporation Limited, was incorporated in October 1989 with an initial authorised share capital of Rs. 5,000 crore with the objective of establishment and operation of regional and national power grids. The transmission systems of all Central sector generating companies were transferred to Powergrid with effect fro April 1992. In the second phase, Powergrid proposes to operate the regional load despatch and communication centres and related operational functions for regional and inter-state integrated grid operation. As on 31 march 1995, Powergrid operated a total of 25,575 ckt km transmission lines consisting of 18,505 ckt km of 400 kv, 4,696 ckt km of 220 kv, 744 ckt km of 132 kv and 1,630 ckt km of HVDC system, over 50 sub-stations with 21,173 mva of transformation capacity. The operational performance of Powergrid transmission system has been very impressive in all the five power regions. Overall regional average availability of transmission lines during 1994-95 was 98 per cent excluding HVDC System.

Presently, 9,521 ckt km of transmission lines are under construction by Powergrid, consisting of 570 ckt km of 800 kv, 7,816 ckt km of 400 kv, 483 ckt km of 220 kv and 652 ckt km of 132 kv to be distributed over 10 substations. Powergrid has drawn up a programme for inter-connecting the various power regions of the country through HVDC inter-regional links and has also undertaken implementation of state-of-the-art United Load despatch and Communication (LD&C) facilities in all the power regions of the country.

Powergrid has developed adequate expertise for hotline maintenance of transmission line. This technique is adopted in southern and western regions. Further, it has implemented a major programme for replacement of insulators of various transmission lines in the north-eastern region, which had been the main reason for transmission lines breakdown.

The Power Finance Corporation Limited (PFC) was incorporated on 16 July 1986 under the Companies Act, 1956 and was declared a public financial institution in August 1990. The main objectives of the Corporation include financing of power generation projects, transmission and distribution of works, renovation and modernisation of power plants, system improvement and energy conservation schemes, maintenence and repair of capital equipment.

The authorised share capital of the Corporation is Rs. 2,000 crore and Paid-up capital is Rs 1,035.45 crore as on 3 April 1995. The Corporation commenced its financial operations in February 1988 and till 300 April 1995, it had sanctioned loans for 731 schemes in the power sector amounting to Rs. 7,731.85 crore and had disbursed Rs.5,224.37 crore against the above sanctions. The Corporation has beenn consistently earning profits since commencement of its financial operations. In 1993-94, it earned a net profit (after tax) of Rs. 147.52 crore and declared a maiden divedend of Rs. 10 crore to the Government of India which owns all its equity. Further the Corporation has been signing Memorandum of Understanding with Government of India each year since 1993-94. The Corporation, for the purpose of institutional development, has evolved an operational and financial action plan (OFAP) for each of its main beneficiaries, namely, state electricity boards (SEBs) and state generating corporations (SGCs) in the country.

The Corporation has also taken up a project on Energy Management Consultation and Training (EMCAT) with a grant from USAID. Under EMCAT Project, the Corporation funds consultancy services from qualified sources to help improve the planning, management and productivity of the power sector and also to hold workshops/seminars to bring about awareness of critical areas of reforms in power sector and to find solutions thereof.

A common symptom of rural poverty which India shares along with other developing countries is the existence of underutilized resources, such as land, water and endemic underemployment of labour. Poverty itself is the lot of about 39 per cent of the population as against about 20 poer cent as per calculations of theearlier government. During the period 1983—84 to 1987—88, rural poverty fell from 45.6 per cent to 39 per cent while between 1987—88 and 93—94, it fell only by a further 1.7 per cent.

In 1987—88, unemployment inperson—years was estimated to be 12.43 million in usual principal status, 15.30 million in weekly status, and 18.95 million on daily status. Even causal labour employment is 38.4 per cent among rural males and 31.4 per cent among rural females.

The above phenomenon has been interpreted from different perspectives. It is regarded as due to the fickleness of the poor and, therefore, the total literacy campaign in India seeks to encnouraged the poor to come together and improvve their lot. It can also be seen as an inherent attribute of the socio—economic structure retarding growth and perpetuating poverty. Land reforms is the answer to this situation. A third perspective is to look at it as a potential for local resource mobilization and its concomitant local—level planning. In this context , the 73rd constitutional amendment conferring constitutional status to local bodies and for greater decentralization in the country is worth noting.

It is this point of view that the present paper has adopted. It is noted that there is an enormous potential for alleviating poverty which such underutilized resources represent. Along side with the resource augmenting aspect, the mobilization of local resources also promises the simultanneous attainment of other adjectives which are apecial to rural development like greater decentralization in planning, increasing popular paraticipation and ensuring a greater degree of self—reliance on the part of local communities. Macro planning embodied in the Ninth Plan alone cannot cope with the highly particularized and the localized problems of identifying development potentialities in the rural communities. Even though the basic criteria of rural development are participation, production, distribution and consumption, participation takes on a different meaning. The disadvantaged people are not to be cast inthe role of the objects of participation, but they are to be integrated as the subjects of the operation. Both human resource development and human development are the objectives in rural development and a World Bank study has shown that there will not be adequate resources for human development if government funds alone are to be depended upon. It is imperative to use local resources and community resources will have to be mobilized. Also the interdependence between eduction, health, sanitation and other social development sectors has to be taken care of because all of them jointly promote rural development.

In this paper, we have discussed, the broad outlines of the Ninth Plan to show the resource constraints. Secondly, the interdependence between agriculture and rural development is noted and it is concluded that there is no alternative except to mobilize local resources. Reference in this context is not only to mobilization of financial resources through imposition of appropriate taxes in agriculture, but also more importantly to mobilize non–financial resources like labour, locally available material and technical expertise.

Backward areas development plan

Tax concession for promoting industrialisation was introduced for the first time in 1949 in the form of tax holiday for the first 5 years of production of new industrial units. This concession was avaliable as deduction from taxable profit, computed at the rate of 6% of capital employed. This incentive was continued till 1980 when, to remove capital bias inherent in it, was reformulated as 80-I to provide for a deduction as percentage of profit rather than capital employed. This provision was modified and renumbered as Section 80-I w.e.f. 1.4.1991. Under this provision any new industrial undertaking or hotel came into business between 1.4.1991 and 1.4.1995 was entitled to a deduction of 25% from the profits (30% for companies for 10 years).

In 1968 Planning Commission set up two Working Groups to evolve a criteria for identification 245 out of 396 districts were identified as backward. Government of India also introduced Investment Subsidy Scheme for identified backward areas. This scheme was, however, discontinued in 1988. States also introduced the Investment Subsidy schemes and these are still in vogue. In 1974, tax concessions in the form of relief in income tax to new units were introduced in Eighth Schedule of Income-tax Act as section 80HH, which was later replaced by notification in 1986. This listed the backward areas.

In 1987 National Institute of Public Finance and Policy conducted a study to evaluate the fiscal concessions for backward areas. This study concluded that while the fiscal incentives for the backward development did successfully promote industrial dispersal, the criteria of identifying backward areas in a state with reference to its development indicators rather than any All India norm favoured developed states.

The NIPFP study as well as the Economic Administrative Reform Commission recommended deletion of Section 80-HH of Income-tax Act which had indicated the backward areas.

Accepting the recommendations of the study the Finance Act, 1993 modified the tax incentive scheme. Full tax holiday was introduced for the initial 5 years of production in case of industrial units starting production between 1.4.1993 and 31.3.1998 and set up a backward state or union territories specified in new 8th Schedule. These states were selected because all their districts were earlier classified as backward in notification issued in 1986.

Following the introduction of the Bill, various representations were received and it was indicated that these concessions were extended to backward districts which would be identified by a Study Group. This has been reiterated by the Finance Minister recently.

Current approach to industrialisation is based on providing industrial infrastructure. Both the NIPFP Study and the Study by World Bank indicated that location decision can only be marginally influenced. The factor which would be crucial in the location decisions could be the availability of physical infrastructure. This has been the rationale of growth centre scheme.

Capital incentive in the form of investment subsidy scheme have not been successful in reducing the skewed industrial growth. Infact it may be a better approach to consider harmonisation of incentives.

While promoting spread of industrialisation, the policy essentially needs to find means of concentration of industries as the complementarity and competitive requirements make such cluster approach more successful. This ensures diversified industrial base and optimal utilisation of infrastructure and other resources. This is the reason why the growth of centres has been in a corridor or cluster of districts which are geographically inter-linked.

In a geographically continuous and ethnic homogenous region, industrial development requires consideration of area specific approach. In these areas besides the problem of markets and non local resources there may be constraint of profit, project identification and ignorance about the resources. This has been the approach for development of backward areas in North East where a North East Development Bank has been set up to cater to the specific requirements of the region, identify areas of investment, infrastructure constraints, technological needs and adoption of a hand-holding approach for the enterpreneurs.

In other backward districts where there is no geographical continuity, growth centres approach which provide the infrastructure and thereby reduces the cost of operation have better chances of being successful. However, regional dispersal is a national issue and rquires discussion at all levels for adoption of a comprehensive policy package.

In the first few months of the current fiscal year, industrial performance—both in production and sales—has not been impressive when compared to the previous year. The Economic Times Investment Bureau has estimated that the average growth in turnover of the sensex 30 companies (excluding IDBI, ICICI and SBI) will be between 9.10% as compared to 24% last year. The net profit growth is also expected to slow down to around 25% as against 46% last year. This along with the relatively poor performance of the infrastructure industries, the depressed stock markets, and slower growth of imports has cast a warning signal about industrial performance in 1996-97.

Improved cities and slums

In most cities and towns of India there are NGOs whose focus is the improvement of the urban environment and the condition of the urbanites.

The Bombay Environmental Action Group's efforts have been focused on Bombay and Maharashtra, but the fallout is expected to be experienced in many urban centres. The group has used environmental advocacy and public interest litigation to bring about a rethinking on siting of failities, unplanned growth and pollution.

The Ahmedabad Study Action Group's activities include programmes for slum children, income supplementing programmes for women, low-cost housing, biogas plants and policy research on poverty-related issues.

The Self Employed Women's Association, Ahmedabad, represents a merger of labour, cooperative and women's movements and has promoted cooperatives of rag-pickers, roadside vendors and hawkers, and has been campaigning for the rights of unroganized workers in the non-formal sector.

The Society for the Promotion of Area Resource Centres (SPARC), Bombay works in training and mobilization of the urban poor.

The KKNSS, Bangalore, is a federation of slum dwellers, one of the few peoples' organizations of thi kind.

The Government has taken several initiatives to cope with the burgeoning problem of urban housing. Slum upgrading became a part of official housing policy in 1972. The rationale of slum upgrading is that in situ improvement of existing communities is socially preferable to relocation or redevelopment. Under the scheme of Environmental Improvement of Urban Slums, water supply including drinking water taps, open sewer drains, storm water drains, street lighting, etc., are provided to notified slums.

In 1986 the Scheme of Urban Basic Services was launched as a centrally sponsored scheme with teh objective of promoting woman and child survival and development, low-cost water supply and sanitation, and other community welfare activities through community participation.

The Government seeks to completely eliminate the practice of manual scavenging by conversation of dry latrines and construction of low—cost sanitation units.

The Government has recently announced a comprehensive Pollution Abatement Policy which seeks to combine regulation with fiscal incentives, encourage clean technologies, make voluntary action attractive and promote people's participation.

A whole economy runs on recycling in Indian cities. In Ahmedabad alone, a hundred factories are exclusively involved in converting plastic picked from the roadside into recycled products. Apart from the used paper which is sold to old paper dealers, 60 tonnes is picked up an recycled. Foundry wastes are ground, undergo magnetic extraction and are made into manhole covers. Rags are sold on a large scale for cleaning machines in factories. The total amount of recycling in Ahmedabad by the informal sector alone is estimated to be 200 tonnes per day, providing employment to 100,000 people, at Rs. 20 to Rs. 30 a day, which is higher than the minimum wage.

Although housing is basically a State level activity, the Central Government is responsible for the formulation of broad policy framework of this sector and overseeing the effective implementation of the social housing scheme, particularly for the weaker sections of the Society.

The Central Government strives to create a conducive environment for generating housing activity so as to meet its growing demand. The Delhi Rent Bill, 1994 has been passed by both the Houses of Parliament and it recieved the assent of the President on 23.8.1995. Soon after the Delhi Rent Act, 1995 was passed by the

Parliament, representations were received from a section of traders-tenants demanding changes in some of the provisions of the Act. On the other hand, some forums representing house owners are pressing for an early notification of the Act and enforcement thereon. All these issues are under the consideration of the Government.

The Indira Awas Yojana (IAY), meant for the poorest of the poor belonging to scheduled castes and scheduled tribes and free bonded labour in the rural areas, had been further extended to cover non-SC/ST poor families, subject to certain conditions. Houses, under IAY scheme are built in clusters so that common facilities can be provided easily. Under IAY, 2,81,754 houses were built during 1996-97 (upto October, 96) as against 8,63,889 in 1995-96.

The Urban Basic Services for the Poor (UBSP) scheme was launched with a total outlay of Rs. 100 crore for the Eighth Plan period. The aim of the scheme is to improve the quality of life of the urban poor specially the most vulnerable sections of the population such as women, children, youth, Scheduled Castes/Scheduled Tribes and minorities. As on 30th November, 1996, more than 8000 Neighbourhood Development Committees comprising primarily of urban poor women have been set up in 318 towns for the provision of basic services. 3877 mini plans have already been prepared and 574 community organisers are in the field working as catalysts for enriching community participation.

In its efforts to enchance the flow of funds particularly in rural areas and its easy accessibility to the needy rural populaltion, the National Housing Bank (NHB) till the end of April 1996, has subscribed to the "Special Rural Housing Debentures" (SRHDs) of State Level Cooperative Land Development Banks (SLDBs) to the tune of Rs.180.91 crore to the cooperative sector institutions, the share of SLDBs works out to 51.1 per cent. Recognising the importance of providing housing to women, particularly those belonging to the vulnerable sections, NHB has announced a "Direct Financing Scheme for Housing for Women". Under the scheme, NHB will directly finance the projects of public agencies and local bodies for the benefit of women belonging tot he Economically Weaker Sections (EWS) and Lower Income Group (LIG) categories.

Water supply and sanitation are important basic needs for the improvement of quality of life and enchancement of productive efficiency of the citizens. Although State Governments are responsible for supply of drinking water in villages, Central assistance is being provided under the Accelerated Rural Water Supply Programme (ARWSP) with 100 per cent grants—in—aid subject to a matching provision (except for DDP areas where matching provision is regular) being made by State Governments under Minimun Needs Programme (MNP). The National Drinking Water Mission (NDWM) renamed as the Rajiv Gandhi National Drinking Water Mission (RGNDWM) is looking into the need for providing sustainable safe drinking water to entire rural population over the next few years.

The coverage of rural population with drinking water supply and sanitation facilities in rural and urban areas increased rapidly. An outlay of Rs.1170.86 crore has been provided in 1996-97 budget for the Rural Water Supply and Sanitation Schemes.

The scheme of rural sanitation is aimed at supplementing the efforts made under different Central and State sector programmes for improving sanitry facilities in the rural areas. It includes, inter alia, construction of sanitary latrines for individual households below the poverty line, village-complexes for women, drains and other sanitation facilities. A total number of 1,66,353 and 37,422 sanitary latrines were constructed for Scheduled Castes and Scheduled Tribes respectively during 1995-96.

Housing is a State subject but the Union Government is responsible for the formulation of policy with regard to programmes and approaches for effective implementation of the social housing schemes, particularly those pertaining to weaker sections of the society. The National Housing Policy is enunciated in the Five Year Plan and the state goverments implement the schemes in accordance with the plan priorities and local requirements.

In tune with the policy of the Government, a National Housing Policy (NHP), taking into account the developments on national and international scene on Shelter Sector after 1988 and also in the light of comments received from state governments and different sections of the community has been evolved. Special emphasis has been given in the policy paper on the specific needs of rural housing. The policy document outlining the strategy under the Eighth Plan has since been endorsed by Parliament in 1994. The long term goal of the NHP is to eradicate houselessness, to improve the housing conditions of the inadequately housed and to provide a minimum level of basic services and amenities to all.

It recognises that the magnitude of housing task calls for involvement of various agencies including government at different levels, cooperatives, the community and the private sector. The policy envisages a major shift in Government's role to act more as a facilitator than as provider. The needs of vulnerable sections of society will continue to be atended to by the Government. It envisages to facilitate housing activity of the lower and middle income groups and to encourage within the framework of housing policy and local planning, the voluntary agencies in efforts to upgrade shelter, extend basic services, augment incomes and promote environmental conservation. The policy has been incorporated in the Housing Chapter on the Eighth Plan.

During the Eighth Plan, emphasis will be on social housing schemes including Minimum Needs Programme projects in rural areas, strengthened role of HUDCO, shelter for the homeless, technology transfer, housing information system and housing for Central Government employees. All the state governments have been requested to formulate detailed action plans for implementation of the policy.

During recent years, the trend towards rural-to-urban migration as well as urban-to-urban migraton is on the increase and the mobility characteristics are particularly strong towards metropolitan cities. Statistics show populaltion increase annually at national level—2%, at Urban level—3% and in metropolitan cities level—9%. As such, the existing areas of these cities are put under much pressure, causing excessive clustering and haphazard urban growth. According to 1991 census (provisional figures), about 65% of the total urban population live in Class-I cities and 50.6 per cent of urban population live in 23 metropolitan cities alone. Even though the rate of growth to over 40% in 12 metropolitan cities during 1971-81 has been less than the growth of urban population of 46%, the absolute addition of about 12 million people representing 24% of the total addition to urban population is distinctly very high. By the year 2000, India's urban population is excepted to be 325 million, twice the 1981 level, and more than half of India's population growth will occur in urban areas only.

It could be seen from this data that the pressure on land in urban areas had increased manifold during the last two decades resulting in further decline in the availability of per capita urban land. Further, nearly 30 to 50 per cent of the urban population in these cities has been living in slum areas with poor and sub-standard living conditions, with civic amenities far from satisfactory. The density of population in slums is also very high. Hence, the imbalance between the rapid growth or urban population in the metropolitan cities and relatively slow process of development of additional land for housing, commercial and other purposes has given rise to the following major problems in the metropolitan cities:

- Acute shortage of serviced land for residential, commercial and industrial purposes, resulting in urban sprawl and invasion on urban fringe.
- Continuous increase in density and loss of open spaces, more demand for land for housing and transportation have resulted in large conversion of land in the fringe.
- High land values due to ever-increasing gap between demand and supply of land for various uses.
- Increasing pressure on physical and social infrastructure due to massive spill-over, population pressure/economic activities etc.
- Acute shortage of housing, resulting in unauthorised construction, squatter settlements, up-coming of slums and even invasion of villages by the spill over population/economic activities etc.
- Inadequate finances/investment in urban infrastructure led to the concomitant problems of unplanned urban development on the green-belt leading to serious environmental/ecological problems.

— Fast urbanisation, coupled with sky rocketing and prices has deprived the poor/low income families to have access to shelter or even serviced land. Hence, not only the weaker section of the society but lower, middle income group of society but lower, middle income group of society have also started on public/ private land, generally on the urban fringe. The Land Acquisition of land have further acted as a major constraint in smooth and expeditious a acquisition of land and making it available for urban development.

The TCPO's study on Management of Urban Fringe Land Development in selected Metropolitan Cities of India namely Madras, Hyderabad, Pune, Indore, Lucknow, and Jaipur was taken up to analyse the efficacy of existing policies and programmes in making serviced land available at affordable prices to the poor for utilisation of land, availability of vacant land, unutilised land for meeting future demand etc. The study has gone into the spatial problems of inner city, density pattern, migration, of various infrastructural facilities like water supply, transport, sewerage, drainage, electricity, roads and other physical amenities in the cities. An attempt has been made in the study to analyse the effects on the management of green-belt, environment and land use transformation, provision of water and transportation for land development. The findings of study are briefly given below:

- The fringe areas of Madras and Jaipur are inhabitated by mostly middle and higher income groups, whereas fringe areas of Hyderabad, Pune, Lucknow and Indore are dominated by poor or low-income people.
- The people living in urban fringe of these six cities are employed in private sector/informal sector. A significant proportion of the total population of these areas are also found to be self employed.

- In case of Madres and Hyderabad, a significant proportion of persons (50-70%) are employed locally. Hosever, in respect of other smaller cities, the majority of the earning members commute to the main city for work or for other purposes.
- Public transport service seems to be the most important mode of transport for work journeys performed by the households of the urban fringe areas. Public transport facilities appear to be good in the fringe areas of Hyderabad, Madras and Pune, wherwas private transport is playing important role in Jaipur, Lucknow and Indore.
- A good proportion of the households who settled in the fringe areas of Madras, Hyderabad and Jaipur have come from the main cities, whereas the households settled in the fringe areas of Pune, Lucknow and Indore have migrated from nearby rural areas.
- Growth of these urban fringe areas has taken place only around mid-1980s.
- Majority of the households in urban fringe areas of these metropolitan cities have their own houses. It shows that the priority of these households has been to have houses of their own .
- Construction in all these urban fringe areas is unauthorised. This may be due to the impression among the people that these construction or pucca houses would be regularised on the intervention of some social or political pressures later on.
- The majority of the households lack municipal or protected water supply and depend on open wells located within their premises. These households are also deprived of sewerage and drainage facilities. Majority of them have water-borne latrines connected to septic tanks.

- Fringe areas of these metropolitan cities lack adequate basic facilities like education/medicines etc. They have to depend for them on the main cities.
- The reasons for living in the fringe areas are the high cost of urban land within city, the city life being unaffordable for the poor.
- Majority of the households of the fringe areas wanted to have domestic water connections and drainage facilities in their localities.
- Land price in the fringe areas started rising around mid-1980s. The price level between 1980-85 was steady. A sharp rise in the price of land, however, occured after 1985. The Urban Land Ceiling and Regulation Act, 1976, instead of being helpful in preventing speculative transactions relating to scarce and precious land, has added to the misery of land-speculation. Thousands of hectares of surplus land that the government proposed to aquire nder the Act was caught in the never ending rigmarole of court litigations. In two decades of its existence, the government has been able to acquire barely 15,321 hectares of the total 2.21 lakh hectares declared surplus across the country.

Urban fringe has been existing since the emergence of urban civilisation. However, its importance in the planning process has been realised only in recent times, particularly in the wake of the Industrial Revolution. No doubt, the concept of fringe is prevalent more in metropolitan and big cities than in small cities and towns.

It is now established that industrialisation and urbanisation are inter-related and irreversible processes. These are two sides of the same coin. A small town grows into a big town, a big town intoa city, and then it acquires the status of a metropolis and a mega city. Rapid urbanisation in the country has been accompanied by the emergence of urban fringe and slums in the cities. The existing areas of these cities are put under much pressure, causing excessive clustering and haphazard urban growth. The study on Management of Urban Fringe Land Development in selected Metropolitan cities undertaken by TCPO indicates that too much pressure on urban land during the last two decades has resulted into a decline in the per capita availability of urban land. As of now, a significant percentage 30% to 50% of population in metropolitan cities live in the slum areas in most deplorable and sub-standard conditions.

The emergence of urban fringe depends on various factors like growth of industrial, commercial and institutional activities in the fringe area, the availability of transportation facilities, proximity to the city, the existing spatial capacity of the city to absorb growing population, increasing economic activities and the basic infrastructural facilities being provided in the fringe areas, as well as in the city, etc. Therefore, it is difficult to assign a spatial boundary to define urban fringe.

According to Lewis Keeble the urban fringe is defined "as the land surrounding the town which is not considered as a part of it but whose use is influenced directly by the town". Richard Mayers considers the urban fringe "as the zone between the country and the city while to Andrews the rural urban fringe outward from the economic city in which there is an interminingling of charteristically agriculture and urban land uses." George Wherewein defines the fringe "as the area of transition between well recognised urban land uses and the area devoted to agriculture".

As such there is no exact definition for urban fringe land. It seems it is not possible also. This is because no one can exactly say as to what distance ithe fringe land should extend from the city boundary. One may say that fringe land should include those areas which fall on the fringe of the city, that is the areas falling just out side the boundary of the city. But the question is upto what distance one should go? Some people define fringe areas as those areas which are not contiguous t the existing built up areas of the city, but those which are likely to become contiguous if provided with the right injection of investment towards the right injection of investmnet towards the development of physical and social infrastructure. The structure plan for the Madras Metropolitan Areas has defined urban fringe as those areas that are experiencing considerable pressure form the process of urbanisation.

During initial staes, the urban fringe land would be mostly under agricultural use. However, once migration of population form nearby areas into the fringe land starts, the available land in taken over for housing, commercial, institutional and industial uses.

Biotechnology is many things to many people. It is the generic name for a variety of biological processes. Biotechnology may be defined as the application of scientific and engineering principles to the processing of materials by biological agents to provide goods and services.

Biotechnology has a long history dating back to the brewers of Babylon. Apart from liquor, other popular applications of biotechnology are cheese and pickles. But modern biotechnology industry was started during the nineteenth century. However, after a lull for many years, biotechnology has achieved many break—throughs during the last three decades.

The vast potential of biotechnology in medicine and agriculture is generally recognised. Heatlh care and pharmaceuticals were the first major areas where biotechnology was used. these were biotechnology was used. These were followed by agricultural and food applications. Now biotechnology is making a mark in the field of environment.

In medical diagnostics and therapeutics, biotechnology is the brightest alternative. Since the commercialisation of human insulin in 1982, the biotechnology industry has accomplished many major achievements in the medical sciences. The major research efforts have been aimed at developing pharmaceutical products for diseases such as heart ailments, AIDS and anemia. There are now over 50 successful products derived from biotechnology.

These include drugs like Epogen and Neupogen, besides Humulin. All three are single proteins performing a specific function in the body. While Epogen regulates the red cell blod count, Neupogen regulates thewhite cell blood count. Humulin is synthetic human insulin which avoids many of the problems associated with the extracted animal insulin.

Biotechnology is intimately related to the traditional pharmaceutical industry. Traditional drugs are discovered by and large on a trial—and—error basis. Biotechnology on the other hand uses biological tools to directly examine and alter the disease process. It thus provides the pharmaceutical industry with the technology it lacks.

The application of biotechnology in cardiovascular diagnostics and therapeutics continues to develop at a rapid rate. The drug Reo—Pro has recently been developed as an adjunct to coronary balloon angioplasty. Another new discovery is the isolation of the AGT gene that may be responsible for one third of the cases of high blood pressure. Tandem PSA has been approved for

The use of specific genes as therapy has been an area of medical research since long. However, the controlled introduction of functional genes into abnormal cells has been a difficult problem for over two decades. Once this problem is solved, gene therapy will emerge as a treatment not only for hereditary deficiencies, but also for non—hereditary diseases as well.

Other applications being studied include cell malignancy, cancer treatment and ageing—related diseases. Emerging technology areas also include a new generation of antibiotics to treat antibiotic—resistant pathogens, anti—viral therapeutics, and treatment of age—related diseases such as Parkinson's, Alzheimer's and osteoporosis.

Biotechnology offers the best hope for medical diagnostics and therapeutics. The industry in this field has just surpassed its infancy and is all set to grow—up and mature. Emphasis on R & D activities by the government institutions as well as private companies will go a long way in giving India an edge in the field.

In the field of agriculture, biotechnology by virtue of recombinant DNA technology can help in controlling the enzymes and hormones which regulate the process of ripening and softening in fruits like tomatoes. Gene technology can also modify the characteristics of certain food products or enhance their nutritive value. In the past few years, many advances have also been made in development of various biopesticides and biofertilisers.

Transgenic crop plants—plants with a genetic trait introduced by a molecular technique—have started finding practical applications. Apart from tomatoes with high shelf life, many other innovations have found their way from laboratory to the fields. These include virus—resistant potatoes. the economic consequences of such improvements will be enormous.

However, apprehensions about the overall efficacy of such innovative techniques continue to plague further developments. The claim of biotechnology to be a catalyst for sustainable agriculture is often questioned. But such apprehensions are but natural for any technical advancement, though these may not always be ill–founded. While new molecular techniques are being introduced since early 1970s, safety in biotechnology has attracted attention over the years.

The market for biopesticides is also growing rapidly. Bio—pesticides contain micro—organisms which prevent insect larvae from developing into adults. Biopesticides may include 'beneficial' predatory insects which eat pests, and pheromones which anc confuse insects and disrupt mating. Adopting a similar technique, Australia has been able to control the growing population of rabbits. Likewise, Japan has been able to successfully eradicate the melon fly on serveral islands through the release of strile insects. In India, the menace of rats and mosquitoes, frequently spreading epidemics like plague, lamaria, dengue fever, etc. can be effectively controlled by indigenous development of such techniques to suit local conditions.

Biopesticides generally pose lower risks to human health and the environment than their chemical counterparts. Thus developing new biopesticides through specific research would help in limiting the growing use of herbicides, insecticides, etc. and providing an eco–friendly solution to most agricultural problems.

After proving its worth in medical sciences and agriculture, biotechnology is now begning to have a significantly impact on the environmental sciences. In fact, biotechnology has quite a large potential to contribute to the detection, prevention and remediation of environmental pollution and degradation.

Even though modern bioitechnology is not new to environmental sciences, it has taken long to have a noticeable impact in this field. One of the earliest and most widespread applications of biotechnology was waste water treatment plants. These plants work by degradation of organic waste with the help of micro—organisms. Developed during the nineteenth century, such plants have seen only minor changes during all these years. One of the main reasons for the slow progress of modern bio—technology in environmental science has been the lack of adequate concern for the environment. On the other hand, medical and agricultural applications have attracted more attention by virtue of more tangible outcome in these cases. But as the concern for the environment increased in the eighties and nineties, environmental biotechnology is now fast gaining prominance.

In US, $ 83.3 million was spent in 1993 on R & D in environmental bioitechnology, which was 2.1% of total biotechnology R & D in the country. Germany and the Netherlands have so far taken a lead in manufacturing and exporting biological technologies for treating waste water and air. Japan is also making efforts to develop export—oriented environmental biotechnology industry. However, the progress in India is lack–lusture as not much attention is being given.

Biotechnology is certainly not the technology to keep the environment clean. But biological clean—up methods are much more sustainable than chemical or physical methods for waste treatment. The simplest procedure adopted for disposal of waste is production of methane by anaerobic digestion. Bio—gas production is one such application.

Environmental biotechnologies utilise micro—organisms and their parts or products. Earthworms, which are among the most widespread natural clean—up agents, are also used in environmental biotechnology to purify soil. In the cleaning—up of air pollution, biotechnological methods such as biofilters are the most effective. Biotechnology is also used to clean—up oil spills.

Global warming can be reduced with the help of biotechnology by improving the photosynthetic ability of plants to fix carbon dioixide. Biotechnology can also help reduce desertification. Bio—polymer molecules help enhance water retention in the soil. Plants resistant to salt and drought can also be developed.

The impact of biotechnology is pervasive. Biiotechnology being a multi—faceted activity can produce many products and achieve many worthwhile claims. Biotechnology needs to be developed to suit local conditions e.g. for a country like India, new varieties using low inputs of water, fertilisers and pesticides to suit local soil conditions need to be developed. Similarly, tackling of plague, malaria, dengue fever, etc. will have to take into account local factors.

Thus the scope of biotechnology is vast and complex, but ill—defined. Only concerted indigenous efforts will help in making use of the full potential of this useful technology.

Various stage trade information should be collected and made available to the villagers. Indigenous knowledge should be documented and made use of. Systems of regeneration, cultivation and harvesting should be evolved. Primary collectors should be helped to get reasonable prices. NTFP based industries should be established near forest. Vrop and market fluctuations should be accurately predicted and displacement by synthetic products guarded against. Comples dynamics of species inter—relationship should be understood and overhead and side light admission should take into account the growth of NTFP yielding herb, shrub and tree layers. In plantations under the inter—cropping NTFP species should be considered.

Commercial scale plantation both inside and outside forests should be raised. Modern methods of vegetative propagation will suit more to NTFP yielding herbs and shrubs. NTFP plantations will suit better to agroforestry NTFP gardens for ex situ conservation should be linked with commercial cultivation in private and corporate sectors. More importance should be given to NTFP in R & D programmes. Long—term and short—term study and research programmes should be drawn and executed. Studies in respect of suitable national, state and grassroots organisation should be taken up as short—term programme. Resource inventory should be prepared. Collection, storage, grading, processing, value–addition and standardisation of measuring units should be studied and improved. Information flow channels should be invented. Corporate sectors should think of raising captive plandations.

Silvicultural systems should be developed for managing forests for sustainable NTFP yield. Canopy manipulation, growing space, regeneration, tending, thinning, SSOs should now accommodate NTFP plants and products. NTFP base should be introduced in RDH programmes. Silvicultural knowledge for herbs, shrubs, climbers and miscellaneous tree species should be developed. Total package approach should be developed for cultivating NTFP species. Arrangements for quality seed and planting stock should be made. Provenance trials and introduction of exotics should also be undertaken. Market survey, demand protection and even demand creation should be done to facititatie profitable trade. Use of modern tools of product development should be experimented. Some non–environment friendly systems should be given up. Rural economic prosperity perspective should be given the maximum importance in forest management.

One simple policy to follow is the communal or collective ownership of forest property. People and technicians should have say in policy and decision making. Banning fellings is not conducive to conservation, regeneration and bioidiversity. There is great scokpe of forest based economy shift in rural India through NTFPs. Management of NTFPs should be taken outside the existing forest departments under separate organisation.

Education and training of officials an non–officials should be attended to properly. Training of gatherers should be given special attention. Political and administrative reasons and convenience should not weigh upon the urgency of executing NTFP management suggestions.

Frogs have been the nature's great survivors—they have hopped about the earth for the past 250 million years, surviving Ice Age, the dinosaurs and the break up of land into continents. They are the link between the fishes and al higher vertebrates. They are the first vertebrates to possess a true voice and tongue.

But in the last 20 years, this ancient link in ecological chain has been decimated due to various reasons. Global warming, acid rain, viruses, increases in ultraviolet light causes by the thinning of ozone layer and clearing of land are advancing the declination of frog numbers. Frogs, probably are the barometers to the environment more than any other creature. Though they do not drink water, they absorb water thrugh their skin and are particularly vulnerable to any changes in the water quality. While agreeing that all of the above theories have some validity, the main cause seems to be the chemical pollution of water, expecially through the use of pesticides.

Frogs inhabit swampy and water-logged irrigated fields. According to one study, in the last 30 years, the irrigated lands are almost doubled and therefore the frog habitat. But this increase means increased usage of pesticides. Frogs seldom escape the effect of pesticides directly applied to their habitat as vector control measures, or as surface run-off and sediment transport from treated fields and soil.

Since frogs breed during rainy season and release their eggs into ponds and other water bodies, the development of eggs itself is affected by the accumulated pesticides.

Paradoxically, frogs are wonderful pest-controllers and their role to that effect is conclusively established. Several important agricultural pests belonging to groups Coleoptera, Hemiptera, Isoptera, Lepidoptera and Orthoptera were found to constitute food of frogs. The millions of frogs that are eliminated every year would have consumed several thousand tonnes of insects and saved a great deal more than several crore of rupees in the pesticide use and several times more in avoidable ecological disruption, where the costle are incalculably higher.

Frogs have become a major source of food for many countries from the recent past. India, Indonesia and Bangladesh were the principal exporters of frog legs to the European countries. India started exporting frog legs a early as 1957, earning a foreign exchange of Rs.5 crore per year. Till 1969, India exported just 500-700 tonnes of frog legs annually, but thereafter it got a dubious distinction of being the biggest frog-leg exporting country, trading on abut 4,000 tonnes per year, earning abut $ 10 million in bargain. However, such export requires the lives of nearly 50-60 million frogs every year. A report says that approximately 60 legs (of 30 frogs) make up on kilo of exportable meat, because only the hind limbs are used to procure meat.

Besides economical and ecological importance, frogs have academic importance too: one can hardly find an educational institution which teaches biology without dissecting a frog. Scientific reports say that utilisation of frogs by education sector is ever-increasing from 2.6 million in 1956 to 18 million in 1980 to more than 25 million in 1990.

Conservation of frogs have been taken up by many countries world wide. Convention on International Trade in Endangered Species in West Germany had placed the Indian Bull frog, Rana tigrina in the protected list. In 1987, the Indian Board for Wild Life had recommended to provide a special status to frogs by including rana species in Schedule 2, Part 2 of Wildlife (Protection) Act, 1972. The 2,9000 and odd species of frogs spread all over the globe are very special to us for, they are least harmful to man of any major zoological class: none of them has inflicted deadly disease upon us as have some invertebrates such as insects and protozoans did; none of them possesses poisonous barbs as some fish have; they do not have poisonous bites as snakes have; they are not destructive as rodents are; they do not rob fields of crops as many birds do; and none of them is ferocious like the scores of carnivores.

On the contrary, frogs are 'scientific wonders': skin glands of some species contain 20-30 chemical compounds used to develop antibiotics (Meganins) and analgesics (one painkiller, epibatidine, isolated from frog skin is 200 times as potent as morphine).

Many other compounds have been used to develop an effective treatment of chronic schizophrenia, gastric ulcers etc.,

Today, the human activity made the frogs disappear. If such unique animals depending on water are on the verge of extinction, what about mankind, which is totally dependent on water for survival? The relatively silent ponds and lakes are telling that something is very wrong with the ecology and, that, unless we reverse this, the outlook for all creatures, humans included, is grim.

Air pollution problem

The immediate environment of man comprises air on which depends all form of life. It has been estimated that a man can live for 5 weeks without food, for 5 days without water, but for only 5 minutes without air. Normally the air is composed of 78.1 part Nitrogen, 20.93 part oxygen and 0.03 part carbondioxide. The balance is made up of other gases which occur in traces. In addition to these gases air also contain water vapour, and suspended matter such as dust, bacteria, pores and debris. Therefore, the term air pollution is applied when there is excessive concentration of foreign mater in the outdor atmosphere which is harmful to man or his environment. Pollution of air has resulted in sickness and deaths. More than 100 contaminants have been identified. The important ones are carbonmonoxide, sulphur dioxide, Nitrogen dioixide, Ozone, Lead, etc. Air pollution is a growing menace to health through out the world.

Most of the pollutants are associated with fossil fuel consumption. Two main categories of outdoor air pollutants are recognised. Industrial smog predominate in large industrial areas. It is a combination of smoke and fog and results from combustion of fuel and consists primarily of sulfur dioxides and particulate complexes. Combustion of coal, oil and other fuel is another source of smoke, dust and sulphur dioxide. Photochemical smog occurs in areas shich a high density of motor vehicles.

Motor vehicles, truck, trains, aircraft and other forms of transport emit hydrocarbons, carbonmonoxide, lead, nitrogen dioxide and particulate matter. In strong sunlight certain of these hydrocarbons and oxide of nitrogen may be converted into photochemical pollutant of oxidising nature. Burning of refuse, agricultural activities e.g. crop spraying, pest control and nuclear energy programmes also contribute to air pollution.

Sulfur dioxide is a major atmospheric pollutant in many urban and industrial areas, produced by the burning of sulfur content of coal and crude oil. The major source of environmental pollution are poer plants, oil refineries, and industries such as smelters, paper pulp mills and wineries. The sulfur dioxide released in the atmosphere is oxidized to sulfur trioxide in the presence of sunlight and high humidity which immediately combines with water to form sulfuric acid. Sulfur trioxide and sulfuric acid are much more irritant than sulfur dioxide.

Nitrogen dioxide is a pollutant generated in the outdoor environment mainly from automobile exhaust. In the presence of flame temperature oxygen combines nitrogen to form nitric oxide, a gas of litlle significance as an air pollutant. However when nitric oxide is vented into the air and cools rapidly, a fraction is converted into nitrogen dioxide. At home wood burning, fireplaces, kerosene heater and improperly vented gas stoves give rise to nitrogen dioxide pollution.

Ozone is a gas which is a key component of a complex mixutre of photochemical oxidant and fine particles called "Smog". It is formed by a series of sunlight driven reactions of nitrogen oxides and volatile organic compounds arising from combustion sources. Indoor sources of ozone include air "purifiers" and ion generators and office equipment with electric motors or ultraviolet lights, such as photocopy machines. In indoor environment (e.g. home, work, school) concentration of ozone are generally lower than outdoor.

Carbon monoxide (CO) duduced in ambient air comes mainly from vehicular exhaust with a bimodal peak corresponding to the morning and evening rush hours. Catalytic converters on motor vehicle decreases CO in exhaust. Indoor air can be contaminated by cigarette smoking and outdoor air that enters building from the street traffic. High exposures are relatively rare and are primarily associated with certain occupations (e.g. fire fighting) and from exposure to the product of combustion in an enclosed space from improperly vented combustion appliances and of charcoal briquettes for barbecuing and space heating. Combustion from fires, stoves, and motor vehicles generates CO at concentrations of 1% to 6% (10,000 to 60,000 ppm).

The leaded gasolines/petrol is the main source of wide spread dispersion of this metal throughout the biosphere. A marked reduction in the ambient levels of airborne lead resulted since 1970s with the use of unleaded gasoline. In countries where leaded gasolilne is still used airborne lead from automotive emissons continues to accumulate in the environment.

Premature infants, newborn, and elderly and people with chronic disease of the lungs or heart are at higher risk. Pre-school and school children appear to be sensitive to air pollution health effects. The traffic policeman, the automobile mechanics, the drivers may have unusually high risk from exposure to community air pollution due to substantial exposures in association with their occupations.

Cigarette smoking is the predominant risk factor in producing respiratory diseases and lung cancer. Air pollution have a more than additive effect. This means that cigarette smokers are at unusual higher risks if they live in areas with substantial air pollution and that the effects of air pollution on chronic disabling pulmonary diseases are more likely to occur in cigarette smokers. During periods of low winds and still weather dissipation of domestic pollution due to heating and cooking will be impaired. In such condition if smoking or cooking occurs indoors, exposures to carbonmonoxide and nitrogen oxides may be quite high.

The problem of air pollution was first brought to a sharp focus when air pollution epidemics took place in the middle of 20th century. In 1952 London Fog epidemic, many people became ill and some 4000 deaths occurred. Since these episodes evaluation of exposed populaltions, have been performed in urban areas around the world to examine the impact of air pollution on human helath. Overall, these studies show a consistent pattern of association between increased sulfur dioxide and particulate concentrations and mortality. The acute bronchonstrictor effects of sulfur dioxide have been well established for more than 20 years. Patients with asthma represent a susceptible subgroup responsive to the effect of SO_2 and H_2SO4 at a concentration that have no effect on normal subjects. Sulfur dioxide is highly soluble in water, nearly all the inspired gas is absorbed in the nasal mucosa and very little reaches to the lungs undernormal resting conditions. Oral breathing reduces the uptake of sulfur dioxide in the nose, but increases pollutant delivery to the lungs. In some patients of asthma oral breathing predominates because of associated nasal obstruction.

Ozone is a powerful oxidant. The respiratory system is the primary target of the ozone toxicity. Inhalation of ozone can result in damage to almost all parts of the respiratory tract, depending upon concentration. Studies on animals have documented the inflammation of the respiratory tract, damage to epithelial cells and marked increase in susceptibility to bacterial infection following acute ozone exposure. Redness and swelling of the airways has been observed after ozone exposure the cytotoxicity of ozone may be largely due to its interaction with unsaturated lipids which generate damaging free radicals. Moreover, long lived radicals could enter the blood stream and exert effects on body temperature of blood pressure or remote organs such as the liver.

The evidence that ozone is determental to health is increasing. The concentration that sometimes occur in urban areas cause modest reductions of lung function both in children and exercising normal adults. There is a wide variation of susceptibility to these effects. Increased symptoms and lung function decrement usually occur in the same subjects. The major mechanism of ozone induced reduction in lung function is the inability of the exposed individual to inspire fully. Ozone exposure potentiate the allergic response and is harmful to asthmatics.

Nitrogen dioxide is less potent than ozone as an oxidant. According to intensity and duration of exposure, respiratory illness ranges from slight irrigation, burning an pain in the throat and chest to violent cough and shortness of breath. Acute Nitrogen dioxide poisoning leading to pulmonary odema and deaths has been recognized. There is a great paucity of information on chronic Nitrogen dioxide exposure because damage develops slowly. Moreover nitrogen dioxide is usually associated with other pollutants, which renders assesment of its action difficult. Indoor sources of combustion add NO_2 to indoor air. The use of gas for cooking might have a small effect on children and asthmatics. Sulfur dioxide has an additive effects on lung functions on healthy individuals.

The exposure to nitrogen dioxide in indoor air might increase the occurrence of respiratory infections because both short and long—term exposures to notrogen dioxide exposures impair the ability to clear inhaled infectious organisms. An increased incidence of respiratory illnesses during childhood predisposes to the development of chronic respiratory diseases in adults. Nitrogen dioxide is also an ingredient of cigarette smoke. Smokers employed in an environment polluted by automobile exhaust are believed to be particularly vulnerable to harm from nitrogen dioixide.

The toxic properties of CO are attributed to its high affinity for oxygen carrying protein (haemoglobin) to form a chemical complex called carboxyhaemoglobin (COHb). The exposure to CO is expressed as percentage of total haemoglobin bound to CO. In healthy individuals who do not smoke or are not otherwise exposed to CO, COHb level ranges from 0.3 to 0.7%. Inhaled CO is thought to be responsible for the further elevation of COHb levels to about 1% in non smokers. A significant proportion of the urban non smokers population has COHb level in excess of 1.5%, suggesting widespread exposure to environmental Co. Cigarettes, cigars and pipe smoking commonlyu commonly result in blood COHb levels of 2-14%. Patients of obstructive airways disease who continue to smoke tend to have higher COHb levels than smokers free of cardiiopulmanary disease.

Acute CO poisoning, with COHb levels over 30 to 50%, results in damage mainly to the heart and brain because less oxygen is carried on haemoglobin secondary to the formation of COHb. Patients with Ischemic heart disease, are particularly sensitive to CO. Earlier onset of angina and ECG changes indicative of myocardial ischemia have been documented during exercise in such pateints at COHb level in the range of 2 to 6%. The adverse effect of maternal smoking on foetal growth and development are now well accepted. CO a major component of cigarette smoke, interfers with the transport of oxygen to the developing tissues. Similar effects have been postulated for ambient CO exposures.

The route of exposure of lead is through both inhalation and ingestion. Most of the lead deposited on the airways is cleared by mucociliary blanket of the lungs and swallowed. Approximately 10% is absorbed in the gastro intestinal tract and gets deposited in the bones. Women with previous lead exposures may have elevated blood levels during periods of high bone turnover (e.g. pregnancy, lactation, or hyperthyroidism). Their urborn children may be exposed transplacentally, and newborns through breast milk to high levels of lead. Foetuses, infants and children are considered to be particularly susceptible to the adverse effects. Early childhood lead exposures has neurobehavioral effects such as various learning dosorders, reading disabilities, poor vocabulary and grammatical reasoning.

Inspite of decades of laboratory clinical and epidemiologic research, however the health effects of exposure of humans to pollutants remain incompletely characterized. Finally most environmental exposures involved multiple pollutants. Control of exposures in life is an important component of appropriate preventive action. Escape of toxic substances into the ambient air can be prevented by an variety of engineering methods such as enclosure, ventilation and air cleaning. A major contribution in this field is the development of arrestors for the removal of contaminants like convertors to reduce automobile exhaust. Use of technology that reduces pollution like use of electricity and natural gas in place of coal. The control of an air pollution is ultimately an engineering problem.

A new twist has been given to the ongoing debate on Global Warming by a recent book titled "The Global Warming Debate" published by the European Science and Environment Forum (ESEF), London. This book has questioned the very existence of the phenomenon fo global warming. The publication is more like a collection of closely argued scientific findings.

In its summary paper release in 1995, the UN sponsored Inter-government Panel on Climate Change (IPCC) had stated that "the balance of evidence suggests a discernible human influence on climate." Thus the IPCC, which is the main proponent of global warming, still does not have conclusive evidence of the phenomenon. The latest development has, therefore, proved to be ecstatic for commercial energy suppliers such as Organisation of Pteroleum Exporting Countries (OPEC), which have been questioning the contribution of fossil fuels to such a phenomenon, fearing a decline in their sales due to conservation measures and development of alternative fuels.

More so because the ESEF book argues that not only are man—made emissions of carbon dioxide failing to raise the earth's temperature, but that a global warming trend does not exist. It says that there is no strong evidence that global temperatures have risen in recent decades. One contributor, Patrick Michaels, has used more objective data from weather satellites, available only for the last 17 years, and finds no trace of global warming. He suggests that since most of the IPCC data are based on on—land thermometers, while two—thirds of the earth's surface is water, the methodology is basically flawed and fails to detect a global phenomenon. On the other hand, satellites can provide a truly global and uniform picture.

Two Danish scientists, Knud Lassen and Eigil Christensen, have argued in the book that much of the observed warming may be due to changes in sunspot activity. Even though few would deny that levels of greenhouse gases concentrations in theatmosphere have increased over the past century, the book's editor Dr. John Emsley of Imperial College, London, and his collegue Dr. Jack Barrett question the basic issue when they suggest that an increased concentration of carbon dioxide is simply incapable of radiating more heat back to the surface of the earth.

Even the impact ofenhanced levels of carbon dioxide in the atmosphere on plant growth has divergent views. While some scientists feel that higher concentrations of CO2 would help plants to grow faster (and also fix some CO2 in the process), others feel that while plant responses differ for different species, plant growth would also be governed by availability of moisture and nutrients.

The origin of the Global Warming theory is quite old. The realisation that the emission of trace gases might change the climate dawned about 170 years ago when Fourier discussed the greenhouse effect in 1827. However, it was not until 1970 that major studies were carried out. As such, no one doubts the existence of natural greenhouse effect. At normal concentrations, the greenhouse gases maintain a protective layer around the earth and trap infra red (heat) radiation emitted back from the surface of the earth. In the absence of these gases, the earth would reflect back most of the heat received from the sun, making it much colder. Thus greenhouse gases maintain the earth's energy balance and made it habitable. However, increase in their concentration may cause global warming due to increased trapping of heat radiation.

Combustion of fuels emits carbon dioxide into the atmosphere. This is the single largest source of man—

made greenhouse gases. Other sources of CO_2 are natural sources such as forest fires, volcanoes, bio—degradation, etc. Thus even in the absence of human interference, greenhouse effect is constantly in operation. However, human activities disturb this balance resulting in global warming.

The Earth Summit of 1992 was the first major event aimed at preventing global warming. The core of the treaty arrived at the summit stated that "the ultimate objective is to achieve stabilisation of greenhouse gases concentrations at a level that wuld prevent dangerous anthropogenic interference with the climate system." Even though India ratified it in November 1993, the UN Framework Convention on Climate Change (UNFCC) came into force only in March 1994, when the fiftieth country ratified it. The UNFCC is based on the broad consensus set out by IPCC.

It has been estimated that global temperatures increased by 0.3 to 0.6 deg Cover the last 130 years and by about 2 deg Cover the last 10,000 years. Latest findings indicate that over the next century the projected rise in global temperatures and the consequent rise in sea levels will be 20–30 per cent lower than what was projected earlier. While global temperature may rise by 2.5 degC as against 3.3 degC projected earlier, rise in sea level may be 48 cms, down from 66 cms. However, this does not mean that the earlier computer models under—estimated the extent of global warming. It only suggests that earlier models did not take into account cooling effects.

However, scientists warm that while the cooling effects of aerosols and ozone depletion will pale over the long term, CO2 is a long—lived gas. Thus any relentless rise in CO2 emissions will lead to increase in its concentrations over the years.

A recent scientific report points out that if the present rate of CO2 emissions continues over the next century, the earth's climate may heat for about 500 years. This study points out that the resultant warming may be as high as 7 degC after 500 years. Just thermal expansions of oceans due to this temperature rise will alone result in an increase in sea level by 2 metres. The effect of melting of ice caps will be extra. Another fallout will be a decrease in CO2 absorption capacity of oceans at higher temperatures. But the most alarming aspect will be stabilising of oceans due to absence of mixing effects of deep waters.

Even if emission rates remain constant at the current level, the concentration of carbon dioxide in the atmosphere will increase from 350 parts per million by volume (ppmv) at present to about 450 ppmv in about 50 years time. Enhanced growth inthe presence of higher CO2 concentration is known as CO2 fertilisation, and may well serve to increase the carbon sink due to enhanced photosynthesis. This is, however, subject to availbility of sufficient nutrients, optimum temperature, adequate moisture, etc. Different plant resonses may lead to a change in compositon of plant species in the ecosystem.

Combustion of different fossil fuels releases CO2 at different rates for the same level of energy production. While CO2 released from liquid petroleum fuels is 1.5 times more than the amount released from natural gas, coal releases almost double the amount than natural gas.

According to IPCC estimates, about 80% of the 7.6 billion tons of carbon released every year comes from combuston of fossil fuels. The balance occurs due to biomass burning. While about half of the 7.2 billion tons per year of all carbon emissions remain in the atmosphere, abut 2 million tons per year of carbon is taken up by the oceans.

Proponents of global warming warm that such changes will afect agriculture. While some regional variations may lead to local conditions more favourable to crop growth, a high proportion of the main food—producing regions in both North and South hemispheres are likely to be adversely affected. Increase in climatic variability will increase the risk of low agricultural yields and potential for crop failures.

For a country like India, which still depend a great deal on agriculture, the implications of global warming, if it does occur, will be profound. While in 1965, agriculture contributed 44% of GDP in India, its contribution is still 30%. Almost two–thirds of the opopulation still depend on agriculture for livelihood. Agriculture in India is all the more climate—sensitive, depending on factors such as the monsoons to a great extent.

Since more than two—thirds of the world's populaltion lives in coastal plains, the impact of rise in mean sea level is particularly critical. Virtually all the land in the Maldives is less than two metres above sea level, and thus the entire nation may be in danger of being wiped out. So are large parts of Bangladesh as also many densely populated and fertile coastal strips around and fertile coastal strips arund the world. Even where the risk of flooding is less, there is a grave threat to the ground water from the ingress of sea water. India is surrounded by a vast coast—linge. Any rise in sea level will have threatening consequences for many low—lying coastal areas.

In the event of global warming, large parts of forest land in India may also get threatened. This may occur not only on account of global warming, but also on account of ndiscriminate deforestation as well as due to rapid rise in population. Since destruction of forest land harms the carbon cycle in two ways—by releasing stored carbon and by reducing CO_2 fertilisation, the implications may be much more adverse for a country like India.

Contrary to popular belief so far, global warming, if it does occur, may not take place gradually over the years. Instead, warming may take place in sudden leaps and the climate may oscillate between stable states. It is doubtful whether our ecosystem would be able to adapt to such sudden shifts.

However, Roger Bate of Institute of Economic Affairs, London, who is also one of the authors of the book, argues that IPCC has a vested interest in promoting fears of global warming. On the other hand, IPCC could counterargued that it has the privilege of contribution by majority of the scientists.

While the debate on occurance of global warming and its causes and effects goes on, it may still be worthwhile to pay some attention to minimise emission of greenhouse gases. Thus, the outcome of the debate notwithstanding, we need to give emphasis on renewable energy sources, energy conservation, etc., not only to counter climate change, but also to save the environment, and averta possible catastrophe before it is too late.

Hazardous waste problem

The Ministry of Enviornment and Forests is the nodal agency for the management and control of hazardous substances which include hazardous chemicals, wastes and micro-organisms. In pursuance of these activities, the following rules have been notified under the Environment (Protection) Act, 1986: (i) Manufacture, Storage and Import of Hazardous Chemicals, 1989; (ii) Hazardous Wastes (Management) and Handling) Rules, 1989; and (iii) Manufacture, Use, Import, Export and Storage of Hazardous Micro-organisms/Genetically Engineered Organisms or Cell, 1989.

A crisis management plan has been worked out to meet chemical emergencies in units handling hazardous chemicals. The plan provides for a three-tier system i.e.establishment of crisis group at the Central, state and district or local levels. A control room has been set up in the Ministry to deal with emergencies caused due to hazardous chemicals. Guidelines for preparation of crisis management plans have been issued to the state governments and financial support is being provided to them to strengthen infrastructure for the purpose. Funds have been released for the establishment of Emergency Response Centres at Bhopal, Baroda and Manali. A Redbook entitled "Central Crisis Group Alert System" which includes names, addresses and telephone numbers of the Central and state authorities and experts to be contacted in case of emergency has been prepared and circulated to all concerned. A Public Liability Insurance Act has been enacted to provide immediate relief to the victims of accidents by hazardous chemical industries.

India is a signatory to the UNEP sponsored Convention on Control of Trans-boundary Movement of Hazardous Wastes which has been adopted at Basel, Switzerland by 126 governments of the world in 1989. The Convention aims at checking the reported illegal traffic in hazardous wastes from one country to another. A scheme on National Register of Potentially Toxic Chemicals (NRPTC) has been started with a view to set up the basic infrastructure for implementing the London guidelines for the exchange of information on chemicals in international trade including the procedure for prior informed consent. Under this scheme the requisite hardware and software have been obtained and elecctronic networking of various Central and state governments and boards has been established through NICNET and SIRNET. An approach paper for establishing a National Inventory of Chemicals has been prepared. It is also proposed to set up a Poison Control Centre at the All India Institute of Medical Sciences, New Delhi. The Ministry has constituted a National Waste Management Council to suggest ways and means for effective utilisation of wastes generated in the country. Three sub-groups have been set up by Council to deal with the major categories of wastes viz., industrial, urban and rural. The sub-groups have been entrusted with the task of identifying wastes, suggesting technological action points including legislation, taxes and incentives. Special emphasis is being laid on promoting the use of flyash in various fields and the state governments have been asked to prepare a perspective action plan for 50 per cent utilisation of flyash by the turn of the century. For the disposal of hazardous wastes, 15 sites have been identified in the country for preparation of secured land fills. The Hazardous Wastes (Management and Handling) Rules 1989 have been amended.

Research promotion

The environmental research programme aims to develop strategies for sustainable resource management and create facilities and trained manpower to conduct research in priority areas. Research projects are supported under three main schemes: (a) Man and Biosphere Programme; (b) Environment Research Programme; and (c) Action-oriented research programme for Eastern and Western Ghats. A number of small, specific research projects are also beng supported. Expert committees and expert working groups make recommendations for undertaking research in priority areas, scrutinise proposals, evaluate progress and recommend suitable mechanisms for implementation of the research projects. Priority areas of research are identified in five fundamental elements viz., land, water, air, space and energy. To strengthen the environmental research and training base, the following Centres of

Excellence have been set up: Ecological Research and Training Centre, Bangalore: Centre for Mining Environment, Dhanbad: Centre for Environmental Education, Ahmadabad: CPR Environment Education Centre, Madras and the Salim Ali Centre for Orinthology and Natural History, Coimbatore.

This Institute, established in 1988, is an autonomous organisation of the Ministry of Environment and Forests for developing strategies, technologies and knowledge base for ecologically sound developoment of the Himalayan region. Besides undertaking action-oriented research projects the Institute has also installed three weather monitoring stations for collecting and analysing climatic data for the Himalayan region. Units of the Institute are also located at UP, Sikkim, Nagaland and Himachal Pradesh.

Forestry research is the primary responsibility of the Indian Council of Forestry Research and Education. It has the following forestry research institutes and centres under it: (i) Forest Research Institute, Dehra Dun; (ii) Institute of Arid Zone Forestry Research, Jodhpur; (iii) Institute of Rain and Moist Deciduous Forests, Jorhat; (iv) Institute of Wood Science and Technology, Bangalore; (v) Tropical Forestry Research Institute, Jabalpur; (vi) Institute of Forest Genetics and Tree Breeding, Coimbatore; (vii) Temperate Forest Research Centre, Shimla (viii) Centre for Forest productivity, Ranchi and (ix) Centre for Social Forestry and Environment, Allahabad. In addition, the Indian Plywood Industries Research and Training Institute, Bangalore, has been transferred to the Ministry of Environment and Forests from the Ministry of Industry. Besides forestry research in wood panel products, this Institute imparts training to workers in optimum utilisation of timber.

Research programmes in wildlife are carried out by the Wildlife Institute of India, Dehra Dun and the Salim Ali Centre for Orinthology and Natural History, Coimbatore. Several projects on habitat evolution, elephant movement, ecology of gharial and turtles, status of endangered species behavioural ecology, bio-diversity, resource study, conservation, ecology and management of specific animals etc., are being carried out by both these institutes.

Then pattern of R&D expenditure calls for a close look. Defence research tops the list with over 28 per cent of the expenditure, followed by Space Atomic Energy while Electronics gets less than one per cent are allotted to R&D that goes into product development for the industry.

More effective R&D is required in health care, agriculture and export-related industial processes and product.

A Major Inrease is called for in Areas for in areas that would Make a big difference to the common peiple. For instance, solar cells (using gallium arsenide) deserves top priority, as it would revolutionize the availability of power. Japan, for example, has made a massive investment on ways to lower the cost of photovoltaic power using amorphous silicon solar cells. However, a radical departure in the expenditure pattern would pose hard choices to the government.

It has become fashionable to cite Japan rather indiscriminately! For instance, Japan is hailed as an example of free enterprise. But there is a vital deffernce. As pointed out by Prof. M.G.K. Menon, the Japanese government interacts closely with Japanese industries and helps them in their production. Japan recently (1995) doubled its budget for scientific research. In contrast, the slight drop in official "initiative" in the US has not been

Primarily helpful to the American industries to compete successfully abroad.

There is a general agreement among scientists that the government should pay to open-ended basic research. No doubt, investments should yield positive results. While the idea of conserving the resources is acceptable, it is against the very idea of the scientific method to insist on positive results in all cases. Those who agrue for mainly industry-oriented R&D cite the Scientific Policy Resolution of 1958 enunciated by Jawaharlal Nehru. It says:

"The key to national prosperity lies in the effective combination of technology, raw materials and capital of which the first is perhaps the most important since the creation of new scientific techniques can in fact make up for deficiency in natural resources and reduce the demand on capital"

Emphasising result-orientd research is laudable but it should not result in the neglect of basic research. There are problems unique to the country and some basic research is necessary. And industry will not support it in a big way in India.

The Department of Science and Technology (DST) has generated a long-term technology vision up to 2020 AD in nine areas: agrofood procesing, waterways, road transportation, electic power, telecommunications, aviation, sensors, intellectual property rights and future technology forecasting. As the modified saying goes, the proof of the pudding is in the casting! It all depends on implementation. Indian scientists should demonstrate the tangible gains of R&D so that Indian industry feels confident and readily accepts their contribution and shares the cost. For example, there is a good case for sharing the R&D cost for development of high performance advanced ceremonies, as India has large reserves of bauxite and black sand minerals.

The Ninth Plan approach paper speaks of the needto restructure and reoreint many of the scintific institutions and laboratories. The emphasis of the research programmes will be on mission mode projects with carefully identified end goals rather than on discipline mode. The vision 2020 initiative will be operationalized.

It must be stted in fairness to our scientists that the Science and Engineering Research Council approved 341research programmes costing over Rs. 34 crore in 1995-96 in various areas of S&T. The plan outlay for DST's programme has increased from Rs. 146 crore in 1991-92 to Rs. 252 crore in 1995-96. The allocation for supporting research in basic sciences has been doubled. A National S&T Management Information System has been set up.

Need for Dissemination of Information: In biotechnology, for instanc, about 591 out of 680 approved projects are under various stages of implementation in different fields such as agriculture, crop biotechnology, plant tissue culture, medicianl plants and biological pest control, though there is very little effort to tell the public about their significance.

The Department of Atomic Energy's gamma irradiation techniques has been successfully applied for preserving onions, potatoes and spices, etc. This work of the Atomic Energy Department deserves wider publicity mong farmers.

Remote Sensing: The Indian remote sensing satellites (IRS series) have become world famous and the imageries of natural resources are sold by an American company. At home, the imageries provide the basic data for recovering wasteland, monitoring crops, flood damage and irrigation patterns and increasing the fish catch from the sea etc. A major application strategy, based on value-added imageries through private sector participation, is called for.

Recently, the Indian Institute of Science, Bangalore and the five IITs were told that their funds would be frozen at the 1993-94 level with an annual 10 per cent nominal rise and that they should attract funding from elsewhere. Only if an industry sponsors a programme, a matching grant will be provided.

It has been recently announced that the Centre would formulate a package of measures to promote greater involvement universities in meeting the needs of industries. Though over four million young people have science or engineering qualifications or 450 per lakh (as of 1990), those engaged in R&D numbered only 15 per lakh.

It would be realistic to reorient the curriculum of engineering colleges and polytechnics, as those engaged in R&D constitute only a small percentage. There are about 450 engineering collegs and 600 polytechnics with 80,000 and 150,000 students, respectively. The coureses need more emphasis on computer science and applications. As Vice Chancellor, Prof R.M. Vasagam explains, the students are mostly going for software applications; it is proposed to make them entrepreneurs so as to enhance the impact on the society of their expertise. Unless technical education is made realistic and financially atractive, students will seek their career uplift elsewhere. As Prof. V.S. Ramamurthy (Secreatary, Department of S&T) says, the country should at least stop, if not reverse the growing trend of a lack of interest in S&T among the younger generation.

According to the Ninth Plan approach, the education sector will be given special attention for upgrading research, education and training in their institutions. Greater emphasis would be laid on training of scientists in modern management techniques. Younger scientists will be attracted to scientific and technological research careers by providing various types of economic incentives and improvement in thier functioning environment.

Environmental Auditing may be defined as the process of examining the records and physical production facilities of an industrial undertaking to identify the extent of compliance of environmental laws and regulations by that undertaking, to verify the efficacy of the system established to ensure compliance, to underline the risks and pollution hazards (known or unknown not yet covered by the regulatory bodies, to report lapses and suggest remedies.

To combat this situaton industrial undertakings should introduce a process which will verify that whether a particular industrial units is complying with the pollution control rules and regulations or not. As financial audit looks into the prevalence of internal control systems, conformity to the accounting standards prescribed by the regulatory bodies etc. by a company, enviroinmental auditing also will take cognizance of theextent of pollution of soil, air and water by an industrial unit through emmission of dangerous fumes and dust or wastes and will also suggest remedial measures to be undertaken. Environmental auditing will make the management aware about the risk associated with the operations of th company causing harm to the environment.

All the threates to environment can be analysed in the following way:

(a) Known pollution hazards which are covered by laws and regulations;

(b) Known pollution hazards for which there are no laws and regulations;

(c) Pollution hazards which can be identified with the assistance of present level of knowledge and resources but endeavour has not yet been taken for their identification;

(d) Pollution hazards which cannot be identified with the present level of knowledge.

Environmental Auditing attempts to resolve the threats of pollution related laws and regulations faced by a manufacturing unit in the following ways:

If the unit has a system to ensure cokmpliance with the applicable pollution related rules and regulations and generating records, then by testing the efficacy of the system.

Whether the uinit is complying with the rules and regulations of the authority vested with the duty to look after pollution related activities. Such as whether the unit has the necessary environmental related permits or licences, whether it is submitting the required reports to the authority in time, disposing hazardous wastes properly or otherwise it may cause future liability and keeping hazardous emissions within the tolerable limit prescribed by the authority.

Test all the discharges and emissions from manufacturing activity and if it is found that the unit is violating pollution related rules and regulations then reporting it to the management suggesting remedial measures. Such as, if on testing it is found that a pollution control equipment is failing to control the hazardous emissions from the manufacturing process within the limit prescribed then steps are to be taken to rectify the situation or if it is needed to install a new pollution control equipment, then recommending the installation of that equipment.

Reporting the hazards which are not yet covered under the present pollution control rules but which may cause harm to the people and environment and suggesting remedial measures for them. These types of hazards may cause immense harm to the manufacturing unit in future though presently posing no threat to the unit. These can be ignored by the industrial unit only at its peril. These are potential devastating risks related with the operations of the factory.

Exploring the possibility of commercial use of wastes effluxing from the manufacturing process, such as using the wastes as raw materials for further processing or selling it to another manufacturer to be used by that manufacturing unit as its innput instead of treating the wastes with the equipment to make them hazards free.

Scokpe of the environmental auditing in a manufacturing unit depends on the following:

— Objective of the company.

— Resources allocated for the purpose of environmental auditing.

— Time frame i.e. the time within which the audit has to be completed.

— Extent of the physical dispersion of the manufacturing facilities to be audited.

— Cooperation from the employees.

— Commitment of the management towards the environmental audit.

Advantages

Environmental Auditing if implemented properly will reap the following benefits to a business carrying on manufacturing operations:

Introduction of environmental auditing in a company shows its responsibility and positive attitude towards pollution hazards. It helps to build up a decent image of that company in the eyes of the employees, persons associated with the company and the siciety at large.

Implementation of environmental auditing reduces the hostile attitude of the authority entrusted with the duty of look after environmental hazards, towards the company. It helps to avoid unnecessary tension between the authority and the industry. The authority may avoid detailed inspection in a company if it is found that the company has already established an adequate procedure of environmental auditing.

It improves the extent of compliance by the company of the environmental rules and regulations. If violations are detected through environmental auditing, remedial actions can be taken immediately on the basis of suggestions of the environmental auditor. Hence the penalties which may otherwise be imposed can be avoided or there will no longer be any threats of closure to the company.

Environmental audit if properly implemented will indicate the pollution control equipment to be installed in future. Hence the company may plan its capital expenditures according to its financial capability. This will enable the company to avoid financial crunch which will be inevitable if the company faces an unexpected capital expenditure in the form of installation of anti-pollution equipment all of a sudden.

In the case of takeover of a company if the purchasing company conducts an environmental audit of the vendor company, then the purchasing company will get information about the environmental hazards generating from the manufacturing process of the vendor company, if there is any, and the capital expenditures needed to render the harmful emissions and wastes pollution hazard free. Then the purchasing cmpany may suitably take its decision regarding the issues related to purchase such as wether to purchase or not, the price to be paid for the purchase etc. In this way the purchasing company may avoid unnecessary future risks and troubles.

Environmental auditing has its disadvantage also. Through environmental auditing information about the environmental hazards of the manufacturing process, harmful emissions and wastes of a company are disclosed. It may cause damage to the corporate morale as well as the morale of the employees. This should be taken care of.

To be successful the environmental audit should be flexible enough to suit the specific needs of a manufacturing unit. There should also be well defined procedures of environmental auditing for the purpose of evaluating the environment related information generated by the company, identifying the violations and recommending corrective actions to cover the deficiencies. the environmental audit report should also be descriptive in nature. Expression of judgements in the report should be avoided as far as possible.